A Beautiful Fight

MUSIC AND SOCIAL JUSTICE

Series Editors: William Cheng and Andrew Dell'Antonio

TITLES IN THE SERIES

A Beautiful Fight: The Racial Politics of Capoeira in Backland Bahia
Esther Viola Kurtz

Hip-Hop Civics: Connected Learning in the Rap Classroom
Jabari M. Evans

Hold Me Down [Online Resource]
Ben Lauren

Teaching Difficult Topics: Reflections from the Undergraduate Music Classroom
Olivia R. Lucas and Laura Moore Pruett, Editors

Improvising Across Abilities: Pauline Oliveros and the Adaptive Use Musical Instrument
The AUMI Editorial Collective

Rape at the Opera: Staging Sexual Violence
Margaret Cormier

Jamming the Classroom: Musical Improvisation and Pedagogical Practice
Ajay Heble and Jesse Stewart

On Music Theory, and Making Music More Welcoming for Everyone
Philip Ewell

For the Culture: Hip-Hop and the Fight for Social Justice
Lakeyta M. Bonnette-Bailey and Adolphus G. Belk, Jr., Editors

Sonorous Worlds: Musical Enchantment in Venezuela
Yana Stainova

Singing Out: GALA Choruses and Social Change
Heather MacLachlan

Performing Commemoration: Musical Reenactment and the Politics of Trauma
Annegret Fauser and Michael A. Figueroa, Editors

A Beautiful Fight

The Racial Politics of Capoeira in Backland Bahia

Esther Viola Kurtz

University of Michigan Press
Ann Arbor

Published in the United States of America by the
University of Michigan Press
First published July 2025

A CIP catalog record for this book is available from the British Library.

Library of Congress Cataloging-in-Publication Data

Names: Kurtz, Esther Viola, 1976– author.
Title: A beautiful fight : the racial politics of Capoeira in Backland Bahia / Esther Viola Kurtz.
Other titles: Racial politics of Capoeira in Backland Bahia
Description: Ann Arbor : University of Michigan Press, 2025. | Series: Music and social justice | Includes bibliographical references and index.
Identifiers: LCCN 2025003800 (print) | LCCN 2025003801 (ebook) | ISBN 9780472077540 (hardcover ; alk. paper) | ISBN 9780472057542 (paper ; alk. paper) | ISBN 9780472905102 (OA ebook)
Subjects: LCSH: Capoeira (Dance)—Anthropological aspects. | Capoeira (Dance)—Brazil—Bahia (State)—History. | Capoeira (Dance)—Political aspects—Brazil—Bahia (State) | Martial arts—Brazil--Bahia (State)—History. | Slavery—Brazil—History—19th century. | Racism—Brazil—Bahia (State)—History. | Cultural appropriation—Brazil.
Classification: LCC GV1796.C145 K87 2025 (print) | LCC GV1796.C145 (ebook) | DDC 796.81—dc23/eng/20250417
LC record available at https://lccn.loc.gov/2025003800
LC ebook record available at https://lccn.loc.gov/2025003801

DOI: https://doi.org/10.3998/mpub.12771665

The University of Michigan Press's open access publishing program is made possible thanks to additional funding from the University of Michigan Office of the Provost and the generous support of contributing libraries.

Authorized Representative: Easy Access System Europe, Mustamäe tee 50, 10621 Tallinn, Estonia, gpsr.requests@easproject.com

Cover image credit: Samba rural of the Angoleiros do Sertão, Feira de Santana, 2023. Photo by Author.

In memory of Anani Dzidzienyo

Contents

Digital materials related to this title can be found on the Fulcrum platform via the following citable URL: https://doi.org/10.3998/mpub.12771665

Figures

Musical Examples

Preface

In March 2016, I was interviewing Iaiá in her apartment in a neighborhood outside of Feira de Santana's city center. I had met Iaiá a few years before, after seeking her out to learn about her perspectives on capoeira, the Afro-Brazilian fight-game played to live music, as it relates to Brazil's Black movement. Although she no longer trained capoeira, she was a prominent Black movement activist closely affiliated with the capoeira group I was working with. She had become a good friend, and I valued how she shared her thoughts with me without mincing words. Toward the end of our interview, I started talking about some of the challenges of conducting ethnography, how I was grappling with the tension between wanting to be critical and honest about problems I had experienced, but also ethical, not wanting to betray anyone's trust. I said, "I have to find a way to write about [these things] without making it all about me. . . . But even so, it's part of it all."

Iaiá responded, "It's part of it mainly because you're coming from another culture. There are moments where you're seen as a person who is there sucking [*sugando*], wanting to know what? Wanting to know too much? . . . And so this thing of the research, too, is also very conflicted. [You're] researching in a space that is not yours, trying to convince the people that this will do good. Remember to give something back to these people because the people expect something in return. What did you write? You're here looking at us. What are you going to do? We want to know what you did."

Here and in other conversations, Iaiá raised fundamental questions that ethnographers have wrestled with for decades: How can my work do something good in the world? How can I repay community members for everything they have given me—their time, thoughts, perspectives, trust? She and

I both knew that I was following in the footsteps of scholars who had studied peripheral Afro-Brazilian communities and cultural practices, researchers who had reduced Black Brazilians to objects, pathologized their poverty and creative expressions, and deemed them less than human. How could I ensure that I was doing things differently? Iaiá was letting me know that I was not the only one concerned about my positionality. She and other community members returned my gaze.

• • •

Over the years of presenting my work at conferences and in classrooms, audience members have asked in numerous ways how I came to this project. Why capoeira? Why racial politics? How did I, a white woman from Newton, Massachusetts, come to write this book? When I was fourteen, I decided to become a professional classical oboist, and it was as an oboist that I first traveled to Brazil, just after graduating high school. In the summer of 1994, I attended a classical music festival in Itu, São Paulo. Along with several other North American *oboistas* and the Brazilian music students attending the festival, we spent the weeks in private lessons, chamber ensemble and orchestra rehearsals, and performances. That summer Brazil won the World Cup for the fourth time, and we watched the thrilling matches huddled around a TV during lunch break. At night, my new friends put down their violins and cellos and picked up *cavaquinhos* (ukulele-sized four-stringed guitars) and *pandeiros* (tambourine-like hand drums), and we played, sang, and danced samba until early morning. Our days and nights saturated with music and dance, it felt at once extraordinary and exactly how it should be. When I returned home to start music school, I resolved to go back to Brazil someday to learn Portuguese and learn more about the music.

After graduating from Eastman School of Music, I continued my studies in contemporary oboe performance in the Netherlands and stayed there after graduating, working as a freelance oboist. In 2006 I met Nestor Capoeira, a capoeira *mestre* who was visiting the country to promote the Dutch translation of his book *Capoeira: Pequeno manual do jogador* (Capoeira: A little manual for the player). As I read it, I experienced an uncanny sense of recognition and felt I had to start training capoeira. Whereas music first brought me to Brazil, a book brought me to capoeira, foreshadowing my academic engagement with all three: music, capoeira, and Brazil. Within a year I had planned a six-month trip to Rio de Janeiro where I learned Portuguese, studied *choro* (an instrumental music genre), and took my first capoeira Angola classes. In 2009 I returned to the United States without a plan, disillusioned with the world of professional classical music but knowing I wanted to spend more time in Brazil. I stumbled upon ethnomusicology and realized that it might be the only field that valued my musical and life experiences.

I had been raised by well-meaning nonracist white parents in a wealthy suburb of Boston, but I first began thinking about racism more closely when I got to the Netherlands. In my first week there, in 1999, I remember my host speaking disparagingly about Moroccans, and soon learned that schools with predominantly Moroccan and Turkish students—whose parents and grandparents had come to the country as temporary laborers but stayed on—were called "black schools." In the decade I lived in the Netherlands, I argued vehemently with Dutch friends about their Christmastime blackface tradition of Zwarte Piet. I insisted that Zwarte Piet's depiction, with a black-painted face, Afro wig, big red lips, gold earrings, bumbling foolishness, and Surinamese accent, was indeed racist. I even directed and played in a multimedia performance to address the topic. I conducted interviews with white and Black residents of Rotterdam, asking them how they perceived and experienced Zwarte Piet, and commissioned composers to write new works using sound and concepts from the interviews. Perhaps that was my first ethnographic project.

I began my graduate studies wanting to learn more about Brazil's racial politics and asking questions about the political potentials of Black music and dance. I was operating under the assumption that capoeira practice changed practitioners' ideas about race and racial politics, and I sought to find out how it did this. At the 2016 Annual Meeting of the Society for Ethnomusicology, Portia Maultsby generously agreed to chat with me about my dissertation ideas and suggested that instead of asking how people change their ideas I might ask what kinds of identities they build through their practice and what kinds of actions result. While I took Professor Maultsby's advice to heart, I feel I only partially applied it in my dissertation (Kurtz 2018). I still wanted to believe that capoeira had a radicalizing potential despite finding that my interlocutors came to capoeira with their politics largely already formed. Put simply, I think I was seeking a mechanism for making white people antiracist but that is not exactly what I found. Reflecting on my own experience, I had to be honest, too. Training capoeira with Mestre Cláudio and thinking about capoeira as an ethnographer had changed me but so had taking classes and earning a Graduate Certificate in Africana Studies at Brown University under the mentorship of Anani Dzidzienyo. In writing this book, I have therefore put aside a generalizing search for change and instead tried to understand diverse group members' perspectives on capoeira Angola as a practice that counters racism and coloniality. Reflecting on which book I could best write, I have sought to leverage my position as a white foreigner to express nuanced critiques of whiteness in the capoeira community—critiques that many members share but that they do not openly voice to one another, out of deference for group cohesion.

As with many ethnographers, I am also concerned with how I have represented my interlocutors' thoughts, speech, bodies, and stories—ethnography's embodied ventriloquism. Recognizing the people I worked with as knowledge producers, I often quote them directly, sometimes in dialogue form to reveal my participation in the exchanges. When possible, I have also shared with group members how I am writing about them, to check with them that they agree with how I am representing their ideas. Over the last several years, I have given semiformal and informal book talks—the most significant one was online during the pandemic, with many group members present, lasting three hours including Q&A. I have also given ten-minute versions, one-on-one, and sent some excerpts to members for feedback. I have received the blessings of community members whose opinions matter most to me, yet I know that others may not approve of my conclusions or critiques. Although I have sought to understand varying perspectives and portray them accurately, I recognize the limits of empathy and good intentions. In sum, throughout my research and writing, I have sought to follow the advice of a capoeira song, one Mestre Cláudio sings on one of his CDs, "*Chega em terra alheia, pisa no chão devagar*" ([When you] arrive on someone else's land, step on the ground slowly) (Santo Amaro and Costa 2003). Yet even stepping slowly, one might slip and fall.

Though I will never experience racism *na pele*—in the skin—I assume the responsibility to approach understanding Black community members' experiences and, ultimately, to work toward the abolition of white supremacist coloniality. Even realizing that this abolition will not happen in my lifetime, I hope to contribute to imagining and creating new ways of being in relation that not only avoid reproducing violence but also put into practice new definitions of being human. I believe that the power of Black music and dance—its healing and life-sustaining force, its *axé*—can empower this radical project, but I know that the axé must be directed with intention, commitment, and care. Under the ethical imperative of call and response, I offer no complete answers but rather responses that must become future calls.

Acknowledgments

In many ways, the process of writing this book has also been a beautiful fight, and I am so grateful I have not had to wage it alone. Starting with the nitty-gritty, day-to-day grind of writing, I cannot imagine what I would have done without the following people in the (virtual) room and on the phone: I thank Dave Fossum for reading every chapter and weathering this journey with me from the beginning; Amy Swanson for providing so much needed motivation, inspiration, and support, and commenting on drafts; Oliver Shao for our intensive writing retreat, providing the exact feedback I needed, and for all our exchanges; Myrta Leslie Santana for strategizing, philosophizing, and plotting together; Adanna Kai Jones, Joanna Dee Das, Elizabeth T. Craft, Saroya Corbett, and Rachel Carrico for providing a lifeline, showing up every day, and sharing ideas, drafts, struggles, strategies, laughs, and tears. Each of your brilliance, grit, wisdom, and love has supported and inspired me along the way.

Se eu conseguir contribuir alguma coisa com este texto é por causa das seguintes pessoas. Este livro não existiria sem a presença, o pensamento, o trabalho, os ensinamentos, e a generosidade do Mestre Cláudio Costa. Obrigada mestre! Agradeço a Rita Eloá Gonçalves, que me acolheu desde o primeiro dia, que toca o coração e a mente de todes que entram no mundo dos Angoleiros do Sertão. Dona Ivannide e Iaiá, não sei como expressar o quanto eu aprendi e ri com vocês. Obrigada pelo seu cuidado e apoio. Todos vocês forneceram informações cruciais para este texto. Qualquer erro é apenas meu.

Também agradeço aos Angoleiros do Sertão, a todes, mas especialmente Mestre Tico, Contramestra Natureza, Pedro Ivo, Contramestre Orikerê, Treinel Solange, Treinel Pernalonga, Treinel Thomaz, Treinel Coragem, e

Treinel Hulluca. Também agradeço ao Contramestre Sapoti e a Elzinha. Seth Hague, I am so grateful to know you, to learn from you, to have experienced your care and hospitality.

I first experienced capoeira Angola in the academy of Mestre Marrom of Rio de Janeiro. Obrigada sempre, mestre! I owe my foundation in capoeira Angola to Mestre Deraldo, Mestre Manhoso, and my brothers Contramestre Calango and Contramestre Toca. To all the CECA-Boston family, love and gratitude! Obrigada também Mestre Iuri Hart Santos.

At Tufts University, where I audited classes to figure out if I wanted to go back to grad school, thank you Jeanne Marie Penvenne, Jeffrey Summit, and my fellow students in the fieldwork methods class: Gordon Alex Dale, Elijah Wald, Tamara Turner, and Christiana Usenza.

Throughout my graduate studies at Brown, I had the privilege of being mentored in the Africana studies department by the late political scientist Anani Dzidzienyo. Anani challenged me to hone my questions about the power of expressive practices to better Black lives and to critically evaluate the politics of white participation in African diasporic communities. His guidance continues to orient me. Also in Africana studies, I was immensely fortunate to have taken classes with Paget Henry, Keisha-Khan Perry, and Tricia Rose, and to have learned from classmates Shamara Wyllie Alhassan, Amanda Boston, Watufani M. Poe, and Nicosia Shakes, among many other brilliant scholars. In the music department, I grew into ethnomusicology under the expert guidance of Joshua Tucker, Kiri Miller, Marc Perlman, Dana Gooely, and Jeff Todd Titon. A great thank you also to Rebecca Schneider, Jasmine E. Johnson, and Stefanie Miller, who each helped shape my thinking and sharpen my ideas in different ways.

My community of colleagues, students, and friends at Washington University in St. Louis continues to support and inspire me. I am so grateful to all of you! In the Department of Music, I have received invaluable feedback and mentorship from Clare Bokulich, Pat Burke, Todd Decker, Dolores Pesce, Paul Steinbeck, Alex Stefaniak, and Christopher Stark. A special note of appreciation to Lauren Eldridge Stewart for reading my work and wading through the "early career" together. I'm also very grateful for the support of librarians Brad Short and Lino Mioni and for the administrative support of Kim Daniels, Jessica Flannigan, Jen Gartley, Samantha Kusnierkiewicz, Laura Perry, Daphanee Rhodes, and Tara Sandretto. Beyond the music department, wonderful colleagues have commented on drafts and puzzled through questions in conversation, including Tili Boon Cuillé, René Esparza, Jonathan Fenderson, Caio Fernandes, Karma Frierson, Elizabeth

Hunter, Ignacio Infante, John Klein, Paige McGinley, John Mundell, Nancy Reynolds, Ila Sheren, Miguel Valerio, Lori Watt, and Eliza Williamson. Also a warm thanks to Shanti Parikh, all my colleagues in the Department of African and African-American Studies, and to Darrell Hudson, Tila Neguse, Diana Parra Perez, and Sheltoria Love at the Center for the Study of Race, Ethnicity, and Equity. I have been fortunate to have research support from graduate students Dan Fister, Felipe Guz Tinoco, Bryce Noe, and Fang Liu.

Other colleagues have supported my work in ways large and small, but all very much appreciated, including Samuel Araújo, Paula Cristina da Silva Barreto, Corinna Campbell, Dasha Chapman, Andrew Colwell, Denise Gill, Tomie Hahn, Megan Steigerwald Ille, Michael Iyanaga, Portia Maultsby, Mario LaMothe, Mika Lior, Angela Lühning, Alejandro Madrid, Jeff Packman, Danielle Robinson, Dan Sharp, Mike Silvers, Ben Teitelbaum, and Elyse Carter Vosen. I am also very grateful for FSP Group#44: Coach Angelique Davis, Alix Johnson, Anjuli Verma, and Courtney Di Vittorio.

My immense appreciation goes to Sara Cohen, who encouraged this project and brought the book under contract, and to William Cheng and Andrew Dell'Antonio for their enthusiastic support of the book. I also thank Haley Winkle, Mary Hashman, Danielle Coty-Fattal, and the other excellent staff at the University of Michigan Press. My deepest gratitude also goes to Keisha-Khan Perry who workshopped the full manuscript and encouraged me to bring more nuance to the book's arguments and critiques of capoeira's political potentials. Three anonymous reviewers also provided excellent feedback and suggestions. I have surely left out names of people who deserve to be mentioned here—please forgive my lapse.

Finally, love and thanks to my family, the Kurtzes, Coffins, and Dickes. My mother, Nancy Kurtz, was my first writing coach, and my father, Dan Kurtz, would have been so proud to see this book in print. While he deserves top billing, I've saved my greatest gratitude for last: throughout the long process, Ben Dicke has kept me laughing, loved, healthy, and sane—at least by our definition—and he's also cared for the best book kitties anyone could ask for, Cozy Cole and Hornbostel.

• • •

Research for this project received funding from the James N. Green Grant, the Global Mobility Program Graduate Research Fellowship from Brown University's Office of Global Development, the International Travel Fund and Music Department funds at Brown, and a Mellon Graduate Student Dissertation Workshop. At Washington University in St. Louis the project received funding from the Center for the Humanities Summer Faculty Research Grant (any views, findings, conclusions, or recommendations expressed in this publication do not necessarily reflect those of the Center for the Humanities); the Center for the Study of Race, Ethnicity, and Equity Faculty Fellowship (this work has been funded by the Center for the Study of Race, Ethnicity, and Equity at Washington University in St. Louis Faculty Fellowship Program but the views remain those of the author); and a BECHS-Africa Fellowship at the University of Ghana, with support from the Mellon Foundation. Chapter 1, which draws from "Community in Syntony: Theorizing *Axé* in Capoeira Angola and Rural Samba of Backland Bahia, Brazil," *Ethnomusicology* 68, no. 1 (2024): 118–49, is published with permission from the Society for Ethnomusicology.

Introduction

A Beautiful Fight examines the possibilities and limits for *capoeira*, a fight played like a game to live music, to cohere a racially diverse community committed to antiracist struggle. Capoeira was born out of resistance to enslavement in Brazil, and today many activists and capoeira players, in Brazil and the world, feel that capoeira counters racism and coloniality. Yet I have found that capoeira often falls short of the radical claims that players make on its behalf. For one, the growing dominance of white participants threatens to divert attention from Black political priorities, even as players forge interracial camaraderie through their practice. Capoeira's economy also functions within a broader system of colonialist racial capitalism, which limits some of its more radical potentials. Despite these constraints, I ultimately argue that capoeira practice can generate liberatory tools for fighting white supremacist coloniality, but the tools must be used with intention, commitment, and care lest they become diffused—and defused—into attractive symbols free to be wielded by the forces that capoeira exists to resist.

A Beautiful Fight (*uma luta bonita*) signals the tension between playing and fighting at the heart of the capoeira *roda*, the circular space of play formed by players' bodies. In the roda, two players face off to play a game that is always also a fight, risking injury at any moment, whether to body or pride. At the same time, they strive to play *um jogo bonito*, a beautiful game, in which they flow together with the music and each other, creatively exhibiting intelligence.[1] Like many African diasporic expressions, capoeira thus holds numerous contradictory elements in tension. This capacity "can be understood as a precept of contrariety, or an encounter of opposites," through which the "conflict inherent in and implied by difference, discord, and irregularity is encompassed, rather than erased or necessarily resolved" (Gottschild 1998, 13). Capoeira's values of "ambiguity, duplicity, [and] oscillation" require that players "associate . . . conceptually opposite categories" with one another, such as "fight and dance," "partner and adversary" (Zonzon 2016, 405). The capoeira roda is a site of both conflict and creativity, competition and cooperation.

A Beautiful Fight also connects the fight (*luta*) in the roda to the broader struggle (*luta*) of Black resistance in Brazil—not to equate them but to recognize that capoeira practice is also a site for contesting and negotiating racial politics. By considering the potential for beauty in struggle, I do not seek to minimize the enduring violence targeting Black lives or to romanticize the suffering it brings. Rather, the beauty refers both to capoeira's musical-corporeal aesthetics and to the collective processes essential to sustain struggle. Historian of US-American Black radical politics Robin D. G. Kelley acknowledged the potential for beauty in continuous struggle in this way:

> If we think of change as an event, we'll never get there. If we think of change as constant struggle, then we live our lives in struggle from the day we're born until we die. And there's something beautiful about that. It's not just the fight, but it's about the struggle to make community, to make new friendships, to make new relationships. (Amanda Seales TV 2023)

The beauty in the struggle comes from building new affective relationships with one another, creating new and necessary ways of being in relation.

Afro-Brazilian scholar-artist-activist Abdias do Nascimento also found a confluence of beauty, politics, and struggle in African diasporic expressions: "Black art is the practice of Black liberation—reflection and action, action and reflection—in all levels of existence: material and spiritual; social and religious; cultural/aesthetic; economic and political" (A. Nascimento 1989, 152). With one multiracial capoeira group in Bahia, Brazil, as a case study, *A Beautiful Fight* explores how each of these interwoven and sometimes contrasting spheres of existence also converge in the Black art form of capoeira.

A Fight That's Played Like a Game

Capoeira is a music-movement practice developed by enslaved Africans and Afro-Brazilians in Brazil. Practitioners talk about training (*treinar*) capoeira and playing (*jogar*) capoeira games (*jogos*), but they know that the game is also a fight that can erupt into violence.[2] The movements are stylized, but

Figure 1. Mestre Cláudio, the third berimbau player from left, plays the berra-boi and sings the ladainha to open the roda. Only the two pandeiros play (to Cláudio's right) while the reco-reco, agogô, and atabaque players rest and listen intently. Video still by the author, 2017.

players rarely talk about "dancing" capoeira even though they move in and against the groove of call-and-response songs and the *bateria* (ensemble), comprised of eight percussion instruments (three *berimbaus*, two *pandeiros*, *reco-reco*, *agogô*, and *atabaque*, see fig. 1). Games are neither won nor lost, and a beautiful game requires both trickery (*malícia, malandragem*) and openness and trust. Playing too open leaves a player vulnerable to attack, but playing too closed, too defensively, prevents a genuine exchange of bodily question and response.

This book focuses on capoeira Angola as opposed to the more widespread contemporary (*contemporânea*) or *Regional* styles primarily because capoeira Angola is known as the more politicized style, and its teachers (*mestras* and *mestres*) are more often vocal militants (*militantes*) of Brazil's Black movement (*movimento negro*) for racial justice.[3] Numerous works have addressed stylistic differences, but briefly, *angoleiros* (capoeira Angola practitioners) colloquially refer to all non-Angola styles as "capoeira Regional," which is represented worldwide by images of muscular, bare-chested, barefooted men in wide white pants performing high straight-leg kicks, flipping their bodies in the air.[4] Capoeira Angola, in contrast, as a song lyric goes, "is played on the ground" (*Capoeira de Angola se joga no chão*). Players wear shoes, tuck in their T-shirts, and maneuver closer to the ground and closer to one another.

In my experience of transitioning from Regional to Angola, I had to develop more upper-body strength, move with more control, and pay closer attention to the music. As "Angola" indicates, angoleiros tend to emphasize capoeira's Africanness, claiming a closer adherence to tradition (Magalhães Filho 2012) and African origins, which they also relate to capoeira Angola's spirituality and politics.[5]

Capoeira as Black Resistance

For *capoeiristas* (capoeira practitioners) and scholars alike, *capoeira é resistência*—capoeira is resistance.[6] As UNESCO declared upon recognizing the capoeira roda as intangible cultural heritage, "Capoeira expresses Black resistance in Brazil during slavery" (Gelbert 2014). Yet perhaps because it is so self-evident, practitioners and scholars rarely explain what capoeira's resistance means today. For instance, in 2013 I first interviewed Mestre Cláudio Costa, the leader and teacher of the group featured in this book, the Angoleiros do Sertão (Capoeira Angola Players of the Backlands). I asked Mestre Cláudio if he thought that capoeira could still function today as resistance for Afro-Brazilians. Immediately he replied, "No, this is what capoeira *is*." For Mestre Cláudio, this aspect of capoeira's identity could not be questioned. He went on to say, "Capoeira *is* resistance because it's not possible that it was but no longer is [resistance]. So capoeira is the resistance of the Afro-Brazilian people [*o povo afro-brasileiro*] and it still is today."

Capoeira's historical resistance is explained in its well-known origin story: enslaved Africans and Afro-Brazilians disguised capoeira's fight as a dance to hide its power from their masters, and they used capoeira as a weapon to resist their enslavement and seize their freedom. Although some historians doubt that this myth can be supported by historical records, clearly enslaved people and their descendants carved out the time and space, against all odds, to play capoeira, or else it would not exist today.[7] Capoeira's endurance over time despite facing suppression is therefore another meaning that resistance takes on in capoeira discourse. In this sense, capoeira belongs among Brazil's historical "alternative spaces of Blackness" such as the Afro-Brazilian religion Candomblé, within which enslaved and free Black people found refuge, cohered their community, healed one another, and resisted their dehumanization (Harding 2000).[8] These meanings persist today when capoeira is described as an "alternative territory," comparable to Brazil's *quilombos*, communities founded by fugitives from enslavement (Couto 2021, 201).

Yet in everyday discourse racial politics often go unmentioned, obscuring the meaning of capoeira as Black resistance. What's more, *resistência* in Portuguese also means physical endurance, and many practitioners use the term in this way, depoliticizing the concept of resistance altogether. Failing to articulate capoeira as resistance "of the Afro-Brazilian people" universalizes capoeira's resistance: capoeira can symbolize anyone's fight against anything. In this way, in capoeira scholarship and communities, capoeira's Black politics often get "invisibilized" (Gottschild 1998). In this book, I take capoeira's resistance as given, but with "resistance" I refer specifically to "the struggles by Black Africans and persons of Black African descent to end racial, economic, and cultural injustice" (Dunkley and Shonekan 2018, 1). The question remains, however, how capoeira's historical resistance against slavery translates into contemporary fights against racism. I address this further below.

After concluding that "capoeira is the resistance of the Afro-Brazilian people," Mestre Cláudio offered a complicating qualification: "Except today everyone does capoeira. White, Indian [*índio*, indigenous Brazilian], Brown, Black, everyone, *mulato*, everyone does capoeira. But capoeira is a product of the Black people. It's *cultura popular* [popular culture]. It's democratic. Understand? Everyone can do capoeira." *Cultura popular* in Brazil, as across Latin America, refers to cultural expressions of "the people" (*o povo*), the lower and working classes (Tinhorão 2001).[9] As the working class in Brazil is mostly Black, cultura popular often implicitly means Black cultural practices, but Mestre Cláudio explicitly claims the Blackness of Bahian cultura popular, which includes numerous other music-dance "manifestations" (*manifestações*) such as the singing, drumming, dancing form *samba de roda*. Yet being of the people means that capoeira is for everyone. Here Mestre Cláudio signals another interpretation of resistance often ascribed to capoeira: it resists racial exclusion because it allows everyone to join. The inversion—Black spaces allowing whites to enter, not the other way around—goes unnoted in the discourse. Capoeira is celebrated as a symbol of racial harmony and a space that realizes Brazil's mythical ideal of racial democracy (Balaguer 2016), which holds that racial mixture makes racism impossible in Brazil.

Herein lies the crux of *A Beautiful Fight*: If capoeira is Black resistance, an alternative Black space, then what happens when "everyone" joins in, regardless of race, ethnicity, regional location, or nationality? From a global perspective, capoeira communities often include more white and non-Black members than Black, though there are growing numbers of Black-majority groups on the African continent.[10] In Brazil, white practitioners likely outnumber Black, especially in groups of capoeira Angola, which tend to be housed in elite spaces like universities, with majority-white student populations (Balaguer 2017, 106).[11] Even in Bahia, where 80 percent of the population is of African descent, many capoeira Angola groups have a majority of white members. Mestre Cláudio acknowledges the racial imbalance in his group, the Angoleiros do Sertão, whose white majority is even larger when including its numerous satellite schools (*núcleos*) throughout Brazil, mainly in São Paulo state, and a few in Europe and the United States. Yet Mestre Cláudio claims that the large white presence does not "whiten" capoeira Angola, but rather that capoeira Angola "Africanizes" white minds.[12] Examining this tension is a major task of this book, and my concern comes in part out of reflecting on my position as a white capoeira practitioner and researcher.[13]

Yet what do "whitening" and "Africanizing" mean? As many have discussed regarding the Afro-Brazilian religious communities of Candomblé, whitening can refer to the dominant presence of white people in Black spaces, but it can also refer to the imposition of white supremacist and colonialist ideologies (França 2018). It is clear that white people predominate in capoeira Angola, but the task is to determine the extent to which racist ideas and behaviors permeate its spaces. Meanwhile, being "Africanized" does not mean being "Blackened," for whites still retain their whiteness and do not suffer from racism (França 2018, 74). In *A Beautiful Fight*, I understand "Africanizing" as I believe Mestre Cláudio means it: politicizing and raising the racial consciousness of white practitioners. Can capoeira Africanize white minds in this way, as some claim (e.g., Griffith 2023)? More urgently, to what extent does capoeira Angola continue to function as resistance for Afro-Brazilians, and to what extent has capoeira become complicit with the systems it historically resisted?[14]

Similar questions can be posed about capoeira as a practice of freedom, as discussed in chapter 3. The phrase *"CAPOEIRA É LIBERDADE"* (Capoeira is freedom) appears carved in relief on a wooden plaque hanging on the dusty, pale brick wall of Mestre Cláudio's training studio (see fig. 2). If capoeira is liberty, who has access to its practices of freedom? Is capoeira equally liberatory for everyone who joins the game?

Capoeira Angola and Historical Black Resistance in Brazil

Beyond legend, little is known about how enslaved Africans and Afro-Brazilians used capoeira to resist their enslavers, but when capoeira entered the historical record by name, mostly in police records, in the early 1800s in Rio de Janeiro and mid-1800s in Bahia (at the time synonymous with the city of Salvador), it was associated with both agonistic and ludic activities.[15] These

Figure 2. "Capoeira is freedom." Plaque hanging on the wall of Mestre Cláudio's training studio. Photo by the author, 2016.

included fights among gangs or individual capoeiristas, conflicts with authority figures, participation in rebellions, and battling as soldiers in the Paraguay war, but it seems capoeira was simultaneously played like a game throughout its early history (Assunção 2005, 70–127). By the late nineteenth century in Bahia, capoeira was a common sight during work breaks, on Sunday afternoons, and on the streets during public religious festivals (106).

Prior to abolition in 1888, Black Brazilians had liberated themselves in great numbers by walking away from plantations, eroding the slavery system, and after abolition the Brazilian state sponsored European immigration to replace the Black labor force, effectively preventing newly free Black people from working (Andrews 1991). During this post-abolition period, with large numbers of unemployed Black men on Brazil's urban streets, some of them playing capoeira, the white ruling class equated capoeira with *vadiagem* (vagrancy) and outlawed capoeira in the Penal Code of 1890 (Assunção 2005, 11). To this day, capoeira remains stigmatized among Brazilian elites as a generally useless activity associated with criminals (*marginais*) or lazy slackers (*vadios, vagabundos*).[16]

In the early 1930s in Salvador, Mestre Bimba, creator of capoeira Regional, opened the first capoeira academy (*academia,* training school) essentially ending capoeira's outlaw status—as long as it stayed indoors (Assunção 2005, 128–41). Soon Bimba's academy attracted white middle-class students, capoeira Regional's popularity grew, and in 1953 then-president (and former dictator) Getúlio Vargas declared capoeira "the only true national sport" (141). By the 1940s, "capoeira de Angola" had come to refer to the traditional style of Bahian capoeira distinguished from the modernized capoeira Regional, and Mestre Pastinha assumed the responsibility of ensuring capoeira Angola's continuation. However, by the 1970s, capoeira Angola practice had declined, and its survival again seemed threatened as contemporary capoeira spread across the United States and Europe.

In 1964 a coup instigated Brazil's military dictatorship, which enforced Brazil's racial democracy ideology by suppressing racial identification and race-based politics (Winant 1992, 184–85; A. Nascimento 1989, xi). However, the mid-1970s began a period of gradual "opening" (*abertura*) initiating Brazil's return to democracy.[17] Under this new climate, in 1978, Black activists founded the Black movement, originally called the Unified Black Movement Against Racial Discrimination (Gonzalez 1985, 124). In tandem during this period, popular culture in Bahia underwent a "re-Africanization." Parading carnival groups with Black cultural themes (*blocos afro*), such as Ilê Aiyê, gave musical, choreographic, and sartorial voice to the Black movement's affirmation of Black-African (diasporic) identity and critiques of racism (Dunn 1992; Crook 1993; P. Pinho 2010; Afolabi 2016). In the 1980s, a cohort of angoleiros in Salvador, Bahia, led most prominently by Mestre Moraes, began to identify capoeira Angola explicitly as an antiracist resistance movement (Araújo 2015). This image of capoeira Angola endures as a counterculture opposing "the system" and promoting a racialized "political consciousness" (Brito and Granada 2020, 17). Yet what does this look like in practice? How effective is capoeira Angola at combating racial injustice?

The Saturday Morning Roda: Black Resistance as Being Human

Mestre Cláudio considers his weekly Saturday roda the group's most powerful contribution to Black movement activism. The roda is significant because it creates a participatory space that publicly celebrates Bahian Blackness of the *sertão* (backlands) in defiance of enduring anti-Blackness. As Black movement activist Urania "Iaiá" do Carmo Rodrigues Santa Barbara writes, the roda exists in tension with the city's authorities, who seem always to be saying "you are not there, we are not seeing you," while the roda responds, "We are here, this space is also ours" (U. Santa Barbara 2019, 38).[18] Mestre Cláudio has secured this space continuously for over thirty years, first inside the Mercado de Artes (Arts Market), a colonial-era building that houses artisan stalls, bars, and a performance stage, and then outside on the median strip of one of Feira de Santana's busiest thoroughfares. The roda consists of roughly an hour of capoeira Angola followed by *samba rural*, the group's style of samba de roda, which is open for public participation. As Mestre Cláudio put it, the people come for the capoeira (to watch) and stay for the samba (to dance).

Karine Damasceno, another of Feira's prominent Black activists, explained in our interview the political urgency of the roda in an atmosphere of increasing religious intolerance.[19] Using the reclaimed pejorative expression "Black thing," she said:

> Everyone who sees a roda of capoeira sees it as a Black thing [*coisa de negro*]. A Black thing [*coisa de preto*]. It is a Black space, Black territory. . . . If you go to Feira de Santana on Saturday, and see them playing there, you know it is a Black thing, even though there are more white people playing than Black! . . . The evangelicals, the Christians, the Catholics that walk by, they cross themselves, they cross over to the other side of the street, because it reminds them of Candomblé. . . . They reject it.

The roda's loud confluence of Black sound and movement declaring the value of Black culture is key to Mestre Cláudio's political philosophy of capoeira Angola. Although, like many capoeira Angola mestres, Mestre Cláudio loves to discuss and lecture, he is adamant that the change he effects in the world comes through doing capoeira, not talking about the problems. The samba is crucial for his project as it invites community members to join in the doing with their bodies: jumping into the samba circle, they immerse themselves in the sound-movement energies of their "Black things." For some moments each Saturday on the street, Black people of the sertão publicly embody their love for Black popular culture and, more importantly, for themselves. Iaiá summarized: "The very space, the very roda, the very event itself is a political act."

However, there are limits to capoeira's resistive potential today. Dona Ivannide, a leading Black movement militant in Feira de Santana (and Iaiá's mother), put it bluntly in our 2015 interview: "Look. Capoeira as resistance, if we are going to define resistance in the most voracious [*voraz*], the most radical sense of the word, from the point of view of confrontation in the class struggle, I don't believe in it. I think [capoeira] no longer fulfills this role." According to Dona Ivannide's Black Marxist critique, capoeira no longer directly confronts racial-economic oppression. She said, "I think that there, in that [historical] moment, capoeira groups were spaces of Black resistance. But to the extent that capoeira turned into a ludic game and became something that was studied by academics. . . . You're mixing the colonized with the colonizer! And I don't know any more what my place is there." For Dona Ivannide, the presence of white players ("the colonizer") compromises capoeira's resistive potential: How can capoeira resist the oppressor if he has become a *camarada* (friend)?

Yet Dona Ivannide was equally forceful about what she felt was capoeira Angola's vital role of bringing self-esteem to Black people. In capoeira, Black Brazilians encounter a form of belonging that is still elusive in mainstream society:

> For you, non-Blacks, non-Brazilians, and therefore non-descended from the enslaved doing capoeira, it is difficult to understand. But for us here, whoever does capoeira here in Brazil, they are not people from the academy, from the university, they are people from the *periferia* [periphery]![20] They're Blacks, they're [pejoratively] called *malandros*, vagabundos, vadios. And so, it seems to me that this space gives them a status of belonging. "I am part of *something*!" . . . This sense of belonging makes it possible that [a capoeira player] can think of leaving that place to construct something because he already *is* somebody. . . . If I am some*body*, I can do some*thing*! For me or for others! And so, I think that bringing self-esteem is the greatest contribution that capoeira gives to Black people: to encounter themselves as individuals, as people, as citizens of the country. . . . It is this valorization of "I," of the humanity [of Black people], to feel like people, to feel human.

Many group members I spoke with confirmed Dona Ivannide's testimony. Some Black members told me that capoeira had literally saved their lives. Growing up in the periphery, life chances are exceptionally limited, and these group members spoke of friends who had fallen into drug trafficking or lost their lives to violence. Capoeira provided another option, confirming their humanity and convincing them that they could pursue higher education or make a career teaching capoeira. Dona Ivannide's understanding of capoeira as a space that valorizes Black humanity thus echoes Caribbean philosopher Sylvia Wynter's call to "put forward new conceptions of the human outside the terms of our present ethnoclass conception" (Wynter 2003, 267). Significantly, Wynter does not call for inclusion, for Black people and others deemed sub- or nonhuman to be allowed entry into the "central ethnoclass Man," but rather argues that we need an entirely new "genre of being human" (261, 269). Capoeira Angola contains the potential to further this project by providing a space in which to imagine other ways of being human.

When Mestre Cláudio continues to hold his Saturday morning roda, rain or shine, year in and year out, delegating its command to advanced students in his absence, he devotes himself to a street-based, sound-movement Black politics. In this way, Mestre Cláudio creates a space in which Black lives from the rural Bahian peripheries are valued. By opening the samba for Black community members to participate in their own culture, the Angoleiros do Sertão counters the violent project of divorcing Black culture from Black bodies, of celebrating the former while exterminating the latter. In these ways, the Saturday roda resists Black people's dehumanization and imagines other ways of reconfiguring the category of the human.

Proceeding from this foundation, the book explores the ways in which the group's capoeira practice both furthers and hinders this radical project. An extensive body of Brazilian capoeira literature, much of it within education studies, has already established capoeira as a socializing pedagogical tool that sustains "alternative logics" (Abib 2004) and empowers students by teaching them autonomy and respect for diversity (Machado and Araújo 2015). Many white group members told me that they, too, have felt empowered, strengthened, and liberated by their capoeira practice. Of course, white people also have issues of self-esteem, and participating in capoeira can benefit them in that regard. However, as Karine Damasceno pointed out in our interview, white people don't suffer from anti-Black dehumanization. Karine explained that while Black players must reckon with capoeira's stigmatization as a Black practice, white players gain social and cultural capital when they associate with Black culture. Referring to the Saturday roda, she said to me, "The people that see *you* there, they say, 'Look! She's cool with Black folks!'" Capoeira may indeed be good for everyone who trains it. However, in a society still ruled by colonialist white supremacist logics, empowering white people does more to reinforce the status quo than resist it—unless they also join the fight for Black humanity.

Racial Ideologies and Terminologies in Contemporary Brazil

Before proceeding, I will explain my use of racial terms and situate *A Beautiful Fight* within the literature on racial politics in Brazil and the Americas. As I address further below, in this book I take a hemispheric approach to race and racial justice movements in Brazil. Although this approach is well supported by scholarship, it nevertheless contradicts claims to Brazil's racial exceptionalism that still hold sway among many academics and lay people. Such scholars contend that race in Brazil is fluid and ambiguous and that racial binaries are imported from the United States.[21] They suggest that Brazil's racial mixture has produced such a wide array of skin tones and phenotypes that "everyone is mixed [*mestiço*]" (Munanga 2020, 149), and it's therefore "impossible to know" who is Black (S. Santos 2006). Many cite as evidence a 1970s survey reporting that Brazilians used at least 135 distinct terms to describe skin color (*cor*). However, scholars have long since clarified that the vast majority of respondents used one of only several terms, and most Brazilians do think about race in binary terms in their everyday lives (Telles 2004, 82; Mitchell-Walthour 2018, 9). The preoccupation with racial ambiguity truly is an "academic problem" (Perry 2013, xviii).[22] As many scholars, activists, and everyday Brazilians attest, authority figures have no difficulty determining who is Black when racially profiling customers at a bank, for instance, or when targeting Black people for police violence (S. Santos 2006; Perry 2013, xi–xii; Smith 2016, 11).

The supposed indeterminacy of race stems from the ideology of *mestiçagem* (miscegenation), the valorization of racial mixture, which provides Afro-descendant Brazilians with alternatives to identifying as Black (*negro/a*). For example, they may opt for terms such as *moreno/a* (brown), *mestiço/a* (mixed), or the more derogatory and now less common *mulato/a*. On the census, they can choose *parda* (brown) instead of *preta* (black), both historically understood more as color than racial terms. In everyday life, however, many people who identify as pardo/a on the census self-identify as negro/a (not a census category), which is why social scientists generally understand both parda and preta to refer to Afro-descendant, Black (negro/a) people (Mitchell-Walthour 2018, 1–29).[23] Meanwhile, white people can also identify as pardo/a or moreno/a (E. Costa and Schucman 2022). For instance, famous "morena" actors Camila Pitanga and Sônia Braga are considered "the female embodiment of brown standards of Brazilianness" (P. Pinho 2009, 47), and yet these women are also often mistaken as white. Moreno/a further becomes a euphemism when applied to dark-skinned Brazilians (McCallum 2005, 115). Yet calling a dark-skinned woman "morena" does not shield her from racism. It merely denies her Blackness, a phenomenon João Vargas calls the dialectical hyperconsciousness/negation of race in Brazil (Vargas 2004). Similarly, although white people can deny their whiteness, their privilege remains intact (Sovik 2009).

After decades of Black movement activism urging Afro-descendants to assume a unified Black identity (Hanchard 1994; Twine 1998; Crook and Johnson 1999; Munanga 2020), recent years have seen a shift.[24] Afro-Brazilians with a wide range of phenotypes and skin shades now more often self-identify as negro/a, and a growing number also call themselves preto/a. For over a century, "negro/a" has been the preferred term among many Black militants, from São Paulo's Frente Negra Brasileira (Black Brazilian Front) in the 1930s (Andrews 1991), Abdias Nascimento's Teatro Experimental do Negro in 1940s Rio de Janeiro, to the Movimento Negro Unificado formed in the 1970s. Now, however, many young people in Brazil, including many of my interlocutors, are reclaiming "preto/a," which they often use interchangeably with negro/a.[25] Meanwhile, more highly educated Afro-descendants are also more likely to identify as Black rather than mixed (Telles and Paschel 2014).

Members of the Angoleiros do Sertão and its community that I interviewed nearly all self-identified as either Black (negro/a and preto/a) or white (*branco/a*), which I believe reflects both the fact that many members have attended university and the group's political-racial consciousness. I translate both negro/a and preto/a as "Black," following numerous scholars (e.g., Perry 2013; Smith 2016), but I indicate when they use preto/a, as it still carries a different political force. I also consider Black to be synonymous with Afro-Brazilian (*afrobrasileiro/a*) and Afro-descendant (*afrodescendente*), though group members used these terms less frequently. Significantly, out of nearly fifty interviewed, only one person identified as pardo and two people declined to identify racially.[26] I refer to them all as "non-Black" because their views aligned more with white members. I recognize that a binary system of racialization leaves some people out—for instance, people with some Indigenous descent but no ties to an Indigenous community are not considered Indigenous in Brazil, but they may appear neither white nor Black. Debates in Brazil are ongoing as to how such people can or should self-identify. However, I generally see moves to avoid self-racialization as either a distancing from one's Blackness (where assuming Blackness is possible) or a refusal to acknowledge one's white privilege, both of which reinforce anti-Black logics (Jung and Vargas 2021, 7–8).[27]

The intersection of race and class also means that a light-skinned Black person who grows up in a poor, peripheral Black community may experience the effects of systemic racism more acutely than a light-skinned middle-class Black person. Mestre Cláudio exemplifies this situation as a light-skinned Black man—note that I use "light-skinned" only to refer to Afro-Brazilians, not to describe white people—who grew up in the poor peripheries of Feira de Santana, immersed in Black cultural practices. Mestre Cláudio also participated in Feira's Black movement for decades, nurturing a close relationship with Dona Ivannide. Mestre Cláudio identified as Rastafari for many years, though no longer, but he continues to wear his hair in locks, now reaching below his knees but almost always coiled into a tam. He has also described suffering racist humiliations and race-based exclusions, both in Brazil and abroad. Mestre Cláudio's life trajectory thus also illustrates the limits of mestiçagem ideology: being "mixed" has not shielded him from racism, but his lived experience has led him to assume a politicized Black identity.

In my interviews, I asked interviewees how they identified racially rather than providing them with terms to choose from. Throughout the book, I provide their self-identification and a brief description of their appearance or a photograph. This should allow readers to see that in Brazil, as in the United States and across the African diaspora, people with a wide spectrum of skin tones and phenotypes identify as Black—and there is variation among white phenotypes, too. After all, as a social construct, race is by definition malleable (not only in Brazil) and has very real, fundamental effects on people's lives (Omi and Winant 2014).

Forming a "Mixed" Nation

Although in broad strokes race and anti-Blackness function in similar ways across the Americas, the formation of racial ideologies in Brazil has followed its own course. Over the twentieth century, the Brazilian state consolidated an official narrative whereby it incorporated Black Brazilian culture into the national fabric to create a "mixed" nation of three "races"—Indigeneity was assumed already to be in the mix.[28] It's important to recognize, however, that Brazil's valorization of Blackness has never contributed materially to improving Black lives in systemic ways; nor has it granted Black people full participation and leadership in the political system; nor has it hindered the state from perpetuating its genocide of Black people.[29] The celebration of Blackness as essential to Brazilianness (*brasilidade*) has always been paired with violent practices of denying Black Brazilians their humanity and lives.

Transitioning from slavocracy to republic, Brazil entered its "high period of racist thought—1880 to 1920," under which white ruling elites pursued "whitening," viewed as both the unavoidable destiny and solution to the population's undesired Blackness (Skidmore 1993, 46). Yet by the 1930s it became clear that Brazil's Blackness would not be whitened away. Sociologist and anthropologist Gilberto Freyre most prominently advocated a new solution. Radically reevaluating the contributions of Africans and their descendants to Brazilian society, Freyre proposed conceiving of Brazil's national culture as mestiço, incorporating Black/African elements rather than seeking to expunge them (Dunn 2001, 24).[30] This new mestiçagem ideology did not replace whitening ideology so much as reframe it to allow the valuing of "Black things" (Vianna 1999, 8–9). Mestiçagem still aimed to whiten or lighten the country, but now this was to occur by incorporating Blackness metaphorically into the national fabric (Munanga 2020). Thus under dictator Getúlio Vargas's Estado Novo regime (1937–1945), "racial and social differences were subsumed by a unitary concept of national culture based on mestiçagem," and the largely Black povo were constructed as a "social and political category" (Dunn 2001, 26–27) that was identified overtly along class not racial lines. Blackness became a symbolic mark of authentic Brazilian identity, but only in abstraction, folded into mestiçagem. According to this narrative, which endures today, "blackness and black people are mutually exclusive," and Black culture can be divorced from Black people and their lived experience (Smith 2016, 13). Mestiçagem ideology thus empowers white Brazilians to claim (some) Blackness while still excluding Black people from the nation (Sovik 2009, 50).

Mestiçagem is also the basis for Brazil identifying as a "racial democracy," in which racial mixture is held as evidence that racism does not exist in Brazil. (Under this system, observed racial inequalities are explained away in terms of class.) The idea that Blackness is essential to Brazilian identity and therefore accessible to all non-Black people continues to have remarkable staying power, as does the embrace of racial democracy as an ideal, even long after it has been proven a harmful myth.[31] As Abdias do Nascimento argued decades ago, the assimilation of Black culture into Brazil's national fabric is a tool of whitening and genocide because it reduces Black people to a "non-entity," the "raw material" used to construct a non-Black nation (A. Nascimento 1989, 61). Following this logic, in Bahia the "re-Africanization" of carnival has been co-opted by the state to uphold the myth of a racially inclusive polity (Paschel 2009), and the production of Salvador as a racially democratic "Afro-paradise" paradoxically depends upon the state's targeting of Black bodies for violence (Smith 2016).

Appropriation and Its Discontents

Within this broader context, *A Beautiful Fight* examines the racial politics of a multiracial capoeira community. Doing so, the book joins a robust literature on white consumption, emulation, imitation, embodiment, and "theft" of Black cultural practices in the Americas and beyond.[32] In the first decades of the twenty-first century these phenomena are commonly subsumed under "cultural appropriation," but they are of course more complex than they often appear in debates in popular and social media, many of which center on hairstyles, clothing, and musical practices.[33] Indeed, scholars have rightly argued that focusing on cultural appropriation can obscure complexities of cultural transmission (Desmond 1993, 57) and stifle other approaches to studying cultural dissemination (Griffith 2023, 8). Yet cultural appropriation remains an issue of vital concern for Black Brazilian activists, intellectuals, and many capoeira practitioners as they see white presence growing in Black practices that remain vitally significant for Black people's spirituality, identity, history, and politics.

A Beautiful Fight intervenes in the literature in several ways. Most significantly, in contrast to studies that examine white consumption of Black culture largely in the absence of Black people, this book addresses a group deeply embedded within a Black community in rural northeast Brazil, in the sertão of Bahia, in which practitioners of diverse racial identities and socioeconomic backgrounds forge deep affective bonds.[34] Moving beyond questions, for instance, of whether white people should wear Black hairstyles or Afrocentric clothing, both of which many white capoeira players do, the book asks what kinds of relationships, allyships, conflicts, and political possibilities emerge when practitioners cultivate community through practicing an African diasporic music-movement form. Contending with the nuanced racial politics of a multiracial community of practice, I heed hip hop dance scholar Imani Kai Johnson's distinction: "There is a difference between staking a claim to a culture (i.e., appropriation) and the culture's staking a claim to you, possessing you, moving you in unfamiliar and possibly uncomfortable ways that become essential to a person's existence" (2020, 192).[35] Echoing Johnson, I ask in what ways "Africanizing" white bodies and minds might move them in relation not only to Blackness but also to Black political movements (193).

A great deal of literature has examined how participatory music-dance practices forge diverse communities, sometimes with the aim of pursuing social justice.[36] Where *A Beautiful Fight* diverges from much of the literature is in its insistence on critique. Though I have tried to tread carefully, I have not let the capoeira group's euphoric sociality divert my attention from underlying tensions and tears in its social fabric.[37] In this way, the book shifts the emphasis from more celebratory claims about the power of music-dance to unify communities across difference. Beyond music and dance studies, similar ideas persist in popular imaginaries around the benefits of racial integration (E. Anderson 2010; Treuke 2020). Both in post–civil rights era United States and under the spell of Brazil's racial democracy, integration (also called inclusion and diversity) is often assumed to automatically counter racism. Yet as Beverly Daniel Tatum cites Dr. Martin Luther King Jr.'s warning years ago, integration alone "cannot bring an end to fears, prejudice, pride and irrationality" (Tatum 2019, 80). Tatum elaborates: "*Empathic* contact must be created. It is not enough to be in the same neighborhood, or even in the same room" (80; original emphasis). Music-dance communities are often taken to be ideal spaces for facilitating this kind of "empathic contact," yet this book reveals that harmful ideologies can persist even within closely knit, politically progressive communities of practice.[38] In this way, the book tempers claims about capoeira's capacity to overcome racist ways of thinking and to politicize practitioners while carefully articulating capoeira's potentials, even if they remain largely unrealized.

The book's examination of white involvement in capoeira is grounded in Black community members' perspectives on capoeira as a political (and politicizing) practice and their critiques of whiteness. Therefore, I ask: What are the consequences for Black community members, and for capoeira's potential to valorize Black humanity, when so many white people join in capoeira's Black movement?

Black Movements: Antiracism and Anticoloniality in the Afterlife of Slavery

Recognizing capoeira as part of the Black movement in Brazil, I also place capoeira among multiple Black movements across the Americas (Colbert 2017). This does not deny the specificity of Brazilian racial ideologies and processes of racialization,[39] but rather acknowledges the hemispheric reach of anti-Blackness and the transnational solidarities forged among activists and scholars who fight against it (Bowen et al. 2017). Across the Americas and regions within Brazil, "multiple racisms" manifest in "heterogeneous forms and guises" (Caldwell 2007, 9). Nevertheless, Black people in different spheres face similar disparities in education, health care, mortality (R. Oliveira et al. 2020), as well as higher chances of suffering police violence and incarceration (Vargas 2008). Black people in Brazil, as in the United States and other sites, confront similarly "skewed life chances" living in what Saidiya Hartman has called the "afterlife of slavery" (Hartman 2008a, 6). Meanwhile, Black movements across the Americas, often led by Black women, continue to organize antiracist resistance, often independently of one another but with increasing transnational dialogue and solidarity.[40]

Hemispheric antiracist mobilizations move within a global context shaped by long-enduring entanglements of anti-Blackness and coloniality.[41] Sylvia Wynter demonstrates that contemporary struggles organized around "race, class, gender, sexual orientation . . . the environment, global warming, severe climate change, the sharply unequal distribution of the earth [*sic*] resources . . . are all differing facets" of a broader struggle of "the central ethnoclass Man vs. Human" spanning oceans and centuries (Wynter 2003, 260–61). Wynter explains that Europeans have consolidated and justified their power by establishing a "descriptive statement" of the human: in the first, theocentric phase, from the fourteenth to eighteenth centuries, Man was defined as Christian in distinction from all non-Christian Others (264). In the second phase, as the church gave way to the state, religion to reason, they constructed "race" to replace the previous description (of non-Christians) and describe Man as human in contrast to subhuman racialized Others (264). In this second phase, Indigenous peoples of the Americas and enslaved Black Africans "were made to reoccupy the matrix slot of Otherness—to be made into the physical referent of the idea of the irrational/subrational Human Other, to this first degodded (if still hybridly religio-secular) 'descriptive statement' of the human in history," and this new "descriptive statement . . . would be foundational to modernity" (266).

Wynter's *longue durée* vision shows how Europeans created a category—that of Other to Man, subhuman to Man-as-human—into which they could insert a wide range of diverse peoples—including not only those racialized as Other but also those whose sexualities, genders, religions, or other deviations from Man disqualified them from being human. Importantly, Wynter's theorizing does not collapse, for instance, Indigenous and Black/African experience into one another. Rather, Wynter and other theorists in this vein recognize the cumulative violence of racism, white supremacy, and coloniality. As Tiffany Lethabo King underscores, the European "conquistador-settler" created multiple, flexible systems of oppression out of the same logic (2019, xi). In sum, "White humanity and its self-actualization require Black and Native death as its condition of possibility" (King 2019, 21).

What is needed to counter this violence, Wynter argues, is a new "descriptive statement" of the human originated by those who live at the margins (2003) or what Black Brazilian activists call the periferia—spaces that are "simultaneously ensconced in and outside the world of Man" (Weheliye 2014, 25). After all, such spaces have sustained Black alternative ways of knowing and being for centuries. Capoeira Angola's most radical, "voracious" potential, I propose, would be to function as one such liminal space, a metaphorical quilombo (B. Nascimento 2023; Henson 2024) within which practitioners could collectively construct alternative descriptive statements of the human. If these statements are a "Black counter-voice" (Wynter 2003, 268), then *A Beautiful Fight* asks what sounds, timbres, or harmonies capoeira Angola adds to a Black counter-voice. And what are the various ways in which Black, white, and non-Black players can contribute to the singing?

Toward a Black Studies Ethnomusicology

The questions that drive *A Beautiful Fight* thus align with the broad political impetus behind Black/Africana studies and hemispheric Black feminist thought. The project of Black studies has emerged over centuries out of social-political movements seeking to undermine and abolish white supremacist patriarchal coloniality, ultimately aiming to create new liberatory ways of being.[42] With this understanding of Black studies as my north star, I undertake my analysis of capoeira's racial politics not only to describe injustice but also in efforts to redress racial harms (Tomlinson and Lipsitz 2013, 13). I have also taken as models the work of music scholars who have developed critical approaches to studying Black music that center issues of racism or social justice.[43] Here I draw a careful distinction between scholarship that is critically concerned with Black people's experiences and political struggles and scholarship on Black music that sidelines issues of racial injustice. For despite its long history of studying Black musics and Black peoples, the field of ethnomusicology as a whole has yet to embrace Black studies or the work of Black ethnomusicologists who engage with its radical project (Harris 2022, 225). A similar critique resounds in Brazil, where a cohort of Black ethnomusicologists is arguing for a "Black Ethnomusicology" that accounts for Black people's experiences and perspectives (M. Oliveira 2018; Rosa 2020; G. Nascimento 2021).[44]

At stake is the timely yet cyclical issue of ethnomusicology's enduring coloniality and racism, recently revisited in Danielle Brown's "Open Letter on Racism in Music Studies" (Brown 2020) but echoing earlier critiques of ethnomusicology's "othering" (Agawu 2003). While ethnomusicologists have grappled with the coloniality of the field in ebbs and flows, they have largely resisted advocating for racial justice in their research (Wong 2006, 262).[45] In 2006, Deborah Wong noted that "ethnomusicologists [had] finally begun to define their research around questions of difference," but were doing so "very cautiously—often with a conflicted avoidance of critique, evidenced by the avoidance of theoretical models focused on social justice issues" (2006, 266). More recently, Maureen Mahon (2019) found that the field still had yet to center the "question of race," despite earlier efforts to remedy the lacuna (e.g., Radano and Bohlman 2000). While more recent studies theorize race and racial formation, many still tend to downplay Black people's "social experiences of race and racism" (Ramsey 2022, 96).

To be clear, I am not suggesting that Black people's experiences can be reduced to racism but rather reiterating that white scholars' failure to confront issues of systemic racism and coloniality—in our scholarship, universities, and lives—only perpetuates harm and trauma (Harris 2022). One practice white scholars can undertake is to engage more, and more robustly, with "the artistic/scholarly work of BIPOC ethnomusicologists" (Harris 2022, 227), and I add that white ethnomusicologists must also engage with Black thinkers beyond music studies.[46] Essentially, I endorse Chávez and Skelchy's proposal that ethnomusicology curricula, pedagogy, and research be grounded in critical ethnic studies (2019), which I understand as a heterogeneous convening of fields, knowledges, and politics that emerged from "critical intellectual traditions and counter-hegemonic struggles" (Shange 2019, 7; F. Harrison 1991, 1) but that does not collapse their "epistemological tensions, ontological discontinuities, and historical-experiential incommensurabilities" (C.E.S.E. Collective 2016, 5). In other words, what fields such as Black, Indigenous, and Afro-Latin American studies share is that they were all founded by collectives of people who were systemically excluded from academia and who fought to tell their own stories and theorize their own practices and politics.[47] Thus part of the problem is not that ethnomusicology retains its "ethno-" modification (cf. Amico 2020), but rather that so many in the field do not engage sufficiently with scholarship whose political imperative is to respond to the calls of racialized people to value their lives and fight their continued dehumanization.[48]

Grounded Theory and Methods of *Convivência*

My questions about capoeira's racial politics emerged in dialogue with capoeira players, interviewees, community members, professors, and classmates and from seeking to determine how I can best contribute to knowledge about Afro-Brazilian music and dance. Reflecting on my position as a white, foreign researcher-practitioner, I have chosen to follow a grounded approach to theory and methods. Technically, grounding theory means "minimiz[ing] commitment to received and preconceived theory" in favor of deriving analytical and theoretical categories from data (Emerson, Fretz, and Shaw 2011, 172), which here includes interviews, field notes, informal conversations, videos, and embodied knowledge passed body-to-body while training, playing music, playing capoeira, and dancing samba. I also understand a grounded approach to include shifting my questions to align with group members' priorities. To illustrate, while I began the project wanting to know how capoeira changed practitioners' political-racial consciousness, I eventually came to focus more on members' critiques of white participation. Thus I have grounded the study in community members' theories, concepts, terms, perspectives, and concerns.

However, I do not exclude theory from beyond the research context, though I engage with it carefully.[49] For instance, I purposefully draw on Black feminist thought from North America, Brazil, and the Caribbean because these ideas also align with community members' intellectual engagements and political commitments (Caldwell et al. 2018). Indeed, a key premise of this book is that subjects already theorize their own practices (Christian 1987) through their sounds, movements, discourse, and political activism: their theorizing is "action and practice already in motion" (DeFrantz and Gonzalez 2014, 7). For these reasons, I try to privilege interlocutors' voices, citing both their spoken and written words throughout (Smith et al. 2021) and using their real names or *apelidos* (nicknames) as they indicated, with some exceptions.[50]

Working from this "commonsense" understanding that capoeira community members were the experts (Hale and Stephen 2013, 3), and learning from the "limited location" of my "particular and specific embodiment" (Haraway 1988, 582–83), I have also aligned my methods with the preferred means of knowledge transmission in Afro-Brazilian cultural spaces: *convivência* (Lühning 1990, 117). Convivência, literally "living with," entails learning through experiencing and spending time with knowledge bearers: listening, observing, adopting the humble posture of apprentice, and refraining from asking too many questions.[51] (Mestre Cláudio often expressed irritation about students who asked for verbal explanations, comparing them to hungry baby birds who needed pre-masticated food fed to them.) As anthropologist Aimee Meredith Cox learned from interacting with Black women activists and elders, "You entered spaces with humility and grace. You observed and listened before assessing and acting" (2020, 119). Convivência also means paying close attention to the wordless ways people make music and move through the roda and their lives. It involves body-to-body learning, watching, imitating (Downey 2008), and listening with the body (Díaz Meneses 2016). Convivência gestures toward a way to "take the thing into yourself but without the avaricious asymmetry of ethnography's past and present" (Wong 2021, 200).

Convivência resonates powerfully with critical ethnographic methods such as "co-performative witnessing," which includes sharing "temporality," putting "bodies on the line," listening to "soundscapes of power," and "liv[ing] in and spend[ing] time in the borderlands of contested identities where you speak 'with' not 'to' others" (Madison 2007, 827–28). This dialogic approach means that while I ground my research in members' meanings, I do not try to remove myself, pulling a "god trick" (Haraway 1988). Rather, I have woven the political concerns of community members together with my own, both in the moments of our interviews and in the text. In our conversations, I not only listened deeply to the people I spoke with but also challenged their ideas. When I was fortunate, they challenged mine, too. Thus our conversations were often intense discussions about issues we care deeply about.[52] By revealing my thoughts, concerns, and politics, in the field and in this book, I open them up to generative scrutiny by interlocutors and readers alike.

Taking convivência seriously also influenced my decision to train exclusively with Mestre Cláudio and the Angoleiros do Sertão. In the capoeira world, when foreign students travel from group to group, training for short times with multiple mestres, this signals that they are only superficially interested in any one mestre's unique understandings of capoeira. It is disrespectful, if commonplace. Though I write specifically about the Angoleiros do Sertão, many of my findings will apply to other capoeira groups and styles, and to other musical or activist contexts, and I try to indicate throughout where I believe Mestre Cláudio's group may be unique. Finally, my ability to engage in convivência again reveals my privilege. A *contramestre* of a satellite group in São Paulo state once remarked that I had probably spent more total time with Mestre Cláudio than he had in over twenty years with the group, because he generally saw the mestre only twice a year, for several days to a week or two at a time.

My in-person fieldwork with the Angoleiros do Sertão spanned twelve months in Brazil, from 2013 to 2023, on six trips ranging from two weeks to four months, with my longest stays occurring in 2015, 2016, and 2017. In Brazil I spent time with Mestre Cláudio at his *roça* (rural property) on the outskirts of Feira de Santana but also traveled with him to train with many of the group's núcleos, mostly in São Paulo state and Recife, Pernambuco. I also visited Mestre Cláudio in 2019 in the United States and brought him to St. Louis later that year. While not in Brazil, I have kept in touch with group members through WhatsApp and social media, and during the pandemic I participated in weekly online classes and group meetings (*bate-papos*) intensively for six months. I conducted forty-nine interviews with group and community members, most of which lasted one to two hours. In this work, I have built on my capoeira training, begun in 2006. Prior to beginning my graduate studies in 2012, I had spent a total of seven months in Brazil.

Dona Ivannide and Mestre Cláudio

Turning now to introduce Mestre Cláudio and his group, the Angoleiros do Sertão, I begin by introducing Dona Ivannide, one of Feira de Santana's most prominent Black movement militants, who has had a formative influence on Mestre Cláudio's political philosophy. Dona Ivannide has oriented Mestre Cláudio and his students in radical Black political thought since he began his group in the mid-1980s. Their friendship, though based on a shared commitment to Black liberation, has also been turbulent as they asserted contrasting visions of how to practice Black resistance and realize Black freedom. While Dona Ivannide's thought is grounded in an organic kind of Black feminist Marxist critique, Mestre Cláudio's views are more (neo)liberal, espousing a bootstraps philosophy of Black people lifting themselves out of poverty through hard, self-sufficient work. The conflicts between the two have sometimes disrupted their collaboration, as when Dona Ivannide criticized Mestre Cláudio for teaching capoeira to whites, and he then refused to invite her to lecture at his events for several years in a row, out of concern that she would alienate his white students. Dona Ivannide is also publicly critical of Mestre Cláudio, speaking at annual events in his presence about his insufficient valorization of the contributions of female group members, including his wife, Rita. Yet while they will surely never align completely in their thinking, they also credit each other with expanding one another's thought, thus revealing their capacities for change and growth. Like many group members, I have gleaned crucial lessons from observing how Mestre Cláudio and Dona Ivannide challenge one another from a place of love, and I strive to emulate their commitments to principled critique, generosity, compassion, and flexibility of thought in this book and in my life.

Dona Ivannide: Black Women's Activism in Feira

Ivannide Rodrigues Santa Barbara was born in 1950 in Feira de Santana. Her mother was a Black domestic worker and her father a wealthy Black doctor, but they were not in a relationship. Her mother, unable to provide financially for Ivannide and her twin brother, gave them up for adoption to a white couple. Dona Ivannide told me she believes that her adoptive mother had intended to raise her as a *criada*, referring to the practice whereby white families "adopt" Black children to be "raised" (*criado/a*) as domestic laborers, thus perpetuating a system of informal enslavement (Hordge-Freeman 2022). However, she said, her mother ended up "falling in love" with her and raised her like a true daughter. (Her adoptive father died when she was only ten years old.) While she was in high school, her biological father was her biology teacher for four years, yet he never acknowledged her as his daughter, even though their resemblance was so striking that her schoolmates constantly teased her about it. Even worse, in class he talked incessantly about spoiling his own adopted (white!) daughter, giving her cars and other luxuries, while Ivannide went hungry when her mother, working as a washerwoman, didn't earn enough to buy food.

As she told her story to me in this way, I sensed that Dona Ivannide was revealing how her critical racial consciousness had grown in part from grappling with painful personal contradictions in her life. She said bluntly, "My mother was a racist." Yet, she told me, they loved each other as mother and daughter. Yet again, despite loving her white mother, in her earlier more militant years, she was extremely "intolerant of whites." She used to criticize Mestre Cláudio ruthlessly for teaching capoeira Angola to whites, for selling Black culture to *gringos* (foreigners) and *Paulistas* (residents of São Paulo state). But she also credited Mestre Cláudio for tempering her views of white people: "Even though I still consider all of you heirs of the colonizers, who therefore have responsibilities, I don't consider you my enemies, individually. I believe that we can construct something different, going forward, in the future." Without him, she said, she would not be sitting here talking with me. Just as Mestre Cláudio acknowledges Dona Ivannide's profound influence on his political thinking, she claims that Mestre Cláudio helped her reconstruct her philosophy of race relations. "It has been very good, our convivência."

Dona Ivannide's narrative poignantly illustrates the complexities of racialized lived experience. The seemingly contradictory details of her provenance—a militant Black movement activist raised lovingly by a poor white single mother, while her wealthy Black biological father disowned her—bring into sharp relief the importance of distinguishing the individual from the systemic. Her story also shows that the messiness of lived relationships does not always map easily onto broader racialized relations of power. Yet it is from within the power of such lived experience that Black women like Dona Ivannide generate radical, necessary knowledge. Black women in Brazil, across the Americas, and in the diaspora, in addition to contributing academic work, "produce everyday knowledge in social movements, community groups and other collective spaces" (A. Mattos and Xavier 2016, 240), and in spaces that do not always identify as "activist" (Caldwell 2007, 170). However, while Black feminist scholars have long recognized the critical-political knowledge Black women produce from the margins, much academic research still often "focuses on public, official, visible political activity," failing to see the "unofficial, private, and seemingly invisible spheres of social life and organization" (P. Collins 2000, 202).[53]

Dona Ivannide's activism spans these spheres: public, private, unofficial, and official. She studied economics at the public State University of Feira de Santana (UEFS) though did not finish her degree (R. Santa Barbara 2007, 2). Prior to studying, she worked as an extensionist (*extencionista social*), organizing rural women domestic workers, then a labor union organizer, where it seems she developed a Marxist understanding of class issues. Noting the absence of racial analysis in these spaces, however, she studied "the racial question" further, eventually formulating her Black Marxist critique while organizing with the Black movement in Feira. Most recently she has served as president of the Workers' Party in Feira, and in 2023 she received an honorary doctorate from UEFS. Dona Ivannide has also mentored generations of activists and cultural actors in the city, including young reggae musicians, first-generation Black university students, and many members of the Angoleiros do Sertão.

When I arrived in Brazil to conduct fieldwork in June 2013, I intended to include as many women practitioners as possible in the study. Most previous capoeira literature focused on male mestres, and when practitioners were the focus, gender was not. Yet there was only one woman training regularly in Feira de Santana at the time. As I visited the group's satellite schools, mostly in São Paulo state, I interviewed women in those groups, but almost all of them were white. I was encountering the "absented presence" of Black women even in capoeira Angola (McKittrick 2006, xxv), a cultural-political space that was supposed to empower all Black people. In Bahia but also across Brazil, the intersecting oppressions of economics, sexism (*machismo*), and racism pose significant barriers for Black women's participation.[54] Many Black women I met worked both outside and inside the home, sometimes as primary wage earners, sometimes studying toward advanced degrees, caring for children and family, which left little time for training. Compounded stigmas also make capoeira a fraught space for Black women. While all Black capoeira players risk further "Blackening" themselves by being involved in capoeira, Black women further risk having their sexuality questioned—often being called lesbians or sluts—thus compromising their respectability.

I soon learned, however, that Black women were very much present in the group's community, just not always as capoeira players. In January 2014, at the annual event on Mestre Cláudio's compound in Feira's outskirts, I met Karine Teixeira Damasceno, a Black woman activist from Feira who had just completed her master's degree in history, writing about Black women's historical "transgressions of social and legal rules" in Feira de Santana, and was about to embark on her PhD, which she has since earned (Damasceno 2022, 2023). She had trained briefly with the group when she was younger but eventually chose to prioritize her academic studies and involvement with local Black movement activism. Still, she stayed connected with the group because she valued capoeira Angola as "a political-cultural movement." When I first met her, Karine spoke highly of Dona Ivannide, her mentor, and founder of the activist group Frente Negra de Feira de Santana (FRENEFE). I soon also met Iaiá, Karine's friend and Dona Ivannide's daughter (see fig. 3). I resolved to interview these women upon my return, and our conversations have profoundly impacted the critiques and arguments of this book.[55]

Mestre Cláudio Costa and the Angoleiros do Sertão

Se eu contar meu nascimento	If I tell you the story of my birth
vocês pode ate chorar	you might even cry
Mesmo antes de nascer	Even before I was born
o meu pai me abandonou.	my father abandoned me
iê! Minha mãe criou três filhos	iê! My mother raised three children
comeu pão que o diabo amassou.	she suffered from deprivation.
iê! Eu nasci na roça	iê! I was born on the *roça*
e não andava de carro	and I didn't travel by car
Era cavalo ou a pé	It was by horse or on foot
Hoje eu ando de avião	Today I go by plane
eu vou pra onde eu quiser	and I go wherever I want
As vezes, eu digo que não vou	Sometimes, I say I won't go
e vocês pode levar fé	and you better believe it
iê! Capoeira cresceu tanto	iê! Capoeira has grown so much
capoeira conquistou valor	capoeira has proven its value
Capoeira me deu tudo	Capoeira has given me everything
Capoeira me educou	Capoeira educated/raised me
Sempre acreditei na capoeira	I always believed in capoeira

Figure 3. Iaiá (Urania do Carmo Rodrigues Santa Barbara), left, with her mother, Dona Ivannide (Ivannide Rodrigues Santa Barbara), after the capoeira and samba rodas in January 2017. Photo by the author.

é pobre de quem não acreditou	Poor is he who didn't believe
Viva Bahia!	Long live Bahia!

Mestre Cláudio Costa was born in 1966 on the outskirts of Feira de Santana. As he recounts in the preceding *ladainha*, the pensive litany-song that begins a capoeira roda, he was raised by his single Black mother, Dona Antônia, along with two siblings. He never had a relationship with his father, who was white or light-skinned. Among other jobs, Dona Antônia sold *acarajé*, the traditional bean fritter snack, but was unable to feed her children some days. Rita, Cláudio's wife, recounted how Cláudio and his friends would rummage through trash bins to find discarded scraps to eat. One of his friends was nicknamed Yoghurt, because he loved it so much. Rita and Cláudio had recently run into Yoghurt. He was in a wheelchair, having survived being shot eight times but left paralyzed. The rest of Cláudio's childhood friends, she told me, were dead, having gone to violence, drugs, or otherwise succumbing to their skewed life chances. This is why Mestre Cláudio sings that capoeira has given him everything—including his life—and this is why he gives everything to capoeira.

Through his mother and her family, Mestre Cláudio grew up immersed in the "alternative spaces of Blackness" of Candomblé and samba de roda (Harding 2000). He proudly identifies as Black, tracing his descent from enslaved people who worked the land of the Bahian sertão, pointing out that his surname, Costa, was given to enslaved people taken from the Gold Coast (*Costa da Mina*, in Portuguese) of Africa. Mestre Cláudio's emphatic assertion that the rural backland of Bahia has its own forms of Black Brazilian cultura popular refutes both academic and popular assumptions that Black culture is centered in Brazil's coastal cities and regions.

Cláudio began capoeira as a young boy on the streets of Feira de Santana, but there were no capoeira mestres in Feira at the time. When he moved to Salvador as a teenager, following his mother, who was pursuing more lucrative work, he dropped out of high school to train at Mestre Dimola's capoeira academy. Returning to Feira several years later, he witnessed an old, worn capoeirista playing "low to the ground" in a street roda during Feira's carnivalesque Micareta festival and thought, *This is the capoeira that I want!* He began to seek it out and soon learned it was capoeira Angola. At this time, in the 1980s, capoeira Angola was undergoing a revival led most prominently by students of Mestre Pastinha's school based in Salvador. But Cláudio learned the style on his own, *avulso*, separately, observing and training in every spare moment. When he was only twenty-two years old, he taught at a capoeira workshop in São Paulo and the older mestres there called him "mestre." As he had no mestre of his own, he could not be officially "formed" as a mestre, but he became a mestre by community consensus, in the way of the old mestres.

Settled in Mantiba, a dirt-road community in Feira's periphery not far from his childhood home, Mestre Cláudio established his school, the Angoleiros do Sertão, in the mid-1980s. Eventually he moved his classes to the University Center of Culture and Art (CUCA), an arts and performance space run by UEFS in downtown Feira, where he still teaches today. To my knowledge, in contrast to Salvador's saturated capoeira scene, the Angoleiros do Sertão remains the only capoeira Angola group in Feira de Santana and the surrounding region.

Mestre Cláudio's decision to stay in Feira de Santana rather than move abroad to Europe or the United States, where he could make much more money, is directly connected to his politics. By founding his capoeira Angola school in Bahia's sertão, Mestre Cláudio intentionally refutes the region's misrepresentations as not only politically and intellectually backward but also devoid of Black culture.[56] He has built an international reputation championing his backland styles of capoeira Angola and samba de roda, which he calls "samba rural." He also vocally contests dominant scholarly narratives that emphasize capoeira's birth in the cities of Salvador (Pires 2004; Abreu 2005; J. Oliveira 2006; Abib 2009) and Rio de Janeiro (Soares 1994, 2001), claiming that enslaved people in rural areas also contributed to capoeira's development, which aligns with origin narratives that place capoeira's birth on plantations. Many of the famous mestres of Brazil, he points out, came from the interior of Bahia state, begging the question of how they learned capoeira if it supposedly existed only in urban areas. He also finds evidence of capoeira's rural origins in its older "traditional" (and public domain) capoeira songs, the ones he privileges in his rodas, which reference cattle, cowboys, and other rural themes. In these ways, Mestre Cláudio claims the sertão as a site of Black cultural production.

By centering the perspectives and critical thought of Feira de Santana's Black cultural-political leaders and their mentees, this book provides a counternarrative to the prolific scholarship on Black culture and politics in Salvador, Bahia, the bordering Recôncavo region surrounding the Bay of All Saints, and other urban centers in Brazil. Doing so, *A Beautiful Fight* underscores the contributions of Black cultural workers and activists that are largely overlooked by coastal elites, academics, and activists.

Chapter Outline

The book's four chapters explore practitioners' interpretations of capoeira's politics from a variety of perspectives. Chapter 1 describes how group members cohere their community by cultivating "axé," a term originally from the Afro-Brazilian religion Candomblé, which they reference to explain their sensations in the capoeira and samba rodas. They talk about axé as an affective, vibrational force that fosters positive energy when transmitted through music, sound, and movement in capoeira and samba. Practitioners experience axé in the music-movement as a "call" (*chama/chamada*) that not only exerts a force on their bodies but also calls them to assume a range of responsibilities in the roda and in their lives. Mestre Cláudio frames these responsibilities as *compromisso* (commitment), another concept borrowed from Candomblé.

Chapter 2 reveals that many Black practitioners sense their *ancestralidade* (ancestrality) in capoeira's axé. For them, the call of axé extends across time and brings the past into the present by evoking visceral images of a lived past under enslavement. When they witness the sounds and movements of the capoeira roda, they envision their ancestral past in enslavement, which in turn reinforces their commitments to create a better future through Black movement activism. I argue that sensing ancestralidade thus fuels community members' dedication to building a world where Black lives have value and Black humanity is redescribed and unquestioned.

Chapter 3 considers how many white Brazilian practitioners also claim to be able to access "Black/African ancestralidade," even though they acknowledge not sharing African descent. The chapter explores how white Brazilian practitioners seek to consume Blackness and Bahian Black culture. They also value capoeira as a practice of freedom and resistance, and they associate capoeira with Brazil's Black movement. However, they often insist that they have no place in Black movement politics. I argue that by reproducing white colonialist consumption of Blackness, white practitioners decline to translate their powerful sensations into a sense of political urgency, and thus they divert energies from Black community members' efforts to confront anti-Blackness in Brazil.

Chapter 4 complicates the critique of white participation in the capoeira Angola group by examining the capoeira group's economic structure. Visiting practitioners—group members, tourists, and researchers, usually white—come to Bahia and pay to experience Black culture and "recharge their batteries" with the energy of axé. Mestre Cláudio has built an international capoeira Angola enterprise around this exchange, and he proudly defends his running of the group as a business. Yet the business operates in an informal economy, with no benefits, job security, or pension. Mestre Cláudio, like other mestres, therefore also uses informal tactics to secure his income, some of which reproduce historical patterns of Brazilian white patronage and others that involve extracting money from white foreigners. While foreigners often interpret these tactics as "deception," I argue for understanding these practices in their larger historical context as a form of reparations, however limited, for past (personal and historical) injustices.

In the epilogue, I revisit key concepts from capoeira discussed in the book to show how capoeira Angola contains valuable wisdom for collaboratively contesting anti-Blackness, but I argue that these tools must be used with intention, commitment, and care.

One

Sensing *Axé*

Sound, Movement, and Commitment in the African Matrix

Capoeira, Candomblé, and samba—*é três conjunto que não se separa* [the three can't be separated].

—Contramestre Orikerê

The Saturday Morning Roda

With repeated triplets on the stringed-bow berimbau, then a downward swipe of his arm striking the wire with the *baqueta* (wooden stick) and a simultaneous "iê!" Mestre Cláudio ends the roda held on the median strip of a main thoroughfare in Feira de Santana, on one of its busiest market days (see fig. 4). The bateria stops playing on cue, and onlookers erupt in applause and whistles. On this Saturday morning in May 2016 the crowd is typical. Capoeira group members wear uniforms of white T-shirts with the group logo and brown pants, and many have their hair tucked into tams of Rastafari colors (red, yellow, green, black). Also in attendance are several mestres from local groups of capoeira Regional, and drummers from local Candomblés in street clothes. Dozens of residents from Feira's peripheries and the surrounding region fill out the circle. Many attend regularly, dressed to impress in colorful shirts, tight-fitting dresses, animal prints, or tanks and short jean cut-offs. Others wear work uniforms, pants with reflective stripes, or T-shirts with company logos; many carry tied-up plastic bags with recent purchases from one of Feira's innumerable market stalls or shops. They flock to the roda to participate in Mestre Cláudio's loud, public, moving-sounding declaration of the value of Black Bahian culture. The roda is an alternative

Figure 4. Mestre Cláudio holding the berra-boi berimbau at a Saturday roda, clutching a caxixi shaker and baqueta stick in his right hand; in his left hand, a coin poised to close the metal wire (*arame*). Photo by the author, 2016.

space, temporarily temporarily formed in the shade of a generous tree, where Black community members show up to be heard, to be seen, and to belong.

Most of the players and audience gathered in the ring are of African descent but not all, and they present a range of skin tones, from darker to lighter brown or tan. I may stand out with my white skin, as I'm lighter and less tanned even than the Bahian group members who identify as white. Onlookers may think I'm European or from southern Brazil, but I am no anomaly. Regular attendees know that white and other non-Black visitors, whether tourists or white Brazilians from São Paulo state, frequently visit this now-legendary roda, especially during the group's annual event in January. Something pulls all of us together, from as far away as the Brazilian state of Amazonas, Europe, North America, and Japan. As Mestre Cláudio says, "*Capoeira agrega*": capoeira assembles unlikely mixes of people from disparate socioeconomic conditions, regions, racial identities, and nationalities.

Immediately when the capoeira music stops, Mestre Cláudio's students, members of the Angoleiros do Sertão, launch into a well-rehearsed choreography to prepare for the samba. They suspend the berimbaus from a nail on the thick tree trunk and gingerly lay the atabaque down on backpacks piled inside the roda's edge, kept safe from opportunistic passers-by. Two *timbals*, tauter tapered drums, louder and higher pitched, are moved to the rim of the roda to lead Mestre Cláudio's samba rural. Drummers (group or community members) tie the twine, secured on either side of each timbal, around their hips to hold the drum fast. Another member places the *bumbo* bass drum on an unfolded stand. He takes out a roll of black electrical tape and bites off a length to wrap around his fingers to protect against blisters, and one of the timbal players leans over to ask for some. Others hand out percussion instruments (see figs. 5 and 6). I take a pair of wood blocks, focusing my attention on the mestre.

Mestre Cláudio begins to sing the call without accompaniment, voice straining above the traffic noise: "*Vou vender meu boi, não tenho troco.*" We respond at a third lower in pitch, bodies taut, listening to the mestre (see musical example 1).[1] As more people arrive, they squeeze into the spaces between bodies, vying for a spot from which to spring into the circle. As he sings, the mestre moves about the roda, organizing the space by gesturing for people to move back or fill in gaps, defining a circle for the samba. When the mestre sings "*Duro bem duro,*" he points his finger to emphasize the lyric, and several group members join him to reinforce his call (see fig. 5 and video 1 at https://doi.org/10.3998/mpub.12771665.cmp.6 and https://doi.org/10.3998/mpub.12771665.cmp.7). When the full chorus responds, "*Vou*

Figure 5. Samba in motion. From left to right, players of cherém-cherém, bumbo, timbal, and atabaque. Mestre Cláudio is pointing his finger to emphasize a lyric. Note the players' gazes are directed intently either at Mestre Cláudio or to the dancer whose shoulder and arm can be seen at left. Video still by the author, 2016.

vender meu boi . . . ," Mestre Cláudio starts clapping the 3-3-2 (x..x..x.) pattern on "*boi,*" eyeing the lead drummer, who cues the full ensemble.

[*solo*] *Vou vender meu boi*	[call] I'm going to sell my ox
Não tenho troco [2x]	I don't have change [2x]
[*coro*] *Vou vender meu boi*	[chorus] I'm going to sell my ox
Não tenho troco [2x]	I don't have change [2x]
[*solo*] *Duro bem duro*	[call] [It's] Hard really hard
Mole bem pouco	Soft very little [rarely]
Toco que é oco	A stump that's hollow
Não bota rama	Doesn't grow branches
Deita na cama	Lie in bed
Que é lugar quente	Which is a warm place
Tapa na boca	A hit on the mouth
Arranca os dentes	Pulls out teeth
Deixa língua na boca somente iaiá!	Just leave the tongue in the mouth iaiá!
[*coro*] *Vou vender meu boi*	[chorus] I'm going to sell my ox
Não tenho troco	I don't have change

Vou vender meu boi	I'm going to sell my ox
Não tenho troco	I don't have change

The roda erupts in sustained explosion, across the widest spectrum of sound, from the bumbo's bass thud to the *cherém-cherém*'s deafening clash of metal against metal, and the wood blocks' sharp snap. Players in the ring sing full-voiced, relishing the feel of the poetry on their tongues, gleefully singing "*Duro bem duro!*" which had become the group's favorite expression that year. A young Black man is pulled into the ring and spins, his rapid steps in perpetual motion. We play, clap, and sing harder to sustain his concentrated vibration, aligning our bodies to his frequency. He smiles radiantly, sustained by the energy and intensity we generate. We respond to his moving call.

• • •

In seeking to understand how members of the Angoleiros do Sertão experienced playing capoeira, I asked them to describe what it was like to be in the roda. As group members tried to verbalize their profound sensations, they often compared capoeira to samba and to the Afro-Brazilian religion Can-

Musical Example 1. As sung in Mestre Cláudio's group, the samba "Vou vender meu boi" is begun by the leader singing the first line as a call and the chorus responding with line 2. The leader sings from "duro bem duro" and then the chorus responds with the entire refrain, usually without the repeat.

domblé. They referenced the other practices to help explain their experiences of simultaneously listening, moving, and playing music; how the sounds of the rodas (both capoeira and samba) moved them bodily, emotionally, and for many spiritually. My conversation with Contramestre Orikerê, source of this chapter's epigraph, was just one of many revealing discussions of the topic. Orikerê is one of the group's most skilled and fluent players. A light-skinned Afro-Brazilian with thick, long locks and a searing critique of race relations in Brazil, he grew up in the aggrieved peripheries of São Paulo city where he seemed destined to become embroiled in drug trafficking and incarceration. As a young boy, he extricated himself from this world and moved to the interior of São Paulo, where he began to train capoeira Angola. In 2005, he moved to Bahia to train with Mestre Cláudio, eventually settling in São Félix, Bahia and founding a núcleo of the Angoleiros do Sertão. São Félix sits across the Paraguaçu River from Cachoeira, a site of the Recôncavo region renowned for its Candomblé communities and located about an hour's bus ride south of Feira de Santana. There Orikerê regularly attends public Candomblé ceremonies, though he is not initiated into the religion. Our conversation began informally, at a red plastic table in a noisy marketplace where we were having a lunch of fried fish and cold beers. When he started to talk about how he experienced and conceptualized capoeira music, I asked if I could record our conversation on my phone and he consented. I asked him about the experience common among capoeira players of hearing the berimbau and feeling compelled to move one's body and play capoeira. He immediately knew what I meant and responded, "It's almost as if you were 'someone of axé' [a practitioner of Candomblé], who can't fail [to respond]. It's the same thing. For us, who surrender ourselves to capoeira, it's the same thing. When the berimbau plays, you must respond. [No matter what state you're in], you respond, you find a way. It's a mystical thing."

When I asked others about sensing music as a "call" (*chama*), some group members also spoke about samba and spirituality. Abusada,[2] a Black practitioner from São Paulo state who also practices Umbanda, an Afro-Brazilian religion derived from Candomblé, said, "I think this question of *chamar* [to call] is very spiritual. . . . When I feel the *toque* [rhythmic pattern] of the *tambor* [drum] inside of me, . . . it seems like I've already samba'ed that samba, that I already was there. The tambor is calling me."

The sense of being called by the sounds of the berimbau, the toque, and the tambor thus summons feelings of mysticality and spirituality, which many players described in terms of axé. Often defined as ancestral energy or life force, axé is so central to Candomblé that it can be synonymous with the religion: "someone of axé" is someone who practices Candomblé. Yet players also referenced axé to explain how the music of capoeira and samba moved them and energized the rodas. When I asked Orikerê how he listened in the capoeira roda, he said, "It's you channeling [the music], directing yourself with it. It's like Candomblé. If you don't play the right toque, you will be playing all night long and no one [no *orixá*, divinity] will come, nothing will happen. When you put in the axé, sing the music—*ê carai!* [wow!]"

As I continued to press Orikerê to explain something that he had declared "doesn't have an explanation," I sensed I was exhausting his patience. Finally, he exclaimed, "To understand capoeira Angola, sometimes you have to go to Candomblé! Then you'll understand why we do certain things!"

• • •

Following Orikerê's suggestion, echoed by many group members, I have looked to Candomblé to understand how the Angoleiros do Sertão experience and understand their practice. Yet rather than conducting ethnographic research of Candomblé ceremonies, I approached Candomblé from the perspective of an angoleiro. Members of the Angoleiros do Sertão community engage with diverse Candomblé traditions to varying degrees. They belong to religious houses (*terreiros*) of various "nations" (*nações*), including Ketu, Nagô, Jeje, and Angola.[3] At least one student I interviewed was undergoing initiation, signaling a deeper commitment, while others participated in ways ranging from more informal "frequenting" of local *festas* (public ceremony-parties), to more dedicated involvement, often as drummers. Still other members expressed curiosity and respect for Candomblé but had little direct experience with its rituals or knowledge. My turn to Candomblé is therefore filtered through the diverse experiences of these angoleiros. I have also attended Candomblé festas, talked with participants and initiates, watched and listened to videos, and read Candomblé literature. While this chapter may open up further avenues for Candomblé research, my aim is to clarify how embodied perception of sound moves practitioners in capoeira and samba. Following the lead of community members, I take a holistic approach that not only sees the three practices as more connected than separate but also recognizes the inseparability of music, sound, and movement. When angoleiros reference Candomblé to explain their experience, therefore, I argue they are grounding their interpretations in a sensorium (Geurts 2002) of bodily orientations to sound-movement shared across the practices.

Capoeira, Candomblé, and samba are indelibly linked in the Brazilian popular imaginary as archetypes of Afro-Brazilian cultura popular,[4] often referred to as *matrizes africanas* (African matrices, or African matrix practices). Capoeira, Candomblé, and samba frequently appear together as symbols of Bahia's "African" identity, both in academic literature and on tourism sites, such as the Bahian secretary of tourism's (Setur) Instagram. However, this facile grouping not only collapses the differences between practices but also renders their association natural and portrays the reasons they belong together as self-evident. Numerous studies address two or three of the practices in one work; however, the literature usually focuses on either music or movement/dance. For example, dance and performance scholar Barbara Browning found that "the body in Afro-Brazilian dance continually cites itself. Gestures from religious and martial dance resonate in the secular samba—and samba infiltrates the circles of candomblé and capoeira" (Browning 1995, xxiv–xxv). Yet no study has addressed the complex multisensory associations between the practices.[5] This chapter explores why and how practitioners experience Candomblé, capoeira, and samba as inseparable. Looking closely at the practices' interrelations not only confirms enduring historical and sociocultural relationships but also reveals that the forms are deeply intertwined at the level of multisensory embodied perception (Iyer 2002).

Bringing music and sound together with bodily movement and perception, I argue that all of the forms cultivate an African matrix sensorium that privileges "aural-kinesthetics"—listening, sounding, and moving "within the all-encompassing aurality" of ritual events (I. Johnson 2012)—powered by the transmission of axé. Oriented by the African matrix sensorium, practitioners experience sound as a call (chama, chamada) that summons bodies—of humans, orixás, and instruments—to respond with movement and more sounds. Learning ways of "listening with the body" (Díaz Meneses 2016), practitioners hone their aural-kinesthetic sensibilities, infusing their movements and sounds with axé and bringing their bodies into *sintonia* (syntony, matching frequencies). As I address below, axé derives from the Yorùbá *àṣẹ*, but in Bahia and across the African diaspora, the axé concept (*aché* in Cuban Spanish) has transcended religion and geographic place to pervade popular discourses and music-dance practices (Henry 2008).[6]

Recognizing that axé energy inhabits music, sound, and movement, I propose that axé also resonates beyond Candomblé ritual contexts literally as vibrations.[7] In Candomblé, drumming the right toques in the right way—with axé—is crucial for summoning the orixás to the festa, where they dance through the bodies of their devotees. In a similar way, infusing the sounds of the berimbau, timbal, and other instruments with axé calls angoleiros to play capoeira and to dance samba. Calling, responding, playing, and moving with axé in the capoeira and samba rodas ensure that axé continues to vibrate through multiple bodies, making something happen. Paying close attention to axé's vibrational properties reveals how sound moves bodies and bodies summon sound-movement within the ritual events. Yet it also reveals much more. From within the rodas, axé resonates outward and pulls bodies centripetally into the ring, and at the same time, it calls practitioners into relation beyond the space-times of the roda. The continuous cultivation and propagation of axé coheres the community and calls members to assume various responsibilities and forms of commitment, or compromisso, to one another, to African matrix practices, and, for some, to Black communities more broadly.

The African Matrix: Candomblé, Capoeira, and Samba

When I asked how capoeira, samba, and Candomblé were related, community members often answered that the forms were all "matrizes africanas." The term "matriz africana" (used both in plural and singular) signifies African origins similar to "African roots," though the meaning of matriz/matrix as "womb" adds the sense of Africa as maternal source ("matriz" n.d.; see also Pinho 2010). Dancer-anthropologist Pilar Echeverry Zambrano explains that the African matrix refers to "practices and discourses [that] revolve around a political and cultural struggle to dignify, reframe, and make visible [Afro-Brazilians'] knowledge and their people" (2018, 75). The concept is thus quite expansive, expressing how Afro-Brazilian music-movement practices holistically incorporate "aesthetic, political, religious, and historical processes that originated on the continent of Africa" that remain inextricable from "concepts of ancestry, identity, and struggle against racial exclusion" (75). Thus, here "African" refers to historical and ancestral connections to Africa while the term "African matrix" signifies specifically Afro-Brazilian (sometimes Afro-Bahian) practices and discourses.

Historically, African matrix practices coalesced in "alternative spaces of blackness," nurtured by Candomblé communities, in which enslaved and free Africans and Afro-Brazilians developed "alternative meanings of human community and black identity within the matrix of slavery" (Harding 2000, xvi–xvii). As capoeira and Candomblé scholar-practitioners Diniz, Sousa, and Lühning put it, capoeira arose in spaces "forged by subjects immersed in a Black cultural environment permeated by Afro-Brazilian religiosity, inscribed not only in ritual situations, but also in bodies and quotidian life" (2015, 196).

Candomblé spirituality pervaded everyday lives, in tangible and often pragmatic ways, revealing the materiality of the "mystical" (Orikerê's term). Many capoeira mestres belonged to Candomblé houses in the nineteenth and twentieth centuries (Abreu 2005, 120; Assunção 2005, 116–19) and served as drummers for ceremonies (Rego 1968, 35–45). Surely many of them played both religious and secular sambas, as is still common today. Capoeira mestres in the past also served as bodyguards to protect Candomblé practitioners against police violence, while *mães-* and *pais-de-santo* (mothers- and fathers-of-saint, the religious leaders) provided shelter and protection for capoeiras by "closing" their bodies to harmful forces (Assunção 2005, 118; Downey 2005, 138). Candomblé comprised the spiritual-social center for Black communities, a veritable "refuge" from white supremacist society, where Africans and Afro-Brazilians defined multiple alternative "orientations," in part through their music-dance practices (Harding 2000).

Many capoeira players today either practice Candomblé and samba or know them well enough to comment on the many overlaps in performance practices between the forms.[8] Practitioners often note that the three berimbaus of the capoeira roda mirror the three atabaque drums of Candomblé (one of which capoeira borrows for its bateria). Both trios consist of instruments of low, medium, and higher pitch: respectively, the *berra-boi*, *gunga*, and *viola* berimbaus and the *rum*, *(rum)pi*, and *lê* atabaques.[9] The capoeira bateria also borrows Candomblé's agogô, a metal double cowbell, though Mestre Cláudio prefers his agogô made from a pair of large hollow Brazil nut pods. In both practices the player of the lowest-pitched instrument (berra-boi or rum) leads the ceremony, choosing songs and directing other instrumentalists and players/dancers (Béhague 1984, 226). Capoeira, Candomblé, and samba all use call-and-response song structures and move within a circle. Capoeira and samba repertoires borrow from Candomblé, using vocabulary or expressions from ritual languages (in Yorùbá, Kimbundo, or Kikongo, depending on the nação), song topics about orixás, or singing Candomblé melodies with modified lyrics (Diniz 2010, 129, 232–33).

The connections also extend to organizational structures, etiquette, and means of knowledge transmission. While Candomblé is more formalized than capoeira, both communities have hierarchical authority structures (Varela 2019, 98). They also both call their communities "family," and they mean this literally. Mães- and pais-de-santo of Candomblé, like some mestras/mestres in capoeira, often become mother or father figures to members. Finally, in all practices expert knowledge and wisdom are passed on primarily through convivência, while text-based and verbal instruction are discouraged.[10]

Mestre Cláudio's Rural Samba and the Cowboy Caboclo

Like many mestres of the past and present, Mestre Cláudio's life story embodies the interconnections of Candomblé, samba, and capoeira. He lived in a terreiro for some of his youth, when his mother was a practitioner there, and he has drummed in local Candomblé ceremonies for many years. Though the group's connection with Candomblé is not exceptional, it is difficult to determine how widespread such ties remain in other groups today. Rising evangelical violence against Afro-Brazilian religions means that "few people have the courage to say, 'I am of Candomblé,'" as Dona Ivannide put it.[11] What may be unique to Mestre Cláudio's group, based in Bahia's backlands, is how explicitly he draws on the music and movements of *Caboclo* rituals to inform both his samba and capoeira aesthetics.[12]

Caboclos are (Afro-)Indigenous deities (Iyanaga 2013, 81) or entities (*entidades*) worshipped in Afro-Brazilian religions. Though *caboclo* is also a racial-ethnic category commonly used to signify Brazilian Indian mixed with European (Portuguese) or African descent, Caboclo rituals are Afro-Brazilian religious practices, not Indigenous ones (J. T. dos Santos 1995). Caboclo worship is associated primarily with Bantu (as opposed to Yorùbá or Fon/Ewe) Candomblé houses, Candomblé de Caboclo (its own nação), and Umbanda, a religion derivative of Candomblé that worships numerous Caboclos (Prandi 2004). However, in practice, Candomblé houses of all nations may include Caboclo rituals (J. T. dos Santos 1995, 78–90).[13]

In the Angoleiros do Sertão, the Caboclo holds special significance as a figure evoking the Black Bahian sertão. In his samba, Mestre Cláudio uses the samba toque of the *samba de Caboclo*, the section of Caboclo festas where the Caboclo dances and sings sambas and welcomes attendees to dance in the roda (Chada 2006, 113–14) (see musical example 2). Mestre Cláudio also borrows samba repertoire played in Caboclo ceremonies, just as these ceremonies play repertoire from samba de roda (113). Mestre Cláudio's rural samba thus directly evokes Candomblé with its sounds.

In our interview, Rita, a longtime group member and Mestre Cláudio's wife, described how the mestre took inspiration from the way people played samba in the Bahian sertão and how his personal life experience with Candomblé deeply influenced his approach. Rita grew up far in the interior of Bahia in Queimadas, a town two hundred kilometers northwest of Feira. With fair but easily tanned skin and large, dark curls, Rita identifies as white, though her mother told me the family has some "gypsy" heritage. Rita recounted that Mestre Cláudio had grandparents, uncles, neighbors, and cousins who played this rural style of samba. When he lived with his mother inside a terreiro, he learned from the Candomblé's *tocadores* (drum players), who played samba both inside and outside the terreiro. Rita explained, "[For] those of us who are born in rural Bahia, rodeos, samba, cowboy festivals . . . you have all of these influences in your everyday life, without even noticing it." For them it was only "natural," she said, to have samba at every party. This is why the weekly samba attracts local Candomblé drummers: "You are attracted by what interests you! The samba is similar to Candomblé, so naturally if a tocador is passing by the samba [she sings the bumbo rhythm *pa-tum, pa-tum pa-tum-pa pa-tum*], it's a call! [*é chama!*] It practically drags you there! It pulls you! Even if you don't want to, you hear it, and you're like, 'But where is it? I need to see! It calls my attention! . . . I need to be there!'"

I asked if this was similar to when people say, "The berimbau called me [*o berimbau me chamou*]," and she replied, "Yeeeeees! This is what I'm saying when I say there exists this whole relationship [among capoeira, samba, and Candomblé]!"

Drawing on his lived experience growing up in the rural outskirts of Feira de Santana, living and drumming in Candomblé spaces, Mestre Cláudio intentionally infuses his rodas with the sounds, expressions, and ludic, agile movements of Caboclos, knowing these elements will call to and pull in residents of the Bahian sertão. He favors songs from the samba, capoeira, and Caboclo repertoires with themes and sentiments about cowboy life, cattle, and the hard life of the sertão, leaving aside common capoeira songs about the ocean, beach, and sailors. He also emulates the nasal vocal tone and characteristic vibrato of the sertão's *aboios*, the songs cowboys and ranchers sing to their cattle to steer and corral them but also to comment on their own life conditions. He even chose the group's brown pants uniform to reference the garb of a typical sertão laborer.

The *Caboclo Boiadeiro* (Cowboy Caboclo) takes on particular salience when understood as an archetype of the Afro-Bahian sertão. A dark-skinned cowboy from the interior of Bahia, the Boiadeiro has also gifted capoeira Angola with one of its most beloved songs. The song "*Quem vem lá*" also exemplifies the interconnections between the three forms. It originated in Candomblé rituals summoning and honoring the Caboclo Boiadeiro, but with altered lyrics it has been canonized within the capoeira repertoire (Diniz 2010, 81; Diniz, Sousa, and Lühning 2015, 199). Comparing musical examples 2 (samba), 3–5 (from Candomblé/Umbanda), and 6 (from capoeira Angola) reveals multiple points of overlap in rhythms, melodies, and lyrics, and some differences. For instance, examples 3 and 4 are also played to the Caboclo's samba toque, the toque Mestre Cláudio uses in his samba (example 2), which in examples 3 and 4 is represented by the same clapping pattern below the vocal line. Example 5, in contrast, uses another rhythm, and example 6 is sung to the toques of the capoeira bateria (see musical example 8).[14]

Musical Example 2. Basic rhythms of Mestre Cláudio's samba. For the timbales, the lower line represents the bass tone, and the top line represents the open tone. The most basic version of the toque would be simply repeating the first measure.

Musical Example 3. Excerpt (0:25—0:41) from video "PONTOS DE BOIADEIRO" (Umbanda let's talk 2017).

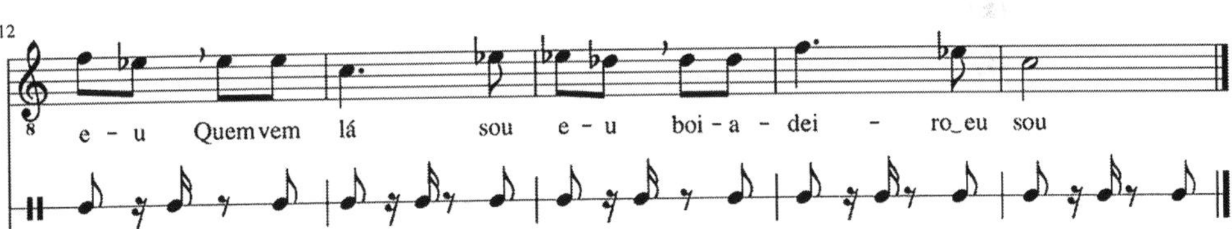

Musical Example 4. Excerpt (00:00—00:19) from video "Ponto de boiadeiro quem vem la [*sic*] sou eu" (Wesle Pereira 2015).

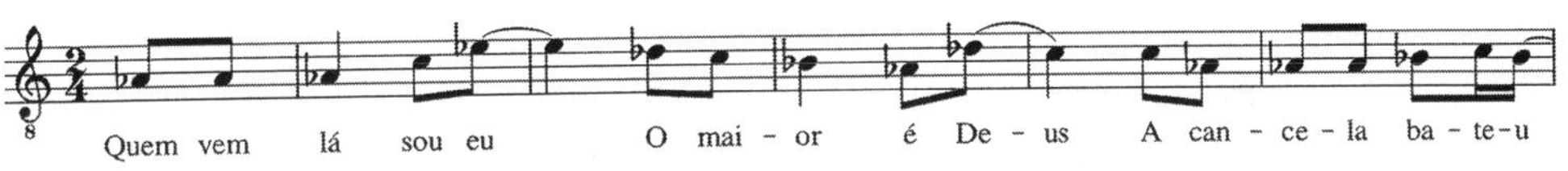

Musical Example 5. Excerpt (00:09—00:31) from video "Quem vem lá sou eu" (Templo Escola Filhos do Mar 2016).

Musical Example 6. First 20 seconds from the capoeira corrido "Quem vem lá," track 31 from CD *Angoleiros do Sertão e do Recôncavo*. First half as sung by Mestre Cláudio, from middle of m. 9 sung by response chorus.

The melodies of the examples share similar rhythmic phrasing, which can be reduced to a basic pattern repeated four times to complete the verse:

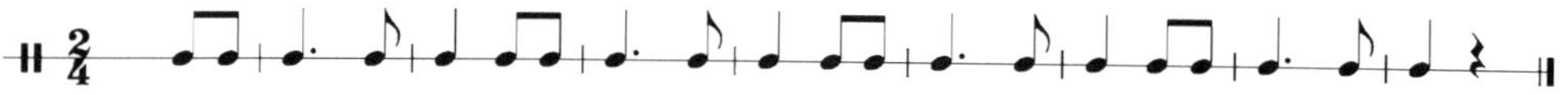

Musical Example 7.

In terms of pitch, the melodies of examples 3 and 4 center on scale degrees three and five, always resolving on the third. Example 6 starts on the first scale degree, ascends the tonic triad, and resolves on the first scale degree, while example 5 begins the same way as example 6 but resolves on the third scale degree. The second half of example 5 varies the melody in ways that are common in capoeira, too. Example 5's lyrics most closely resemble the capoeira version of the tune, yet note how the gate slamming (*A cancela bateu*) becomes the berimbau striking its wire cord (*Berimbau bateu*), sharing the verb *bater* but shifting its meaning. Most significantly, who "I am" in the song shifts from Boiadeiro to angoleiro.

A direct embodied result of this borrowing is the spark of recognition I felt in my chest upon visiting a Candomblé de Caboclo on Ilha de Itaparica and hearing a "Quem vem lá" version that evoked the song we sing in capoeira. I felt immediately summoned into the energy of the ceremony's call and response. Even though I was a newcomer, I felt at home and I knew how to respond.

Candomblé/Umbanda	*Candomblé/Umbanda*
[Musical Example 3.] *Quem vem lá? É ele!* [x3] *Boiadeiro é!*	[Musical Example 3.] Who goes there? It's him! [x3] It's Boiadeiro!
[Musical Example 4.] *Quem vem lá sou eu* [x3] *Boiadeiro eu sou*	[Musical Example 4.] Who goes there it's me [x3] Boiadeiro am I
[Musical Example 5.] *Quem vem lá sou eu* *O maior é Deus* *A cancela bateu* *Sou eu boiadeiro sou eu*	[Musical Example 5.] Who goes there it's me God is the greatest The gate slammed shut It's me, Boiadeiro am I
Capoeira Angola	*Capoeira Angola*
[Musical Example 6.] *Quem vem lá, sou eu* [x2] *Berimbau bateu* *Sou eu, angoleiro sou eu*	[Musical Example 6.] Who goes there? It's me [x2] The berimbau [was] struck It's me, I am an angoleiro

Axé and the African Matrix Sensorium

Although historical connections and overlapping performance practices go far toward explaining the relationships among African matrix practices, they still cannot fully account for practitioners' powerful sensations—physical, emotional, and spiritual—of the three forms' inseparability. What has been missing is a consideration of how axé energizes simultaneous music and movement in the practices. As capoeira scholar Greg Downey found in his phenomenological study of capoeira players' perception of music "with a trained and responsive body" (2002, 490), I also found that angoleiros "do not seem to hear musical sound as a conjuncture of abstractable, purely sonic qualities, like rhythm, tone, or melody" (496). Rather, practitioners speak about musical elements (such as toque) in terms of their bodily experience of sound, as Abusada, who said, "I feel the toque of the tambor inside of me." Guided by practitioners' "sensational knowledge" (Hahn 2007), therefore, I have taken a multisensory approach to considering practitioners' holistic experience of the "sound body," a resonant and porous body that "transforms according to the vibrations of its environment, and correspondingly transforms that environment" (Kapchan 2015, 38). However, in contrast to Downey's phenomenological bracketing, his Husserlian attention to "the things themselves" ("cartwheels, kicks, rhythms, songs, exercises, and rituals") at the expense of attending to "deeper ideas" behind immediate everyday experience (2005, 19), I have worked with the understanding that "sensory values are social values and social interaction is sensory interaction" and vice versa (Howes 2019, 22). Thus my approach is closer to what Csordas called a "*cultural phenomenology* concerned with synthesizing the immediacy of embodied experience with the multiplicity of cultural meaning in which we are always and inevitably immersed" (1999, 143; original emphasis). Taking a holistic approach, I seek to account for the ways in which energies, sensations, and perception take on interwoven social, spiritual, and political meanings and inform practitioners' experiences and interpretations.

In this way, the chapter contributes to scholarship theorizing the interdependence of music/sound and dance/movement in African diasporic forms (Nketia 1965; Daniel 2005; Gaunt 2006). Studies of music and dance have so often been siloed in their respective disciplines, resulting in partial accounts that not only partition the senses but also further marginalize African diasporic ways of knowing.[15] By treating sound and movement holistically, I respond to hip hop dance scholar Imani Kai Johnson's productive call in her *Sounding Out!* blog post to attend to the "visceral, embodied, kinesthetic response to dance music in a particular social space, which is not [necessarily] explicitly directed by the lyrics or a set of moves but by the feel of a song as a whole" (2012). Johnson proposes "aural-kinesthetics" as a framework, asking scholars to "engage more than just the sensory response of moving to what one hears" in order to develop new ways of exploring "the all-encompassing aurality of an environment" and the ways in which sound comes "at you from all sides" and produces social space (2012). Paying attention to the kinesthetic aurality of the capoeira Angola roda reveals how the sounds and movements generated there reverberate through practitioners' lives, calling community members into the ring and thereby calling community into being.

Although Downey did not discuss sound as a "call," he described players' feeling of being called in a similar way: upon hearing "the distinctive sound texture of the berimbau . . . practitioners feel the swaying movements [of capoeira play] . . . either as an outward movement or an inward quickening, a readiness to move" (2002, 500). Downey's interlocutors claimed that "bodily movement is immanent in the sound of the berimbau itself," but he ultimately finds this "implausible" as he concludes that this way of listening-moving is learned (503). However, Downey's theory cannot explain why many practitioners I spoke with reported experiencing visceral, emotional responses—an "inward quickening"—to the berimbau's sound when first hearing it, prior to any capoeira training. This was how Orikerê described his first encounter with capoeira: He was only eleven years old on November 20, 1999, when he heard the "tong-tong" of the berimbau playing the Angola toque and got goosebumps all over his body. He ran to the person playing the berimbau and asked how he could do it, too, and the next day he showed up to train and has never stopped. The berimbau called him, even though, as he said, "I didn't even know what it was! I heard the berimbau, and I just went in. Once I heard that shit [*porra*] I was already inside of it. There was no way to get out anymore." Candomblé scholar and ethnomusicologist Xavier Vatin has also observed that people "completely external" to the religion frequently fell into a trance upon hearing the "atabaques and sacred songs," leaving open the possibility that the music possesses some kind of "supernatural power" that induces or triggers the trance (2013, 259).[16] From an African matrix worldview, then, it appears that movement's immanence in sound—sound's power to move bodies and shift bodily states—is indeed plausible.

Members of the Angoleiros do Sertão explained sound's ability to summon movement in terms of the power of axé, leading me to consider practitioners' ways of listening, sensing, and moving as comprising an African matrix sensorium energized by axé. Geurts defines "sensorium" as "a pattern of relative importance and differential elaboration of the various senses" within a cultural group and suggests that sensory experiences are "encoded and *performatively elaborated* in their rituals and cultural traditions" (2002, 5; original emphasis). The African matrix sensorium orients practitioners to produce and respond to aural-kinesthetic calls that transmit axé through movements and sounds. Collectively cultivating axé fosters belonging not only among practitioners of capoeira Angola, samba, and Candomblé but also among lay participants who are called to enter African matrix spaces. In this way, axé can be understood as an energy that calls together and coheres community.

Capoeira and samba foster sociality through their fully participatory natures (Turino 2008). Everyone present may switch from playing instruments, singing, and clapping to playing capoeira or dancing samba. Participants get into the groove of the toques, entering temporal and affective entrainment (Phillips-Silver and Keller 2012). However, this begs the question, "What is this groove," this "vital drive" that players feel is "so

Figure 6. A samba dancer in the roda. To the left, two wood block players and one shaking a caxixi. To the right, players of triangle, cherém-cherém, and pandeiro. Photo by the author, 2016.

important to get into?" (Keil 2005, 59). Something more is at work in the roda beyond, or perhaps permeating, the discrepancies in micro-timing—"and it is the *something* that fascinates" (Floyd 1995, 97; original emphasis). I suggest the something is axé. Focusing on axé, moreover, reveals that practitioners orient their bodies toward sound-movement in efforts to produce axé. Far from a passive state, experiencing capoeira and samba requires active, energetic call and response: putting in the axé (see fig. 6 and video 1 at https://doi.org/10.3998/mpub.12771665.cmp.6 and https://doi.org/10.3998/mpub.12771665.cmp.7).

Putting Axé into the Roda

When Mestre Cláudio speaks about how to play capoeira, he uses terms such as "expression, spirit, intelligence" (*expressão, espírito, intelligência*) and, above all, the "sense of the game" (*sentido do jogo*). Significantly, "sentido" means not only "sense," as both perception and reason, but also "spirit," "thought," "intention," "attention," "orientation" (as in direction), and "signification," all of which apply to playing capoeira well ("sentido" n.d.). A game makes sense when the two players communicate fluently, and thus move fluidly, with one another. Yet when teaching how to play with intelligence, Mestre Cláudio emphasizes the details of bodily expression: bending deeply at the knees, opening hands with flexed extended fingers, shifting between weight on the ball of the foot versus flat on the ground. A movement's meaning (sense, intelligence) is inseparable from its expression (spirit, sense).

Mestre Cláudio revealed what he meant by "espírito" in one informal training session at his compound in Feira in 2013, though I would appreciate the significance of the lesson only many years later. I was practicing an assigned movement with one of his sons. When we performed it back for him, he stopped us, displeased. He said we had failed to grasp the espírito of the movement. To get the espírito of capoeira Angola, he told us, it was essential to get the espírito of the Caboclo. He explained that the movements, gestures, and expressions in capoeira came from Candomblé and samba. As he spoke, he bent his joints with supple, loose control, masking the muscle of his kick, shifting his weight easily but unpredictably. As he moved, he said, "Orixás do this. You see orixás doing this, too."[17] He was demonstrating how the Caboclo lends his "attitude" and "gesture" (Diniz 2010, 153) to capoeira Angola.

While angoleiros' movements differ from those of Caboclos (the Caboclo is not playing capoeira, sparring with an opponent), they share similar "loose" and "broken" aesthetics, such as when a Caboclo "stumbles and catches himself with a wave up the spine and a fall to the front" (Lior 2021, 183). The Boiadeiro's wide-legged stance while dancing samba, evoking the bowed legs of a cowboy who makes his living on his horse (23), is also echoed in the wide steps of capoeira's *ginga,* the swaying side-to-side, front-to-back basic movement. The following description of the Caboclo Boiadeiro could also describe an angoleiro at play:

> He kicks his feet and legs outward in various directions, sometimes propelling his body high in the air, or shuffling himself rapidly across the floor. Through the caboclo's body, spiritual power is . . . dramatically exhibited—or perhaps generated—through athletic movements, astonishing endurance, speedy footwork, and spontaneous delivery of one song after another. (Piper 2007, 57)

If the Caboclo's body generates spiritual power (axé), then moving like a Caboclo may do the same in the roda. Yet it is not the movements alone that

Figure 7. Mestre Cláudio playing in the foreground with deeply bent joints, extended fingers. Compare to the samba dancer's angularity in figure 6. Photo by the author, 2023.

create axé. To put axé into the movements is to play with the Caboclo's spirit (see fig. 7).

Playing capoeira music also requires putting in the axé, as Orikerê said above. Simply playing the right toque is not enough. After all, the basic rhythmic patterns are easily grasped by novice players (see musical example 8). Moreover, in Mestre Cláudio's group, as in most groups today, the same basic toques are used in every game. Yet they do not always produce good, exciting games. Players often comment after a disappointing roda that it lacked axé. While more advanced participants play variations of the toques (Downey 2005, 91) that can excite capoeira players' movements, even potentially cuing attacks (Díaz 2017), regulating the game's energies still involves more than technical virtuosity. Beginners who struggle with the movements but exert themselves with genuine effort are also complimented as having axé. What is necessary, above all, is "the intention that players put into it and the resulting energy . . . conveyed via the music (which is supposed to bring in *axé* . . . to the roda)" (Robitaille 2013, 192). Playing with axé means playing with the proper intention, whether calling an orixá in Candomblé (Cardoso 2006, 237–38) or an orisha in Cuban Santeria (Hagedorn 2001, 132–33) or bringing bodies into sintonia in capoeira Angola.

How does one play music with intention? Detailed verbal instruction on playing music is rare, but Mestre Cláudio often tells his students to play the instruments with "attitude," which he demonstrates with his bodily posture:

he stands upright with weight on both feet, no slouching or hip jutting; eyes are open, watching the game. Mestre Cláudio gets more explicit when someone makes a mistake. One time he got quite upset with a student who was playing timbal in the samba with closed eyes and head down. He explained to me later that "you must look the horse [*cavalo*] in the eyes!" In Candomblé, the person who incorporates the Cabloco is called a "horse": "Caboclos outwardly refer to their mediums as 'cavalos' or horses on which they ride in to a festa from their villages and ranches, arriving 'montado cavalo' or on horseback" (Lior 2021, 23). Mestre Cláudio demonstrated, saying, "Not like this!" while bending his head downward. Singing a samba, "*Eu vou mandar de lado de lá pra cá!*" (I'm going to send it from that side to this side), he looked up and stared into my eyes with such intensity that I recoiled. I had seen this look on his face many times as he drummed, watching the samba dancer—his eyes bore into my head. But in that moment, I realized that his intense gaze was not one of anger, intimidation, or desire—it was impersonal. He was sending axé "from that side to this side," to the dancer in the roda. What binds together these explanations of how to play (both music and game), combining effort, intention, spirit, sense, and effectiveness, is playing with axé.

Multiplicities of Axé

Àṣẹ in Yorùbá Language

Axé is a term/concept from the Yorùbá language (spelled *àṣẹ*) that has migrated across the African diaspora to become a "Pan-Africanist term" (Abiodun 1994, 71). While it retains connotations with spirituality, aesthetics, expression, life force, and Africa, axé (also spelled *ase*, *àse*, *àshé*, *ache*) "consistently escapes full meaning" (Davies 2008, 118). This is axé's *esquiva*, the cunning capoeira move of evasion. As such, I resist trying to pin it down. Instead, I consider axé's "multiplicity" (Sodré 1988, xxi), reviewing common definitions of àṣẹ/axé, without insisting on any one, while also addressing the ideologies that accompany them.[18]

In Yorùbá language and culture, àṣẹ has been defined as "performative power; the power of accomplishment; the power to get things done; the power to make things happen" (Drewal 1992, 201). As àṣẹ has migrated, however, it may have remained "almost intact" (Abiodun 1994, 71) or retained some meanings, added new ones, and shed others (Matory 2005, 123). Members of Nagô Candomblé houses, who conduct their ceremonies in Yorùbá, often say that "àṣẹ" is a religious concept while "axé" is a separate, secular term meaning simply good energy or vibe. Or they may claim that axé is àṣẹ, but the uninitiated do not understand its true meaning. One's relationship to Yorùbá/Nagô Candomblé in particular, with its ideology of Nagô superiority based on claims of "African purity" (Matory 2005, 225–29), will thus significantly shape one's understanding of axé.[19] Ultimately, I am less interested in what axé is than what axé does for angoleiros. My interlocutors did not provide Yorùbá definitions of àṣẹ like those found in academic texts, but they nearly all spoke of sensing axé in the roda. They understood axé with their bodies.

Axé among the Angoleiros do Sertão

Most practitioners and community members I interviewed thought of axé as a holistic force that permeated sacred and secular spaces.[20] Dona Ivannide, who belonged to a house of Jeje Candomblé (a Fon/Ewe nação), stated firmly, "For me, the same *vital force* that *sustains* the *religion* of *Candomblé sustains capoeira!*" emphasizing each word with a sharp slap of her palm on the table. She was careful to frame this as her opinion, thus acknowledging the validity of contrasting viewpoints. Many group members defined axé simply as "good energy" (*energia boa*) or "force/power" (*força*). In Bahia and across Brazil, "Axé!" is also a casual greeting and a common expression of well-wishing, as in, "*Axé pra nós!*" (Axé for us!). Dona Ivannide explained, "When I say to you, 'Axé, Viola!' I am wishing you light, peace, positivity. All of this is axé!" "*Axé music*" (using the English word) is also a genre of Bahian pop, "the featured soundtrack of Salvador's carnival" (Packman 2010, 250). Still, some members expressed concern that the term was used too casually, without recognizing its spiritual weight. When I asked Orikerê, he said that axé in capoeira was the same as axé in Candomblé: "It's força, just that!" But then he added, "Now, when we say [that] something *really* has axé, it's when you sweat, it's different. . . . Not 'força' as in [physical] strength [but] spiritual. . . . It's the same in capoeira, it's also ancestral. . . . Axé is when you give your body, you sweat for it, you really throw yourself, break everything [*quebra tudo*]!"

Hearing Orikerê describe how playing with axé meant leveraging spiritual-ancestral energies with one's whole body, I prompted, "So it's a physical force?"

"It's spiritual." He corrected me.

Trying to understand, I asked, "But it also has a physical side?"

"[It's] everything! Yes, body, spirit, and mind. It has to have it all. You have to channel the energy, sacrifice yourself, and feel."

Throughout our interview, Orikerê spoke about doing capoeira out of "necessity." He acknowledged that his ancestors had a different need, to liberate themselves from slavery, but he still felt that he participated in capoeira out of necessity. He explained, "I'd be fucked without the mestre. He's already helped me with many things . . . especially in terms of direction. When I first saw him, I thought, *porra!* [damn!], I know it's you, you are a capoeira [player], too! But it's difficult, you're always liberating yourself. . . . I believe that the majority of capoeira professors [do capoeira] because they didn't have any other choice in life. It was the only solution. So they embraced capoeira and got away."

He said that after he played, he often heard onlookers say, "Wow, that guy plays really well!" (*Po' a cara joga muito!*). I recalled how he throws his entire body-spirit-mind into his game: shirt drenched, springing to land lightly on both hands, elbows bending to catch his inverted torso as it descends, legs folded in the air, cheek pressed to pavement, then pushing himself up and out again with such ease masking effort. Or playing the timbal and singing in samba, veins raised through the moisture on his arms as he slaps the drum, voice scratching the air, callused hands. It was impressive! He was one of the most beautiful players I had ever seen.

"But," he said, "it's not that. It's because you're there out of necessity, feeling the desire to do it. I learned a lot [about this] from the mestre. I don't go to capoeira because it's cool. I go because I *feel* something ancestral." For Orikerê, playing with axé incorporates everything: body, spirit, mind, sweat, sacrifice, and feeling. Axé energizes his movements, but the force of axé comes from its spiritual, ancestral power.

Axé in Candomblé

Within Nagô/Yorùbá houses of Candomblé, axé (àse) is an elaborate, formal, and foundational concept:

> the force that ensures dynamic existence, that permits happening and becoming. Without *àse*, existence would be paralyzed, deprived of all possibility of realization. It is the principle that makes possible the vital process. (J. E. dos Santos 2012, 40)[21]

Axé—and its correlates in other denominations—is necessary for Candomblé practices to function and for practitioners to thrive. Indeed, the primary purpose of Candomblé rituals is to cultivate, accumulate, and (re)direct axé.

Much Candomblé literature has focused on the material objects that are depositories of axé: offerings of food and sacrificial animals, herbs, beaded necklaces, and blood (e.g., Opipari 2010, 85–86). The material bodies of instruments also contain axé. The atabaques "are believed to have a 'voice' of their own, irresistible to the gods, and their *axé* needs to be reinforced through 'nourishment'" (Béhague 2006, 98), their regular ritual "feeding" with macerated herbs, blood, salt, palm oil, and honey (Béhague 1984, 223–34). Moreover, axé can refer both to the "container" and the "content" (Wafer 1991, 18), and thus the food, herbs, blood, and drums all contain, and can be referred to as, axé. Yet containing/being axé are not fixed states but part of a "dynamic system" of building and maintaining axé (J. E. dos Santos 2012, 40). Axé's "mobility," its ability to be accumulated but not kept indefinitely, necessitates its regular renewal through repeated rituals (Wafer 1991, 91).

Axé in/as Sound

In Candomblé literature, attention to the material objects of axé tends to overshadow the central roles that simultaneous music-sound and dance-movement play in cultivating and transmitting axé. Santos briefly touches upon sound as a "conductor of *àse*" primarily through the sounded word (sung or recited) but also through the sounds of instruments, which are "formidable invokers of the supernatural entities" (orixás) and "effective inducers of action" (J. E. dos Santos 2012, 50; see also Cardoso 2006, 216). In other words, musical sounds "transmit a power of action and mobilize the ritual activity" (Béhague 2006, 95). The movements of the dancers in turn also "invoke and maintain . . . *axé*" (Daniel 2005, 84). As Vatin noted in his study on Candomblé rituals, music, and possession, "it is through some sort of successful interaction between music and dance that the axé arises over the course of the ritual ceremonies" (2005, 111).

Capoeira studies likewise contain only fleeting allusions to the notion that axé "circulates . . . through the instruments, the songs," and the moving bodies in the roda (Barbosa 2005, 94). Flávia Diniz (2010) cites Mestre Decânio's (2002) theory of a "capoeirian trance" (*transe capoeirano*) that is "triggered" by a specific berimbau toque. Yet rather than the toque's rhythm, Diniz explains that what "triggers this 'incorporation' is the 'energy' or the 'axé of the roda,' . . . which depends extraordinarily on its musical aspect"

(Diniz 2010, 163). When my interviewees described their experience, music transmitting axé seemed to act less as a trigger and more as a call. The toque may trigger an initiate's trance in a Candomblé ritual, but it calls the orixá to the festa. Thus I find that in capoeira, the angoleiro occupies a position more like that of orixá than initiate (though only concerning their felt relation to sound). The music calls to the angoleiro, who responds with movement and sound. Across the practices, axé as sound calls bodies (of orixás, capoeira players, samba dancers, instruments) into vibratory movement. When I hear the berimbau and want to move, or hear the samba drums and want to clap or dance, it is a surrendering, as Orikerê said, "You must respond." I give in and give over to the call of axé.

The Aural-Kinesthetics of Axé: Being in Sintonia

Many group members described the state of experiencing axé as "being in sintonia." When I asked one member, Pernalonga, why he had moved across the country to train with Mestre Cláudio, he said, "Man, there's no explanation! You feel it and you want to feel it forever, the axé of the Angoleiros do Sertão!" When I asked him about axé, he said, "If you have various people, energies, with the same intention, it will become axé. . . . They must be in the same sintonia." Another member said that "axé is to be moving well . . . to have everyone in the same sintonia." When players move together with the performative intention of axé, they enter sintonia.

More common in Brazilian Portuguese than its cognate in English (syntony), "sintonia" is a term from radio technology that refers to a matching of frequencies, with colloquial meanings similar to "being on the same wavelength" and "being in sync." What I find compelling about syntony is the way in which it describes being "responsive to and in harmony with the environment; resonance" ("syntony" n.d.). A body receiving vibrations could be imagined as passive, but sintonia expresses the active state of responsiveness necessary for two bodies to seek and find the same frequency—imagine tuning in: turning a radio dial until the frequencies align, and you hear a clear signal. Sintonia evokes the "resonating and reciprocal nature" of sound vibrations, such "that every mechanism capable of expressing them can also receive vibrations" (Henriques 2010, 75). Thus sintonia reveals that in order to transmit axé, one must be able to receive axé, and vice versa. Sensing, receiving, and producing axé, bodies in sintonia must achieve sympathetic resonance collaboratively, thereby collapsing distinctions between transmitter and receiver, actor and acted upon. Sintonia expresses not only a state but also the dynamic aural-kinesthetic processes of simultaneous hearing, listening, moving, sounding, and giving-receiving axé in the capoeira roda.

Sensing Sintonia in the Saturday Morning Capoeira Roda

Rewind to an hour or so before the opening scene of this chapter. The capoeira roda is about to start. The cement brick ground is speckled with sunlight diffused through the leaves of the massive tree that provides shade from the brutal sertão sun. Buses, cars, and motorbikes rumble by, but the sphere formed by players' bodies and arching tree branches contains the sound. The mestre plays a slow, unadorned toque on the berra-boi joined by the other berimbaus and pandeiros, while the reco-reco, agogô, and atabaque remain silent (see fig. 1). The tong-ting of the berra-boi playing the Angola toque hangs in the air, its hollow ring punctuated by the buzz of coin on wire and the sharp shake of the *caxixi*'s seeds (see musical example 8). The berimbaus' tone clusters prickle the surface of my skin. We all look to the mestre as he calls out, "*Iêêê!*" to start the ladainha, the solemn opening song.

Na fazenda do sertão [2x]	On the farm of the sertão [2x]
ai ai ai já vi muita covardia	Ay ay ay I've seen a lot of cowardice
já vi negro massacrado	I've seen Black people massacred
e jogado no porão	And thrown in the cellar
eu vi tocador de gado	I've seen the cattle driver
que vinha de Serrinha e Riachão	Who came from Serrinha and Riachão
dessa Feira de Santana	From this [here] Feira de Santana
montado no alazão	Mounted on a sorrel
para vender o boi ai ai ai	To sell the ox ay ay ay
ao mandado do patrão	At the orders of the master
Iê! Num dia que vem a seca [2x]	Iê! On the day the drought arrives [2x]
não encontramos solução.	We don't find a solution.
A tardinha o sol se põe	In the evening the sun sets
vai embora o clarão.	the brightness departs.
A notícia próxima	The next news
vem trazendo a solidão.	Brings solitude.
Me lembro das vaquejada	I remember the rodeos
e as cuida de mourão.	And mending [cattle] fences.
Me lembro da capoeira	I remember capoeira

Os Angoleiros do Sertão, camarada.	The Angoleiros do Sertão, dear friend.
Iê, viva Bahia!	Iê, long live Bahia!
[*coro*] *Iê, viva Bahia, camará!*	[chorus] Iê, long live Bahia, friend!
Feira de Santana!	Feira de Santana!
[*coro*] *Iê, Feira de Santana, camará!*	[chorus] Iê, Feira de Santana, friend!
Viva o sertão!	Long live the sertão!
[*coro*] *Iê, viva o sertão, camará!*	[chorus] Iê, long live the sertão, friend!

The mestre's voice carves out a channel within the stillness, penetrating the air with the nasal timbre of an aboio. The berimbaus' micro-intervals, with their richly clashing harmonics, might even evoke the crunch of gravel on parched earth, under the cart's wheels. As the pandeiros plod ahead, the

Musical Example 8. The basic toques of Mestre Cláudio's bateria. The top three lines are the berimbaus: the lower note is the open string, the higher note is the string closed by the coin, and the *x* represents either the shake of the caxixi (clutched in the same hand that holds the baqueta stick), the coin-loose-against-wire buzz tone, or both simultaneously. The berimbau staves represent Mestre Cláudio's preferred relative tuning, where each second represents an approximate major second, and the open tone of the berra-boi is approximately a fourth below the viola's open tone. In practice, pitches vary, and the berimbaus play variations on these toques.

tempo steadily increases. I catch only certain lyrics filtered through the traffic, but I hear how they invoke the afterlife of slavery (Hartman 2008a), the violence that still takes the lives of descendants of enslaved and freed Black people who populated the drought-ridden sertão (Ferreira and Tambascia 2021). In a mournful inversion of the samba yet to come, quoted at this chapter's start, the ox seller's bravado is absent. Now he conducts his commerce "at the orders of the master." The mestre folds slightly at his waist, bending his knees on the beat to emphasize the emotion of his poem.

Just before he sings the group's name, he steps into the roda's center to signal the coming call-and-response section (*chula* or *lovação*). Immediately, as we sing, "*Iê, viva Bahia, camará!*" the bateria releases into full volume: the atabaque's thud, the wooden agogô's "tock," the scrape of the reco-reco; the pandeiros' slap. As if we'd been holding a collective breath, we now let out our voices. Some students jump in place or lift their arms, "Long live Feira de Santana!" (See video 2 at https://doi.org/10.3998/mpub.12771665.cmp.18 and https://doi.org/10.3998/mpub.12771665.cmp.19)

My pulse begins to pound in my neck as the mestre transitions to a *corrido*, the running call-and-response songs that accompany game play. He sings, "I am an angoleiro who comes from the sertão!" (*Sou angoleiro que vem do sertão.*) The roda stirs as the corrido calls, players shift right and left, bouncing slightly in anticipation, for their turn may come next. The bateria resounds in and around us, summoning spectators, increasing the roda's density. As the pace picks up, frequencies align and muscles loosen, games get faster, and energy accumulates. At over one hundred beats per minute, the bass *boom ba-doom* of the atabaque drives the bateria, the players' movements, and the surge of blood in our hearts and limbs.

When the mestre lowers the berimbau toward me, calling me to play, a shock snaps me out of listening and singing. As I stand up, any lingering fatigue evaporates from my limbs, replaced by something akin to what Pernalonga called a mix of anxiety and joy, a "cold [pit] in your stomach." I kneel at the foot of the berimbau, my blank expression masking giddy nerves. To start the game, I place both hands on the ground, balance my torso on one elbow, and lower my head toward the feet of the berimbau player, touching the pavement with my temple. I prop my bent legs on my other elbow, watching my opponent perform the same movement (*queda de rins*). We push back up toward the center of the circle, eyeing one another, everyone's eyes on us, heads down, and our legs swoosh through the thick air. There is much to describe of the bodily dialogue of attacks and defenses, but the axé also enters as a partner, facilitating our split-second calculations, anticipations, and evasions; manifesting tangibly as a "felt *push* of the possible underneath the surface of the perceived and unfolding present—a push that can be felt on the skin and in the ear" (Garcia 2015, 72; original emphasis). Vibrations amplify in the berimbau gourds, the atabaque's wooden barrel, stretched pandeiro skins, fist-size nut shells of the agogô, otherworldly shimmers of the pandeiros' tin discs, and the heterophonic voices.

Playing in the middle, I feel the full-bodied voices energize the air, touch my skin, and urge me to put in the axé. For me, games often pass in a blur, with only certain details surviving, but what remains is a buoyancy from the joyful effort of throwing my body-spirit-mind with full força. Sensing axé in the sound-movement means giving-receiving and giving in to sintonia. At the end of our game, I embrace my partner in genuine gratitude for having shared the game with me. When I return to sit in the ring, I realize I played the entire time with an ecstatic grin splashed across my face. As one group member put it, "I can only be grateful to be part of the Angoleiros do Sertão and to have a little of this sintonia." (See video 3 at https://doi.org/10.3998/mpub.12771665.cmp.20 and https://doi.org/10.3998/mpub.12771665.cmp.21 for a game played at the same roda by Contramestre Tico and Hulluca.)

The Call of Axé: Compromisso

Sensing axé in the rodas of capoeira and samba, practitioners feel called to participate, to move, dance, sing, and play. However, there are other consequences that follow from responding to axé's call. In my interview with Rita, mentioned above, I was struck by how forcefully she described feeling pulled by the sounds: "*É chama!* It practically drags you there! It pulls you!" Seeking to hear more about the embodied experience, I prompted, "And you'll *feel* it, too—?"

"You will get *involved*," she interjected. "You'll feel the energy, the involvement of this movement. You'll perceive that it's not only the three berimbaus and the *rum, pi* and *lê*. . . . It's the *formação* [the way people are educated], it's the energy, it's the *comprometimento* [commitment] with the work. The *ogãs* [Candomblé drummers] are *extremely committed* to the terreiro of Candomblé. Just as we have to be very committed to capoeira, to take care of the instruments, not to leave them without someone watching them. It is this same responsibility."

Using Candomblé as a reference, Rita described how aural-kinesthetic responses gave way to greater responsibilities and commitments, which

Mestre Cláudio often calls compromisso.[22] Compromisso can mean obligation, promise, or commitment ("compromisso" n.d.), or obligations one has promised to fulfill. For an initiate in Candomblé, their compromisso includes commitments to fulfill certain obligations (*obrigações*), specifically referring to rituals performed after initiation, but also more broadly gesturing toward "a way of constructing and caring for [affective] ties over time, which is characteristic of candomblé" (Rabelo 2020, 1). Mestre Cláudio's use of "compromisso" resonates with the latter, more general understanding: his students' range of responsibilities and long-term commitments to capoeira, the group, and its community. Indeed, the compromissos that members have in both capoeira and Candomblé "families" are very similar to the obligations commonly assumed among family members (Baptista 2007, 4). When the Angoleiros do Sertão say they are a family, it means they embrace the lifelong challenges and responsibilities that family brings. For Mestre Cláudio, compromisso also means assuming ongoing commitments to capoeira itself, as he often warns: "*Capoeira dá, mas ela cobra*" (Capoeira gives, but it charges, demands payment). The benefits practitioners receive from capoeira incur an obligation to give something in return. Yet very similar to the compromisso an initiate has with their orixá, this is not a debt to be canceled with a single payment. Rather, the compromisso is unending.

It is unusual for Mestre Cláudio to give detailed explanations of what he meant by "compromisso," but he went into some depth on the subject during a master class he gave to his newly formed satellite group in Recife in 2016. Perhaps wishing to impress upon his new students the seriousness of their decision to join his group, he explained how in Candomblé there was something they called "*surra de caboclo*," the whip of the Caboclo. When things are not going well in an initiate's life, it is because their Caboclo (or orixá) is displeased. To remedy the situation, the initiate must make the proper offerings to the Caboclo. It was the same in capoeira, Mestre Cláudio said, only the obligation is not paid to an orixá but to capoeira. In this way, Mestre Cláudio rendered capoeira a kind of entity with the power or agency to punish a devotee. This sense was reinforced by a story Rita told me: As a young man, Cláudio was visiting with a mãe-de-santo, likely someone he knew through his mother's involvement with the religion. She charged him with an obligation, perhaps to make an offering to a protecting orixá, but Cláudio defiantly refused. He told her that he had only one compromisso in his life, and it was with capoeira Angola. Mestre Cláudio did not specify all that group members' compromisso entailed, but he models his compromisso with his own life. Clearly his students' responsibilities also include committing to ongoing introspection, continually asking themselves if they are giving enough (back) to capoeira.[23]

The actions of the group also reveal the forms compromisso can take. As discussed in the introduction, maintaining the Saturday morning roda is perhaps the group's greatest, most serious compromisso, their commitment to the Black community of the region. As Dona Ivannide described it, "It's beautiful to see! Elderly people, Black people, crowding together there in the roda and feeling comfortable to samba in public!" When Black men and women samba in the middle of the street, she said, when they get home, they will be able to help their impoverished peripheral communities and "think themselves free" (*pensar-se livres*). To maintain the weekly roda, students are expected not only to train capoeira three nights a week but also attend the roda every Saturday, showing up ready to participate with their full bodies, minds, and spirits. They also spend hours, usually alone at home, practicing the berimbau, learning to vary the toques, and building the stamina to play a berimbau (its thin taut string balanced on a single pinky finger) for hours on end. Playing the pandeiros, timbals, and bumbo drums in the samba likewise requires tremendous endurance. Group members rarely mention their bodily commitment to playing instruments, but their sweat and blistered fingers speak more than words. Leading the song, especially in the samba, also requires the vocal force to project the call over thundering drums and street noise. Over the years, Mestre Cláudio's voice has grown hoarser from the effort. Other weekly duties include making and maintaining the instruments. While I often heard the mestre berate his students for not taking good enough care of the group's bateria, still, every Saturday there are at least six berimbaus (two of each), well-tuned and fully resonating, strung to Mestre Cláudio's exacting specifications. There are multiple pandeiros and extra berimbau wires, baquetas, and coins, because wires snap, baquetas break, coins can fall and roll away. Several of Mestre Cláudio's students can often be found hanging around his instrument workshop on his compound, observing and assisting him in his skilled craft of making atabaques, berimbaus, pandeiros, and other percussion instruments.

As Henriques (2010) has proposed about the vibrations of the dancehall session and scene in Jamaica, capoeira's and samba's frequencies repeat, even as they vary, every beat, every measure of each song, every week and year. As the frequencies spiral outward from within the vibrations and toques of the roda, from the micro-moments of training and play, they broaden to encompass years and eventually generations. Henriques's sound-based model of "repeating vibrations in material, corporeal and sociocultural wavebands"

(2010, 73) beautifully illustrates how sound coheres community in moments of body-to-body encounter that continue to resonate beyond those spacetimes. If the Saturday roda is the culmination of the weekly cycle, then the group's annual event in January is the culmination of a year's worth of work, preparation, and anticipation. Here, too, group members commit themselves to assisting with all the necessary preparations for the annual event, from clearing the ground of Mestre Cláudio's compound of overgrowth so that event participants can pitch their tents, to organizing the logistics of transportation and lodging for visiting guest mestres, to cleaning the floors of training spaces, and preparing and serving food during the event. Assuming a compromisso with capoeira requires attending to these material logistics, but it also exceeds them.

As Orikerê's story illustrates, having a compromisso with capoeira Angola can also alter the course of one's life trajectory. His sense of necessity, his obligation to be in capoeira, derives from his certainty that capoeira saved his life. When he first encountered the sound of the berimbau, he had already fled the violence of São Paulo city to the state's interior. There he trained with a satellite group of the Angoleiros do Sertão for seven years before Mestre Cláudio brought him to Bahia. Or, perhaps more accurately, capoeira brought Orikerê to Bahia. As he put it, "Really, it was more [like] capoeira itself chose me, because I didn't know shit about anything."

Capoeira has called other members to change their lives, too. Pernalonga sold all of his belongings and moved to Bahia from Rio Grande do Norte.[24] Thomaz, a white engineer from the interior of São Paulo, began training in 1998 in a satellite group in Bauru, another interior city of São Paulo state, and moved to Bahia to be closer to Mestre Cláudio in 2007, forfeiting more lucrative career opportunities. When I asked Thomaz why capoeira was so important for him, what he felt capoeira brought to his life, he answered, "It's hard to explain. After you have a certain involvement with capoeira, I think it's hard for you to let go of it. The mestre says it's not even you who lets go of capoeira, because it's bigger than you are. It's capoeira that lets go of you. If you're not on the right path, not making the right choices, capoeira will end up letting you go." When axé calls, some players end up reorienting and restructuring their lives in response.

Yet this is only the beginning of compromisso, for when they achieve a certain proficiency in capoeira, it is also expected that practitioners will begin teaching groups of their own, under Mestre Cláudio's supervision. Orikerê teaches in São Félix, Thomaz in Salvador, and Pernalonga taught with his partner, Solange Couto, in a periphery of Feira de Santana before they moved away for Solange to pursue her PhD. Since our interview in 2015, Rita has also begun teaching in Salvador and as a guest at events throughout Brazil. Many of the group's teachers intentionally establish groups in underserved Black peripheral neighborhoods with the express purpose of bringing capoeira's empowering valorization of Black culture and Black ways of knowing to the youth who can benefit from it the most. Continually experiencing the life-altering effects of surrendering to capoeira's axé, these group members devote their lives to passing on capoeira's liberatory lessons to Black community members, to people whose ancestors sustained the practices centuries ago.

Conclusion

Members of the Angoleiros do Sertão experience axé as a sounding, moving force that brings bodies into sintonia, coheres community, and calls them to assume a compromisso with capoeira and Black communities of Bahia and beyond. Orienting their bodies with an African matrix sensorium, the Angoleiros dissolve the sensorial boundaries between capoeira, samba, and Candomblé, gesturing toward a broader sense of community that extends beyond the group and beyond capoeira. Axé as vibration blurs boundaries not only between practices (Gidal 2016) but also between sound and movement, mystical and material, aural and kinesthetic, and among participants from disparate backgrounds. The force of axé calls together practitioners, communities, and practices, creating a new entity that is at once corporeal and collective, a "singular-multiplicity" (Henriques 2010, 67), bringing individual bodies into relation without erasing their differences. Capoeira, samba, and Candomblé remain distinct practices, only they cannot be separated. Focusing on axé's vibrational properties thus allows a conception of community not as something forged or bound but rather syntonic. Axé summons bodies to actively participate in the intentional seeking, finding, and aligning of frequencies in sintonia.

Although axé seems to possess a certain autonomy and even agency, bringing bodies into motion and sounds into vibration, making something happen, axé cannot act alone. For it to keep resonating within and beyond African matrix spaces, players must continually renew and regenerate axé. As this chapter has illustrated, "putting in the axé" requires more than simply playing the right rhythms or performing the right movements. Playing with axé demands effort and intention. It does not happen automatically or even easily, even though when vibrating in sintonia, players' movements may feel or appear effortless. Indeed, so much of the labor required to keep the group charged with axé happens outside of the rodas, before and after the moments of playing, dancing, singing, and clapping. This is why group members' compromisso is so wide-reaching and never-ending. Ultimately, by joining the group and collectively generating and sensing axé, members commit themselves to sustaining capoeira, not only in terms of their personal practice, or the group's practice, but also ensuring that capoeira Angola continues for future generations.

As this book proceeds, I will temper what may seem like a utopian claim that axé unites across difference. When axé calls bodies together, diverse players and community members experience and incorporate axé, which they recognize as an African matrix force. In this sense, axé is always already racialized, understood as an energy and concept originating in African and African diasporic practices. Yet even though everyone involved in capoeira and related practices can sense axé, each player interprets capoeira from the ground of their lived experience. As the following chapters show, patterns emerge in practitioners' interpretations, and these tend to diverge along racial lines.

The following chapter explores how the calls and responses of axé reverberate not only across space but also across time, as forces of ancestralidade. Accessing their ancestralidade, some practitioners consider what they owe to generations future and past.

Two

Accessing *Ancestralidade*

Spiritual Memory and Embodied Fabulation

When you play berimbau, when you play samba, it's as if the force is internalized as part of you. As if an ancestral energy, something from your past, becomes internal, and calls me to it.

—Bolinha

On November 19, 2020, one day before Brazil's Day of Black Consciousness, João Alberto Silveira Freitas, a Black man, was brutally beaten and murdered by two white security guards outside a Carrefour supermarket in Porto Alegre, the capital of Rio Grande do Sul, Brazil's southernmost state. A delivery man filmed the scene on his phone. The video also shows a white woman in a Carrefour uniform hovering close to the two guards. As people exit the store, some try to intervene, and the woman pushes them away, seeming to threaten them if they try to film the attack, actively preventing anyone from stopping the violence. The guards, one of whom was an off-duty "temporary" military policeman, beat João Alberto with their bare fists. The video shows João Alberto's blood splattered across the yellow floor. At one point, one of the attackers kneels on his back. The video records the victim's call for help, saying it hurts, that he is dying. An eyewitness heard him crying out that he couldn't breathe. João Alberto died of asphyxiation.

A few days later, on Saturday, the Angoleiros do Sertão held a *bate-papo*, an informal discussion session. Early in the worldwide lockdown, which began in March 2020 due to the global COVID-19 pandemic, Mestre Cláudio had started holding online capoeira classes twice a week. Then in May 2020, George Floyd, a Black man, was murdered at the knee of a white policeman in Minneapolis, Minnesota. A video of the scene captured Floyd calling for his mother, saying that he couldn't breathe, and as the video circulated on social media the world erupted in protest. In early June, Mestre Cláudio held his first Saturday bate-papo in response to the violent event, which reverberated across Brazil. He recognized the need group members felt to be together, to talk things through, and the bate-papos continued weekly throughout the summer of 2020 and frequently through the end of the year. Although the gatherings were informal, Mestre Cláudio invited speakers and discussants, and some featured Black activists from Feira de Santana.[1] This provided a structure and offered various community members an opportunity to share their stories and experiences with the group. The bate-papos partially filled the hole left by the absence of the weekly Saturday roda.

The bate-papo following João Alberto's murder featured Karine Teixeira Damasceno, one of Feira's most prominent Black movement activists. Group members, including Mestre Cláudio, were visibly and audibly shaken by João Alberto's death. It was acknowledged that this kind of violence happens all the time in Brazil, that the only thing that distinguished this case was the video. At one point Clara (pseudonym) spoke. A Black woman who had trained for many years with the group, she now lived away from Feira de Santana and was raising her children and working toward her PhD in women, gender, and feminism studies. She grew more emotional as she spoke, cautioning us to remember all the other assassinations of Black people. She said, "The violence doesn't begin with the assassination of João. It begins when we are children." As children they are instructed to believe that Black people are bad, that they have no history. "We are never seen as humans." Stridently, she reminded us, "Today we're outraged about João, but we can't forget the assassination of Marielle Franco"—her voice started to break—"who was violently assassinated . . . because she was the voice of the periphery, the voice of Black women, of LGBT people. We can't forget Evaldo, who died of so many gunshots at his car." Speaking through her pain, she went on: "We can't forget Miguel, whose Black mother cried over the death of her son because the white employer couldn't see him as a *child*! Because the white gaze doesn't see a Black child as someone who needs care! . . . We can't forget Cláudia, who was shot by the police and then dragged [by the police car]!" Clara continued:

> And so, for a long time we have been dehumanized and assassinated. And when I speak of ancestralidade and capoeira, I am referring to people who came before us and who died, who gave their blood so that we can be here today, debating. So that today we can be there in the

university, breaking into the master's house. So that we can say today, "I am a Black [preta] professor, a Black intellectual . . . a *feminista negra*; that I want to break with this university, with this white epistemology. And I want to help my camaradas with capoeira, to affirm their identity as a people."

As the poet said of our ancestralidade:

Who birthed me was the belly of a ship,
Who heard me was the wind in the void,
From the dark bowels of a hold
I will bow down in your terreiro!

And so, "I'm going to learn to read in order to teach my camaradas!"

With these lines, Clara quoted the stirring song "Yá Yá Massemba," now a classic of *música popular brasileira* (MPB), sung by Maria Bethânia on her album *Brasileirinho*, which gives musical expression to Brazil's racial mixture (Bethânia 2003). "Yá Yá Massemba" recounts the perspective of enslaved Africans who survived the Middle Passage. When Maria Bethânia sings the lyrics Clara recited, the song moves from major to minor and Bethânia's voice quietens, plunges, and darkens, marking the depth and darkness of the slave ship's hold and the solemnity of the memory. The wind that heard her—pleas, prayers, laments?—powered the ships as they sailed through the terrible void of the Middle Passage.[2] Birthed from this horror, Bethânia's voice rises in defiance when she sings, "I will bow down in your terreiro!" Born of unspeakable violence, she summons strength—to survive, to exist, to fight—through participating in the embodied rituals of Candomblé.

As Clara indicated, these lines capture the essence of ancestralidade, the subject of this chapter. "Ancestralidade" literally means ancestry, referring to a person's lineage. However, ancestralidade can carry deeper significance especially for Black Brazilians, because thinking about their ancestors means grappling with their ancestors' enslavement and contending with the numerous ways in which their forebears' stories, histories, and experiences have been denied and suppressed. Ancestralidade also has a religious connotation, for according to some definitions, Candomblé's orixás are "divinized ancestors"—that is, "great ancestors" who were transformed into divine entities (P. Johnson 2002, 36). Thus Afro-Brazilian religions are said to be permeated with ancestralidade, evidenced also by axé being considered "ancestral energy." Sensing ancestralidade, whether in a capoeira roda or listening to a

Maria Bethânia song, therefore means sensing something spiritual, deeply moving, and connected to the past. For many Black people I spoke with, the concept of ancestry is inherently significant because the term invokes centuries of both unfathomable suffering and improbable survival of their ancestors.

Clara ended her recitation of the lyrics by skipping to the final verse of the song, a new section returning to the major key of the opening, which repeats defiantly, over and over, "I'm going to learn to read in order to teach my camaradas!" With the history condensed through Bethânia's song, Clara's emotional testimony declared the power of ancestralidade as a force in her life that has empowered her to earn advanced degrees and use her knowledge to benefit Black people, her camaradas. This illustrates how ancestralidade operates like a force in so many Black Brazilians' lives. Whereas the previous chapter showed that axé, the force generated by sound-movement, calls practitioners to participate in African matrix practices and assume commitments to their communities, this chapter explores how the forces of capoeira and samba rodas also call across time. Sensing their ancestralidade, I argue, some practitioners access their past and feel summoned to take on political commitments to combat anti-Blackness in the present and future.

As Bolinha's epigraph above and the testimonies that follow show, many Black angoleiros and activists sense ancestralidade as a force that calls them to respond. In this way, ancestralidade is related to axé: axé may transmit ancestralidade or at least help practitioners access it. As with axé, angoleiros sense ancestralidade with their bodies when perceiving the sounds and movements of African matrix spaces. By accessing ancestralidade, Black community members, activists, and scholars recover the past in order to alter the present and future. Building on Black feminist methods of recovering the past to understand the present and future, I propose that some community members perform a kind of "embodied fabulation": a bodily sensory means of imagining and experiencing an otherwise inaccessible past in order to transform the present and future. Indeed, as Black feminist writer and activist Elizandra Souza put it, ancestralidade "is a marvelous and very advanced technology" (2023, 276).

When Clara referred to those "who came before us and who died, who gave their blood so that we can be here today," she includes her distant ancestors on slave ships and, tragically, more recent ones like the assassinated Rio city councilor Marielle Franco and João Alberto. This continuity of Black death, the enduring fungibility of Black life, is what Saidiya Hartman has called "the afterlife of slavery." In an oft-cited passage, Hartman defines the afterlife of slavery as the enduring impact of slavery's past on our present:

> If slavery persists as an issue in the political life of black America, it is not because of an antiquarian obsession with bygone days or the burden of a too-long memory, but because black lives are still imperiled and devalued by a racial calculus and a political arithmetic that were entrenched centuries ago. This is the afterlife of slavery—skewed life chances, limited access to health and education, premature death, incarceration, and impoverishment. (2008a, 6)

Clara urged us to remember that skewed life chances and anti-Black violence plague Black life in Brazil, too, where every twenty-three minutes a young Black person is killed, many by police (Escóssia 2016).[3] The afterlife of slavery spans the histories and spaces of the Western hemisphere and beyond, signaling the "persistence of the past . . . not as a repetition but as a continuation" (Colbert, Jones Jr., and Vogel 2020, 16). Clara and many other Black community members face slavery's afterlife every day, living "in the wake" of the slave ships (Sharpe 2016). Yet by accessing their ancestralidade in and around rodas of capoeira and samba, they conjure embodied fabulations of their ancestors' past enslavement and struggles, and this calls them to continue to fight for bettering Black lives in the present.

Ancestralidade in the Literature and Capoeira

Numerous Brazilian scholars have theorized the concept of ancestralidade in depth. In his dissertation, based on auto-ethnographic research on capoeira Angola, philosopher Eduardo de Oliveira (2005) put forth a "philosophy of ancestralidade" as the ideal basis for Brazilian education. In poetic-philosophical language, Oliveira summarized:

> Ancestralidade is a category of relationship, connection, inclusion, diversity, unity and enchantment. At the same time, it is an enigma-mystery and revelation-prophecy. It indicates and hides paths. Ancestralidade is a way of interpreting and producing reality. This is why ancestralidade is a political weapon. It is an ideological instrument (a set of representations) that serves political and social constructions. (2005, 258)

As a philosopher, Oliveira elaborates new meanings of ancestralidade that transcend everyday usage, but there is some overlap with the ways I encountered the term.[4] Like Oliveira, community members often connected their experience of ancestralidade to their politics. Oliveira also claims that "the body both is ancestralidade and is governed by it" (2005, 125). While my interlocutors did not equate ancestralidade with the body, they clearly sensed their ancestralidade through embodied perception. Moreover, their practices of accessing ancestralidade—one of which I call "embodied fabulation"—seem to be ways of interpreting and (re)producing reality. In other words, community members leveraged their sensations and understandings of ancestralidade to make sense of their past and its political meaning in the present. Along similar lines, anthropologist Alexandre Emboada da Costa, in his ethnography of a cultural center's antiracist activism in São Paulo state, found that his interlocutors saw ancestralidade as "a form of Afro-diasporic decolonial politics" (2014, 47): a "lived theory and cultural practice" that "mobilizes the past not as legacy or 'tradition,' but as a project for contemporary transformation" (46).

Although ancestralidade, much like axé, takes on a variety of meanings in Black activist contexts, among angoleiros, and in the literature, common threads emerge connecting the past to present and future politics. Niyi Afolabi, a scholar of Afro-Brazilian cultural politics, expansively defines ancestralidade as both "source" and "force": "that vital source of kinship and heritage" that Afro-Brazilians access through their religious, music, and dance practices (2009, 239) and a "resourceful, imaginative, adaptive, and progressive force [that] has sustained African peoples throughout their turbulent engagement with Western modernity" (198). Ancestralidade as *source* thus describes shared connections of descent fostered through music-dance practices, while the *force* of ancestralidade fuels Afro-Brazilians' creative cultural and political movements.

In capoeira Angola communities, common understandings of ancestralidade are assumed though rarely made explicit. Yet ancestralidade clearly signals the past and invokes ancestors. After all, a fundamental aspect of capoeira Angola practice is experiencing how "the past is intentionally summoned through ritual, music, and song" (Downey 2005, 116), not least through lyrics, which contain numerous references to history. Frequent themes include Africa and African languages, slavery, and notable historical events and figures, especially wars and capoeira fighters (Assunção 2007). In some groups, capoeira students are taught to "worship" previous capoeira players as their ancestors (Varela 2019, 103–122), or at least claim and remember capoeira ancestors by praising them, displaying their photographs on studio walls, or reciting one's capoeira "lineage" (Abib 2004, 187).

Capoeira scholar-practitioners Sara Machado and Janja Araújo draw at length upon Oliveira's philosophy of ancestralidade to argue for capoeira Angola as a "transformative and liberatory educational praxis" (2015, 99). Citing Oliveira, they explain that ancestralidade spreads "its 'dynamics' to any racial group that wants to assume the identity of 'African.' Thus [ancestralidade] becomes the authentic bearer of an African 'logic' that organizes the lives of its practitioners—white or black—and engenders social structures capable of maintaining and updating 'African values' forged in pre-colonial Africa" (108). Ancestralidade in Candomblé also transcends biological lines of descent. When one enters Candomblé, one assumes a new kinship with the *família de santo*, the family of one's Candomblé house, and therefore also assumes their ancestors. This flexibility of ancestry to be "real" (biological) or "imagined" (adopted or metaphorical) reflects a similar "logic operative within African societies," which enslaved Africans brought with them to Brazil (Parés 2013, 50). For instance, Africans who survived the Middle Passage on the same ship considered themselves a brotherhood (49).

For now, I set aside the question of whether white angoleiros also feel that ancestralidade organizes their lives (see chapter 3). But it is widely accepted that angoleiros, regardless of their race or spirituality, inherit deceased capoeira mestres as their "ancestors" when they make deep, embodied, long-term commitments to capoeira Angola. Thus ancestralidade can evoke different meanings of "ancestors," from enslaved Africans (some of whom created capoeira) to past capoeira players and mestres. It is no surprise that Black practitioners often merge these meanings, for they can claim descent, imagined or real, from all of these ancestors.

Spiritual Memory and Ancestral Retrieval

Bolinha grew up in Feira de Santana in the historically Black neighborhood of Rua Nova in the 2000s, where as a teenager he encountered Dona Ivannide Santa Barbara, the militant Black movement activist and community organizer, who lived there with her family. It was Dona Ivannide who put Bolinha and many other Black youth "on the path of the fight, the resistance," by encouraging pride in their African descent and empowering them to participate in antiracist activism and politics. Bolinha said, "If I believe that the

Black population can have another way of living, it comes, in addition to my ancestralidade, through meeting Ivannide de Santa Bárbara." For Bolinha, joining capoeira came later, and at the time of our interview in 2017, he was in his early twenties and had been training capoeira for three years. Yet despite his relative newness in capoeira, he already considered capoeira Angola his "greatest instrument of militancy."

As Bolinha described his entry into capoeira in our interview, he explained that he had chosen to start training when he realized capoeira's importance to the Black movement. Echoing his words back to him, I asked, "Can you speak more about how you understand capoeira as 'resistance,' as 'part of the Black movement'? Because this is my biggest question: What is it that capoeira does, that capoeira contributes, and what are the limits? . . . Why do you feel it's important to be in capoeira?"

He paused for a moment, smiled, and asked, "Can I smoke a cigarette?"

"Of course!" I laughed, slightly embarrassed at my torrent of questions. Bolinha collected his thoughts and then spoke:

> This question is very emotional for me. Because what I understand is that we call it capoeira Angola because the majority of slaves came from Angola. But it could have been called capoeira of Haiti, capoeira of Guinea-Bissau, capoeira of the Congo. When you say "capoeira Angola," I don't think it means only Angolans. Capoeira Angola is capoeira of the slaves.
>
> And so imagine that against all of this suffering, you have your body as an instrument of liberation. It's as much a defense against the whip of the overseer, a defense of *mandinga*, so you can escape the oppression the slave master wants to impose on you, as it is a ritual, to say, "No, our ancestralidade must be kept alive!" Capoeira Angola must fulfill this role, to keep this ancestralidade alive. Today, to do capoeira Angola for me is to keep all of this suffering alive, and all of the courage of a people, all the dignity, all the respect this people had in order to still be alive today. So many people died so that capoeira could still be here today!
>
> So when I go to a roda of capoeira, when I see the toque [sounded rhythm] of the berimbau, when I see all the energy involved in capoeira, in various moments in my life, when I'm in a roda of capoeira—I perceive it all as happening back then, during slavery. Many times I see this, in my mind, when I close my eyes. I can discern the sugarcane field, and I can discern Black folks playing capoeira.

For Bolinha, capoeira is an embodied instrument of liberation for anyone descended from enslaved Africans. Practicing capoeira, angoleiros not only train physical moves of defense and mind games of trickery and manipulation (*mandinga*), but they also keep alive the memory of their ancestors' struggles for life, survival, and beauty; their suffering, courage, and dignity; and their capacities to defend, escape, create, and ritualize. By locating capoeira's liberatory potential in his body, Bolinha's understanding also resonates with Oliveira's idea of the body as ancestralidade. This further recalls how scholar-activist Beatriz Nascimento centered her quest for history in her body (more on this below).

When Bolinha "sees" the sounds and energy of the roda, the colloquial use of the verb "to see" (*ver*) takes on a more expansive sense of perceiving, gesturing toward a multisensory perception. When he closes his eyes, he discerns (*enxergar*) the past, perceiving sound, movement, and imagery across time with multiple senses. Later in our interview, Bolinha returned to this idea of perceiving the past while hearing the toque of the berimbau and emphasized that he felt this was something Black people alone experienced in capoeira:

> Black people are going to perceive in capoeira, aside from the spirituality, the call, the toque of the berimbau, how all this involves their spiritual memory. This is the best word for it. It's spiritual memory. Because it's undeniable that we are not only material, only body, we are spirit, too, and this spirit has already walked other paths. And Black people have this ancestral retrieval—something that whites don't have.

I will return later to Bolinha's claim that only Black people have ancestral retrieval, leaving open whether white people may be able to retrieve another kind of past—though no white people I spoke with claimed to do so. For now, I understand Bolinha as referencing both the ancestry and lived experience that he shares with other Black people. Unlike white people, Afro-Brazilians are descended from enslaved Africans and today suffer the daily injuries of racism and prejudice. If white people did retrieve a past of enslavement, this might mean conjuring images of enslaved people (who are not their ancestors) or their ancestors (who were not enslaved). In short, white people are positioned differently in relation to the concept of ancestralidade, and as the next chapter addresses, they described sensing ancestralidade in distinctly other ways. This reveals that shared sensations of sound and movement can generate multiple, overlapping, and divergent experiences. Significantly, these divergences often meant different interpretations of capoeira's politics.

When Bolinha senses the toque's ancestral call, he re-calls, re-embodies, and reimagines his past, revealing another layer of experience in the roda. In addition to sensing the axé vibrating in the roda, aligning frequencies, and entering into sintonia, while listening to the berimbau with his body, Bolinha also synesthetically sees a past that his ancestors lived.[5] When he says that his "spirit has already walked other paths," he suggests that he carries within his body a connection to his ancestors' experiences of suffering enslavement, which he recognizes was shared across geographies. Saturated with the sensations of the capoeira roda, Bolinha brings to body-spirit-mind his "spiritual memory" of that past. He calls this process "ancestral retrieval": perceiving ancestral energy that calls across time, from past to present, and reaching back, from present to past, to retrieve what was left behind. To emphasize the body's role in ancestral retrieval, I call this *embodied fabulation.*

Embodied Fabulation

Embodied fabulation refers to the ways some Black community members creatively (re)imagined and conjured an unrecorded or "forgotten" past through sensing sound and movement in capoeira Angola and samba rodas.[6] Seeing the scenes of their ancestors' enslavement, they also experienced the emotional impact of those scenes. Many talked about this as a kind of memory or remembering, even while acknowledging that they had not personally lived through those days. This remembering is therefore a kind of fabulation: a re-creation of something that they know happened but that they never experienced. Experiencing embodied fabulations, community members recall both the suffering and resilience of their ancestors. However, they do not inhabit the past. Rather, they summon the past into the present, which in turn summons them to assume responsibilities for countering anti-Blackness in their lives today. Listening with their whole body-spirit-minds to the toques of the berimbaus, atabaques, and other sounds of the roda, they respond to the calls with movement(s)—physical, sounded, expressive, and political.

Scholars have explored music and dance's profound relationships to memory from a diverse range of viewpoints, but with embodied fabulation I refer to a way of leveraging bodily sensation to recover a silenced past and summon it into the present.[7] Like Apache listeners hearing certain popular songs, Black community members immersed in the sounds of the roda experienced a "rediscovery of something that one thought had been lost forever, the recoverability of the past" (Samuels 2004, 138). When Bolinha hears the toque of the berimbau and sees "the sugarcane field, and . . . Black folks playing capoeira," he recovers and reexperiences moments that no written record captured, in which enslaved people stole away (Hartman 1997, 65–70) from the eyes of the overseer, temporarily eluded capture, and sequestered time and space to flex their limbs and play.[8] Heidi Feldman also described how Afro-Peruvian choreographer Victoria Santa Cruz leveraged what she called her "ancestral memory" to rediscover and recreate movements, gestures, and meanings linked to an African past (Feldman 2006, 49–82). Such sensory, affective, and imaginative responses to sound-movement do more than reach across time to remember. They reorient temporality and summon an unknowable past into the present.

Saidiya Hartman proposes "critical fabulation" as a method for redressing "the violence of the archive" of transatlantic slavery by writing imaginatively "at the limit of the unspeakable and the unknown" (2008b, 1). The past of slavery is unspeakable because of its horrors and unknown because little record exists of the "interior life" of enslaved people (T. Morrison 1995, 92). While this appears at first to be a project concerned primarily with the past, Hartman insists that her concern with "narrating counter-histories of slavery has always been inseparable from writing a history of [the] present, by which I mean the incomplete project of freedom" (2008b, 4). A history of the present, she explains, "strives to illuminate the intimacy of our experience with the lives of the dead, to write our now as it is interrupted by this past, and to imagine a *free state*, not as the time before captivity or slavery, but rather as the anticipated future of this writing" (4; original emphasis). Critical fabulation is therefore also future oriented, a creative way to tell an "impossible story" (10–11) of the inner lives of the enslaved so that we may imagine a better future. Thus, while fabulation embraces fiction, it not only reaffirms that all histories are fictions to a degree, but it also pushes historical methods further, out of political and ethical necessity. In the embodied fabulations of Black community members, I sense a similar yearning to encounter enslaved people as full beings and to redefine the humanity of those who have been excluded from the category of the human for centuries (Wynter 2003; Hartman 2008b, 3).[9]

Black Brazilian women writers have also grappled with "a past that is not past" (Sharpe 2016, 13), merging forms of "autobiography, autofiction, and fiction" in efforts to "look at the past to understand the present time, through a process of revisiting and extolling their ancestral matrices as fundamental to their existence and re-existence" (Sousa and Freitas 2021, 215). Though her work was long overlooked, Afro-Brazilian activist-scholar Beatriz Nascimento's primary concern was with recovering a "History of Black

People," a challenging, difficult project that would require rethinking ways of doing history, as history has almost exclusively been written from white men's perspectives (B. Nascimento 2023, 86–87).[10] To this end, Nascimento undertook extensive research on the quilombo as a historical institution in Angola and Brazil whose sociocultural and political systems, she argued, continue to manifest in contemporary peripheries (Ratts 2007; B. Nascimento 2021). In her essay "Kilombo and Community Memory: A Case Study," she provides a telling alternative title: "Memory and the Hope of Recovering Usurped Power," revealing the political aim of her project (B. Nascimento 2023, 236). Nascimento's concept of quilombo thus bends temporalities, connecting past, present, and future. Tracing how quilombos of the past—communities and territories to which enslaved people escaped—nurtured "dreams of freedom" (B. Nascimento 2023, 253) throughout Brazilian history, Nascimento gestures toward a present and future return to quilombo's ruptures and "cracks" within oppressive systems (252). Yet Nascimento also located the quilombo in herself: "The Earth is my quilombo. My space is my quilombo. Where I am, I am. When I am, I am" (Ratts 2007, 59). Wherever she goes across time and space she brings quilombo with her, carrying and sustaining quilombo's "historical continuities" (Ratts 2007, 109–110) in her body.[11]

In this way, Beatriz Nascimento located continuities of spirituality and freedom in "the Black body" (Smith, Davies, and Gomes 2021), positioning the Black body not only as a site of identity construction, for reclaiming senses of pride and beauty, but also as a territory unto itself. For Nascimento, the Black body moves, migrates (forced or voluntarily), escapes (enslavement, oppression), and forms a space of refuge, continuity, and memory: "The body is also memory. Of pain—that the images of slavery will not let us forget, but also of fragments of joy" (Ratts 2007, 65–69). As Smith, Davies, and Gomes note, in Beatriz Nascimento's conceptualization, the "Black body is not dehumanised, un-feeling flesh, but an extension of the spiritual terrain of the earth as it is defined by Afro-Brazilian cosmological understandings" (2021, 286), such as those cultivated in Candomblé. By receiving orixás, Caboclos, or other spiritual entities of Afro-Brazilian and Afro-American religions, "the Black body can exceed its geographical boundaries . . . to become something that defies both space and time" (287).[12]

As their testimonies show, Black community members' embodied fabulations similarly transcend spatial and temporal limits. Thus with embodied fabulation I recognize resonances between written and embodied archives, and I draw parallels, though not equivalences, between various modes of interpretation and expression—written, oral, sensory, and emotional. Because the lived experiences of their ancestors have largely been flattened or ignored in historical archives, Afro-Brazilian community members turn to what could be called "alternative archives of Blackness":[13] the embodied knowledge (Daniel 2005), or what Beatriz called the "corporeal memory" (Ratts 2007, 68), transmitted through the sounds, movements, bodies, and repertoires (Taylor 2003) of African matrix forms. Experiencing these embodied archives, they sense their ancestralidade.

Sensing Ancestralidade

I conducted a joint interview with Igor and Papagaio, two young Afro-Brazilian group members and friends in their early twenties in Feira de Santana. We met for the interview before capoeira class one weekday evening at the CUCA, the University Center of Culture and Art of UEFS, where the group's classes are held. In the bright fluorescent lights of the foyer where we sat, Igor's lighter brown skin contrasted with Papagaio's darker tone. At the time, Papagaio wore his hair in short locks while Igor's hair formed large, shiny curls close to his head. When I asked how they self-identified, both young men firmly asserted their Black identity. Perhaps to clarify, implicitly acknowledging his lighter skin, Igor added, "I'm Black [negro], *cotista*, with Black skin.[14] To assume a Black identity is to assume it in everyday life, in the way I walk, wear my hair . . . and to affirm my Blackness in capoeira Angola." Papagaio said with a laugh, gesturing to his darker skin, "I'm already Black, everybody knows!"

Igor said he had sought out capoeira Angola expressly to access the ancestralidade and "because it was a movement of freedom, of resistance." I found it notable that he had associated ancestralidade with capoeira before he started training, so I asked him if he had grown up knowing about this connection. He responded, "I think you only know what it is when you have contact, when you're practicing, day to day—you feel it, you *feel* more than you *know*."

"How?" I asked.

"It's how you feel part of the movement, you feel you belong to it, as if it was always going to happen in your life." Here the movement (*o movimento*) refers to capoeira Angola as a social movement, though this includes taking part in its bodily movements.

I had heard other students describe their sensations in the roda like this, so I asked Igor, in order to clarify, "Like seeing it and feeling like you've already done it?"

"Yes, and thinking of capoeira Angola also as a philosophy of life, a way of thinking—"

Papagaio jumped in, saying, "The freedom of your body, too. When you start to practice capoeira Angola, you feel a liberation, bodily movements go naturally. With time you learn the *molejo* [smooth, swaying quality of movement]. . . . You figure out your own ways [of moving], and it's as if you'd already practiced it before, as if you'd already seen it. And you see that there, the body already wants that—"

"And not only the body, but it's the connection between the body and mind and spirit!" Igor added.

"Exactly!" Papagaio confirmed emphatically.

Igor went on: "All three work together. The music, too, conducting the game, the music conducting the movements of your body. You're in sintonia with the music and at the same time with the partner who is playing with you."[15]

"That exchange of axé," Papagaio added, "of positive energy, it's always good. When we're in the roda, and we let the music enter our thoughts, we let ourselves be carried away with the movements of capoeira Angola, and the music takes us, carries us to do movements, to make new friends, this is capoeira. Bodily and mental liberation."

Answering my questions about ancestralidade led Igor and Papagaio to insist that ancestralidade was something that had to be felt and sensed, with body, mind, and spirit, through the music conducting the game. When I asked them to describe "a moment of the game," trying to better understand what they felt in the roda, Papagaio returned to the past:

> It's an energy that will take care of us. And entering the roda to play, damn! It's a marvelous sensation! To be there, representing the group, doing what you love, feeling that freedom, knowing that you fought, you sweated to be there—it's like in the old days. The Black folks, they worked hard during the day. They suffered, suffered, but never stopped practicing capoeira, never stopped practicing samba. Because for them, it was their life. It was there they wanted to live. Night would come and it was a moment of liberation for [them], to feel at ease, to bring a little of their ancestralidade, where they came from. . . . It was distant, but it was close. Capoeira brings this to us, too. When we are in the roda, we go to a world that isn't ours, that when we enter to play—you liberate yourself. . . . It's a world where we have our freedom.

Papagaio's testimony evokes Hartman's "*free state* . . . as the anticipated future" of those moments in the roda (2008b, 4)—an imagined future experienced in the present. As he speaks, the roda emerges as a parallel world of care, respite, and freedom continuous with a past in which Black laborers (his ancestors) carved out time in the day and space in their lives to practice capoeira and samba. Doing so, they connected with their ancestralidade, which was both far (across the ocean) and near (in their bodies). Numerous early capoeiristas worked hard labor jobs, as stevedores on the docks lifting heavy crates, as porters carrying goods across the city all day in the heat (Abreu 2005; Abib 2009). Reading these histories, I've tried to imagine the soreness and stiffness of their muscles and joints after days of labor, and then how they recovered their strength by swaying in *ginga*, side to side, forward and back, knees bent deeply and torso leaning forward, then springing lightly on their feet, lifting their legs in the air, and bearing the weight of their musculature on their arms in *bananeiras* and *aús*.[16] When they summoned the stamina to play capoeira even after so much exertion, they must have been countering the physical and emotional strains of their long days. They were healing themselves with what we might now call "active recovery."

Yet as Igor and Papagaio insisted, the benefits of training far transcended the physical. Entering a "world that isn't ours," they experienced (momentary) freedom from the pressing concerns of daily life, freedom to do what they want and love. Sensing their ancestralidade is liberating for these Black angoleiros, and ancestralidade liberates because it bends time and awakens a different future of the past, that which was going to be, as Igor responded when I asked what ancestralidade felt like: "As if it was always going to happen in your life." Perhaps in the roda, Igor and Papagaio anticipate "future anterior freedoms" (Weheliye 2014, 130): new ways of being free that are as inevitable as they are yet unrealized.

Igor's and Papagaio's descriptions of experiencing ancestralidade also illustrate how closely it relates to axé. In a conversation I had with Mestre Cláudio, I asked him if the axé in capoeira and samba was the same as the axé in Candomblé. He answered yes, explaining that ancestralidade is there in all of them and that axé comes from ancestralidade. He went on to say that the ancestors were present in all the practices, capoeira, samba, and Candomblé. The axé that emerges from ancestralidade, he told me, comes from the rhythm, the drums, the music, and the movement. It is no wonder, then, that players often sense ancestralidade and axé together. Ancestralidade also seems to manifest vibrationally, transmitting the vital force of axé, through the music and movement. Yet axé and ancestralidade are not the same thing. It's possible, for instance, to sense axé and not sense ancestralidade, which is how I would describe my own experience.

To avoid collapsing axé and ancestralidade into each other, I note two ways in which they differ: First, ancestralidade expresses an explicit relationship to temporality. Second, in the afterlife of slavery, this bestows upon ancestralidade a racialized political significance. While axé, too, endures across time (transcending individual humans' lifetimes), ancestralidade more specifically effects a "layering of present and past" (Samuels 2004, 46), bringing different times and spaces to rest upon or even merge with one another.[17] Its energies call and respond "back and forth among bodies across different times and different spaces," opening up the "possibility that the past may yet have another future" (Schneider 2018, 288). In sum, whereas axé signals angoleiros' (direct and indirect) associations of capoeira with Candomblé, ancestralidade evokes particular relationships between temporality, (African) descent, and racial politics. Ancestralidade, as source and force, connects Black community members to their past and summons them to carry on the struggles of their ancestors. Sensing ancestralidade can therefore be understood as a practice that takes many forms.

Ancestralidade in Practice

Before our interview, Bolinha gave me a tour of Rua Nova, located downhill from the central bus terminal in Feira de Santana. As we walked through the gently sloping streets, Bolinha explained Rua Nova's significance in his life and in Feira as a center of Black movement organizing. The streets were mostly paved with cobblestones peering through gaps in the pavement. One- or two-story buildings with storefronts and residences wedged against one another, with red clay roofing tiles showing various degrees of wear (see fig. 8). Whereas I saw nothing remarkable about the neighborhood, Bolinha clearly wished to impress upon me the deep significance the place held in his life and the development of his thought. He explained that Black residents had owned the land on which they built Rua Nova, and their self-determination lived on in the cultural and political life of the neighborhood today.

Bolinha led me to a small triangular plaza wedged between the streets, a few trees lining its borders, and he paused at the bust of a woman. We had arrived at Praça Dona Pomba (Dona Pomba Square). Bolinha explained that Dona Pomba (Lady Dove), depicted in the bust, had owned the land that now makes up Rua Nova (see fig. 9). In an act of legendary generosity, she had parceled it out to the Black people who already lived and worked in the community.[18] These gifts had enabled the residents, now Black landowners, to build and shape their community as they wished. Rua Nova residents today retain a fierce pride in their independent Black origins, and the neigh-

Figure 8. Street view of Rua Nova. Photo by the author, 2017.

borhood continues as a site of thriving social, cultural, and political Black movements. By telling me this history, Bolinha was countering the way the neighborhood is portrayed from the outside, stigmatized as crime-ridden and poor (F. Santos 2016a, 15).[19] As I'm sure he was aware, I had often been warned not to walk alone on the street at night in that area. Bolinha wanted me to see beyond this flattened image and understand Rua Nova's important legacy as a site of Black culture, organizing, and activism in the city. By peeling back the layers of time and stigma from this nondescript neighborhood, Bolinha was putting ancestralidade into practice. Walking beside him, listening to his stories, I felt his pride surge in my chest, too.

Bolinha told me that his sister, Flávia Santana Santos, had written a children's book about the community's unique origins, titled *An Urban Quilombo Called Rua Nova* (F. Santos 2016b), for her master's degree in the history of Africa, the diaspora, and Indigenous peoples. In her report, she explains that her primary sources were the "memories of residents" collected through interviews, for there was little written record of how the neighborhood developed (F. Santos 2016a, 23). Santos describes each interview as an intimate "moment of reminiscing about the lived experiences and testimonies" of

Figure 9. The plaque, dedicated in March 2002, reads, "In homage to D. Pomba, an example of the love of the Feirenese woman." The turqoise building in the background is what remains of Dona Pomba's residence. Photo by the author, 2017.

events that led to the formation of the neighborhood (23). She crafted her book as a "historical novel, in order to approach all of that symbolic universe that was embedded in the experiences of the interviewees, who became characters who told their own stories" (31). Santos's methods emerge as a kind of critical fabulation: she drew on both her lived experience and the interviews to narrate what Rua Nova's first residents might have felt, thought, and said to one another. In these ways, Santos's approach resonates with that of other Black women authors, like Hartman and Toni Morrison, who have sought to reconstruct an inaccessible past. Santos's choice to call Rua Nova an "urban quilombo" (2016a) also echoes Beatriz Nascimento's theorization of quilombos. Santos affirms that "the link between the quilombo of yesterday and that of today is and has always been the psychosocial and historical capacity to re-signify the painful experiences of racial discrimination" (29). By writing *An Urban Quilombo Called Rua Nova*, Santos has recovered Rua Nova's history as a way of sustaining popular memory and nurturing contemporary racial-political consciousness in the community's young minds.

I've lingered with Rua Nova because I see both Bolinha's tour and his sister's book as forms of ancestralidade in practice: thinking, sensing, and remembering to recover the past, shift the present, and summon a future of flourishing Black life.

True History

At the time of our interview in 2016, Abusada was one of the few Black women training in her capoeira group, one of the satellite schools of the Angoleiros do Sertão in the interior of São Paulo state. A dancer and teacher of *dança afro*, an Afro-Brazilian dance form that draws on the dances of Candomblé, Abusada was in her early twenties and wearing her hair woven with gray wool into long, thick braids that draped down her back. The light gray of her braids next to the dark tone of her skin had a stunning effect, signaling her astute fashion sense that she has since leveraged in her hair care and braiding business. In a second interview, in 2017, she explained her *apelido* (nickname), Abusada. Although the English cognate of "*abusada*" is "abused," this is not the primary meaning of the word. Abusada explained that she had immediately identified with the apelido and embraced its positive meanings of "courageous" and "brave," unafraid to enter into confrontation, both within and outside of the roda. At the same time, Abusada noted its gendered-racial significance and the way it evokes stereotypes of strong Black women. She said, "It's messed up [*foda*] because you'll see that the white women in the group all have names of flowers and jewels, like Flor, Flor do Oriente, Natureza, Esmeralda. And the Black women get names like Atrevida [cheeky, petulant], Ousada [brave, daring], Abusada. So there's this thing of the white woman here, she's white, pretty, a delicate flower."

In 2016, as I began to ask questions, Abusada answered with alacrity and detail. It seemed as if her fearlessness also manifested in her rapid speech as she narrated and analyzed her experiences. I felt my mind whir as I tried to keep up with her but was grateful that she was offering so much in our limited time together. When I asked how she had started training capoeira Angola, she described it this way:

> The moment I entered the [capoeira] class, I knew *this* was what I wanted to do! Only later did I realize why it was such a strong experience for me, the first time I saw capoeira Angola. Today I understand that it is directly connected to ancestralidade. When I'm in the roda, in the capoeira Angola environment, it's as if I've already been part of

it for a long time. And today capoeira Angola is part of the formation of my identity as an Afro-Brazilian woman.

Abusada had brought up ancestralidade in the context of doing capoeira, so seeking to understand what she felt in the roda when she sensed ancestralidade, I said: "Talk more about the ancestralidade, what you feel in your body, in your mind." I expected her to talk more about her sensations in the roda. Instead, she began by describing her childhood and her earliest experiences with racism as one of few Black children in her school in the interior of São Paulo:

> Since I was little, before capoeira came to me, before I understood capoeira as a form of ancestralidade, there was the fact of being Black [*negra*] and being a Black woman. This is very strong for us since infancy, because in school, in the classroom, we suffered *a lot* of racism. Racism from the other children, from the teachers. And we were in public school, so being a little Black girl and poor, from the periphery of the city, we were always in a situation of not knowing what we were, of feeling inferior. We saw how the girls at school who have smooth hair and lighter skin were the ones everyone flirted with, and so we suffered from that time on because we didn't know our history. Because the history taught in school is a Eurocentric history. . . . When the older teachers talk about Black people in the class, it's only in reference to [using air quotes] "slavery."[20] And so we feel really bad because the only time we see people with our color in the classroom, it's in the sense of being something bad, of being something black [*preta*], being dirty, and all the other stereotypes. . . . And so we don't learn what is good [about us], from our point of view.
>
> After we grow up and learn *just how* important Black people were for Brazil and for the entire world, how important Africa is for the whole world, after we started learning about this side, we were able to assume [the identity of] being Black. . . . And so, since I learned about my true history, . . . I was able to recognize myself as Black and see the good side of it. And included in all of this is capoeira Angola, dança afro, and various other dimensions of Afro-Brazilian culture here in Brazil. And it's in *this* context that I use the term "ancestralidade." . . . So when I look at my history, I see the enslaved Black people who began capoeira Angola as role models. So this thing of ancestralidade is a thing of familiarity, really, to be close to the Africans. . . . It's in this sense that I talk about ancestralidade.

Like Bolinha, Igor, Papagaio, and others, Abusada emphasized the continuities between her experience and that of her forebears. As she went on to explain, her understanding of her African descent includes knowledge of her family's story. She told me that her direct ancestors on her mother's side labored as *bóias-frias*, seasonal laborers who worked (and in some cases still work) long hours of hard labor on sugar or coffee plantations. They were named after the food/chow (*bóia*) that they brought to the fields for lunch, which they had to eat cold (*fria*) because they had no way of heating it up. Though these family members were several generations removed from slavery (abolished in 1888 in Brazil), the conditions they endured had barely improved since then.

As Abusada grew aware that she had been taught a false history, in which Black people were always only "slaves," subhumans without will or culture, she began to seek out her "true history." This enabled her to contextualize the struggles of her relatives within slavery's long afterlife, revalorizing the enslavement of her ancestors. Recovering her true history, Abusada saw how these suppressed histories continued to shape her lived experience of gendered racialization. Confronting racist perceptions of her self and her body, Abusada began developing her "double-consciousness" and her "second-sight"—knowing and seeing herself both with her own eyes and through the eyes of white others and recognizing the falsity of the latter viewpoint (Du Bois 1986; G. L. Mitchell and Hordge-Freeman 2016). Abusada came to value herself as a "*mulher preta*," a Black woman, and now she claims as role models her enslaved ancestors who created capoeira, against so many odds, as a way of cultivating their strength and resisting their subjugation. I had asked Abusada to speak more about sensing ancestralidade because she had said she felt it in the capoeira environment. Yet she answered by narrating a richly layered personal, familial, ancestral, and political history, merging her sensing, thinking, knowing, and being. This reveals that sensing ancestralidade encompasses the sensory, affective, intellectual, spiritual, and political simultaneously.

When we conducted the interview, Abusada had recently joined a terreiro of Umbanda, an Afro-Brazilian religion that shares many characteristics with Candomblé. As in other interviews, my questions about the music of capoeira elicited responses about other African matrix practices. When I asked her to describe what it was like to play in the capoeira roda, or to participate in Umbanda, Abusada said, "It seems as if I've already heard that tambor, a long time ago. It seems like I've already samba'ed that samba." She described her experience as a process of "remembering" a past she had already been a part of:

> When I start playing, it's the same in capoeira as in Umbanda. It's as if I'd already played this someday before, but in this incarnation I'm—I'm remembering [*relembrando*] what I've already done. The capoeira is very different, it's changed a lot over the course of time, so I'm learning how it is today, but it's this thing of—I'm playing with my partner in the roda, but there's very much something beyond just playing, which is my ancestralidade, really. In the roda, it's like this: I feel the presence of my ancestors very strongly. I feel that they are with me. You know? I feel that I'm never alone! Because they are there with me, playing, they're orienting me, they are a part of me in that moment of the roda.

Abusada clarified that she was not claiming to incorporate spirits or entities into her body like initiates do in Candomblé or Umbanda. Rather, she explained:

> The thing about my ancestralidade is that there have already been Black people—an enslaved Black woman—who did capoeira and who constructed capoeira. And when I'm in capoeira Angola, I feel this connection with these people who have already been there. Not necessarily that there is an entity present there in the moment, but rather the feeling of knowing that they have been there and knowing that I am closely descended from them and feeling that I'm in a space where I already was.

Abusada's use of "relembrando" implies repeated acts of remembering: this is not the first time she has remembered doing what she has already done. Her sensory re-remembering is also an "emotional memory—what the nerves and the skin remember as well as how it appeared" (T. Morrison 1995, 99). Abusada recalls the Black women progenitors of capoeira, although they have largely been written out of the history books (J. Oliveira and Leal 2009) and all but ignored in the stories told about past capoeira players. Responding to the call of her ancestralidade with her body in the roda, Abusada fabulates the true history of an enslaved Black woman playing capoeira so that Abusada could practice it today.

Memory-Imaginary

One need not practice capoeira to experience corporeal immersion in the sounds and energies of African matrix practices. Other community members participate by singing or clapping at the edges of rodas, dancing samba, or in Candomblé festas. Dona Ivannide has never practiced capoeira Angola, but she regularly attends the Saturday roda of capoeira followed by samba in support of the group's street activism. She also belonged to a terreiro of Jeje Candomblé for many years, prior to the passing of her mãe-de-santo. In our 2016 interview, we were talking about the connections between capoeira and Candomblé, and she was reflecting on how she had come to know about these connections. She said:

> And so—I don't know, I keep imagining—I never studied any of this more deeply—but I keep imagining—I close my eyes and *think* about moments in Brazil's history, and as a person who lived in Candomblé for some time, I keep thinking about moments where, in the terreiros of Candomblé, after the big festas, I see the capoeiristas there, on the day of rest, playing capoeira in the terreiros of Candomblé. This is what I see in my memory—not my memory, in my imaginary. I keep thinking like this. Because capoeiristas were nothing more than sons and grandsons of the mães-de-santo, brothers of the *ialorixás* [Yorùbá for mães-de-santo]. They were the people of the community. And the communities during this time of slavery were communities of *santos* [Candomblé practitioners]. Generally, they began as a *roça de santo* [rural area where they built the house of worship], and then they organized themselves afterward into quilombos. But it was a *preta velha* [literally, an old Black woman, a spiritual leader], a mãe-de-santo who called the community together to bless them; as we say in Candomblé, to *fechar o corpo* [close the body]. To bless the individual and free them of dangers. So it was out of this that they constructed Black unity.

A self-described skeptic, Dona Ivannide chose her words carefully, first describing seeing the past in her "memory" but then calling it her "imaginary." Yet alongside Bolinha's spiritual memory, Beatriz Nascimento's community and corporeal memory, and Abusada's relembrando, "memory" seems apt. Memory-imaginary and relembrando also recall Toni Morrison's "rememory," ways in which undying events, places, and experiences of the past can haunt the present (2004). Dona Ivannide's self-correction also reveals the limits of our languages (English and Portuguese) to name this imaginative process of sensing what came before one's lifetime and fabulating an inaccessible past.

When Dona Ivannide closed her eyes and remembered the past in this way, she drew on her experience of many years immersed in the calls, sounds, and energies of capoeira and samba rodas and Candomblé rituals and festas. Her experiences of the rodas inform and are informed by her life beyond the spaces of African matrix practices, including her perspective as a Black woman who grew up in poverty in Feira's peripheries and who for years has organized with labor unions and mentored successive generations of local Black movement activists. The sum of her experiences comprises the embodied archive of her (re)memory, which enables her to see how her ancestors labored to build Black unity in alternative spaces of Blackness of the past. Like Abusada and others, she used her fully sensing body-spirit-mind to fabulate a past of which she has no other record.

Any Body Accessing Ancestralidade

In our 2016 interview, Dona Ivannide was talking about capoeira and Candomblé sharing the same "cosmic energy" (axé), and she mentioned that practitioners could sense and respond to this energy even unconsciously. This made me wonder if she meant that axé and perhaps even ancestralidade could be sensed by anyone, regardless of race and background. I had heard white practitioners suggest something to this effect, so I said, "I was struck, talking to many people, by how many white capoeira players also talked about *feeling* ancestralidade."

"Indeed [*pois é*]."

Dona Ivannide was unfazed by my observation, so I went on. "And it makes sense, what you're saying—it could make sense, because if the energy is ancestral, can it be transmitted through *any* body [*qualquer corpo*]?"

"Any body," she confirmed. "This is my belief. First, I think like this: not just anybody, white or Black, will be a capoeirista or go to Candomblé. Someone goes because . . . they are close to the kind of energy that lives inside of them, and the energy calls you to capoeira or to Candomblé. I believe this, you know? And so—" Her voice breaking, she continued:

> You talked about white people feeling this—it makes me emotional. Because I've already seen rodas of capoeira with [white] people who were quite skilled. I felt a great prejudice in relation to this: [There are] as many white people in Candomblé as in capoeira! [She let out a short, bitter laugh.] Until I understood that this ancestral energy doesn't choose . . . only us Black people [*pretos*]. It may be that we, *pretos e pretas*, have *amos* [slave masters] brought here. But [the energy] inhabits whoever is open to perceiving it. . . . If you open your mind to

> perceive this, it manifests itself, from the point of view of emotions, of sentiments. I've already seen very beautiful things in capoeira, people playing capoeira, that I say to myself, "That's not what's-her-name playing there! There is an orixá!"

Dona Ivannide said she thought that the white player would call her "crazy" if she suggested they had incorporated an orixá, but she said that those who had made a commitment to Candomblé and had a relationship with the orixás would see it: "Sometimes there's a spontaneity, a lightness, that we perceive that on another day the same person doesn't have the same lightness. So—it's energy."

I wonder if Dona Ivannide's emotional response to recalling a white angoleiro playing with orixá energy arose not only from witnessing her beautiful game and sensing a powerful presence but also perhaps from a kind of emotional cognitive dissonance. Was it painful to see a white woman inhabited by the energy of an orixá? Can white players also access ancestralidade in the capoeira roda?

Other group members acknowledged this possibility. When I asked Binho, who identified as "totally Black," about white angoleiros reporting they could feel ancestralidade, he responded, "It's because, for me, it's energy. Ancestralidade has no color. So this thing of Black, white, it doesn't exist because if it's in your blood, it is inside of you. It doesn't matter [what] your color [is]." Here Binho's use of "blood" referred not to an essentialized idea of race (cf. Pinho 2010, 153–55) but to its visceral opposite, the notion that blood flows through all human bodies and therefore any body can resonate with the ancestral energy. From this perspective, ancestralidade, like axé, is accessible to anyone who can sense its vibrations.

This may seem to contradict Bolinha's claim, cited above, that only Black players can perceive their spiritual memory in the roda, accessing ancestral retrieval. White players also experience powerful sensations in the capoeira roda, and as the following chapter explores, they also claim to sense ancestralidade. Yet none of the white practitioners I spoke with described anything like the embodied fabulations narrated here. Still, if the ephemeral moments of rodas generate energies and sensibilities that both recover the past and continue to reverberate into the future, and if these energies are at least theoretically accessible by anyone open to them, then this suggests the possibility that white and non-Black players could also be summoned by ancestralidade to re-embody their ancestral past. This could include remembering the violence committed by their ancestors and recognizing how it reverberates in the present. As I address further in the epilogue, fabulating such a past might move white practitioners to ask themselves what they could do in the present to interrupt the afterlife of slavery.

Conclusion

In the rodas and at their edges, ancestralidade manifests as an embodied force that calls Black community members to summon the past of enslavement in the present. Accessing their ancestralidade, these members renew their compromisso with their ancestors, who inspire them to continue to care for one another and fight for a future in which Black lives have value and Black humanity is unquestioned. By calling attention to embodied fabulation—the ways that sounds and movements summon practitioners to fabulate their past—I gesture to possibilities for conceiving of slavery's afterlife in sonic-vibrational terms. What if the violence of past regimes is a kind of reverberation? If the past continues to vibrate, in ongoing re-percussions and re-soundings; if slavocratic coloniality resonates in the present, entering and violating our bodies (albeit in disparate ways), then the ancestralidade that moves bodies in capoeira and samba rodas could be a counter-force to the violence of slavery's afterlife—a vibrational companion to Hartman's counter-history. The way in which Bolinha described capoeira Angola keeping Black people's ancestralidade alive also supports this sense of ancestralidade as counter-force: as with axé, the rodas of capoeira and samba continually renew the ancestralidade so that it may continue to move people in their lives.

If, as Bolinha suggested, the force of ancestralidade carries and calls forth both "all of this suffering" and "all of the courage" of enslaved people, then this also recalls capoeira's capacity to hold seeming contradictions in tension, the beauty and the fight. The process of embodied fabulation, in response to sensing ancestralidade, brings into the present both the ancestors' trauma and the physical, emotional, and political resources they developed to mitigate the violences they endured and survived. Afro-Brazilian community members' embodied fabulations therefore disrupt ideologies of a teleological progression of history (Thomas 2016, 177), a linear concept of history that would relegate both slavery and the necessity for Black resistance to a best-forgotten past. Accessing ancestralidade and embodying fabulations of a violent past are therefore also actions of restoration and repair (Colbert, Jones Jr., and Vogel 2020, 8). These are the possibilities they offer all of us in the afterlife of slavery.

This raises the question of what happens when white practitioners access ancestralidade through capoeira and samba. Do they also feel summoned to fight the violence of slavery's afterlife? Does their immersion in African matrix spaces call them to assume a compromisso with Black communities in Brazil and the diaspora, imagining together other ways of being human? The following chapter addresses these questions by examining how white and non-Black practitioners describe and interpret their experiences of participating in capoeira.

Three

Consuming Bahia

The Politics of White Participation

> I don't have any Black genealogy, as far as I know. But I *feel* the ancestralidade anyway, just as other people also can feel the Black ancestralidade.
>
> —Beija-flor (pseudonym)

Echoing the capacity of ancestralidade to summon the past into the present, this chapter opens by once again circling back to November 19, 2020. Recall that on that day in *novembro negro* (Black November), the month of racial consciousness, João Alberto Silveira Freitas, a Black man, was assassinated by two white security guards outside a supermarket in Porto Alegre.[1] Several days later, the Angoleiros do Sertão held an online bate-papo, a semi-informal discussion, to process the event and simply to come together (virtually) as they had nearly every Saturday afternoon in 2020 during the pandemic. Black activist-scholar Karine Damasceno was the invited speaker, but the discussant had also arranged for Dona Ivannide, Karine's mentor, Black movement leader, and beloved community member to speak at the end of the session.

On the screen during this bate-papo, we could see that Mestre Cláudio was visiting one of the group's long-standing members, Raul (pseudonym), an older wealthy white Paulista man, at his home. Other group members from São Paulo state joined them, and they were attending the bate-papo poolside, drinking beer, joyously reveling in one another's presence—recalling the raucous post-roda celebrations Mestre Cláudio held every Saturday, now on hiatus. However, their alcohol-fueled lightheartedness jarred with the seriousness of the subjects being discussed. Several times, Raul interrupted a Black woman speaker, once declaring that he was "white, male, rich" (*branco, macho, rico*) as a kind of disclaimer before asking his question. When it was finally Dona Ivannide's turn to speak, Raul interrupted again to express his admiration for Dona Ivannide. He sent kisses and hugs. He missed her! He loved her! And then Mestre Cláudio asked him to repeat something he'd said off-screen, and he obliged, declaring, "If I could, I would buy ten Black women just like you!"

There was an immediate audible response, voices jumbled in protest, but soon Dona Ivannide once again commanded everyone's attention and responded, "Look, Raul: You cannot, Raul! Fortunately, you cannot. This is no longer possible. It's over. IT IS O-VER!" Emphasizing each syllable, Dona Ivannide was referring, of course, to slavery.

• • •

The Angoleiros do Sertão cohere their deeply affective community by generating axé, joining together in sintonia, and responding to the call of compromisso to commit to their shared practices and one another. However, as in other communities and families in the more traditional sense, animus, tensions, and conflicts—including racial ones—can be embedded within loving relationships.[2] Still, even though racialized power relations haunt group sociality of the Angoleiros do Sertão, they rarely disrupt the camaraderie as in the scene above. Until the summer of 2020, though individuals had privately expressed to me their concerns about the predominance of white members, racial matters in the group were rarely discussed in group settings. In the years I've known them, the community's sociality has conformed to the Brazilian norm of racial cordiality, tending to default to cross-racial "affection," which Sovik identifies as "the Brazilian way of dealing with [nationally] internal difference" (2009, 34). When expressions of racism do manifest, they are often more "veiled," "cordial" (Costa 2016, 31–32; Folha de S. Paulo 1995), or "camouflaged" (Mestre Cláudio's term).[3] Thus, in the group as in Brazilian society, the "tenderness, affection, friendship and love" purported to characterize race relations does not so much prevent racism as effectively secure Brazilian racial hierarchies in place (Sovik 2009, 53). This is the case even though the Angoleiros are more politicized, racially conscious, and left-leaning than average Brazilians.

Camouflaged racism is by definition difficult to observe—especially, one could argue, by white people, who are not on its receiving end. I witnessed problematic racial jokes go unremarked, for instance, in the group chat, but surely other microaggressions and racial slights took place when I was not present, or I failed to notice them. This underscores the invaluable contributions of Black scholars writing about their personal experiences of racism in Brazil.[4] Yet white researchers can contribute in other ways—for instance, by observing what white people say when no Black people are present (Schucman 2020, 38) or reflecting auto-ethnographically on their process of "becoming white" by recognizing their whiteness (G. Mattos and Accioly 2023). In our interviews I found that white community members expressed racist ideologies most openly when they expressed their desires to consume Black culture.

White consumption of Black culture has played a crucial role in the broad project of defining the Brazilian nation. In the early twentieth century, grappling in the wake of slavery with the undeniable influence of African culture in Brazil, Brazilian modernist artists sought to create art of value (music, literature, poetry, etc.) that was uniquely Brazilian. In 1928, proto-ethnomusicologist Mário de Andrade published his "*Ensaio sobre a música brasileira*" (Essay on Brazilian Music) (M. de Andrade 1972), in which he "exhorted Brazilian composers to draw on popular elements to create a distinctive national art music" (Dunn 2001, 22). Although Mário, of mixed race, was more ambivalent about African contributions, poet Oswald de Andrade (no relation) positioned Afro-Brazilian popular culture at the center of the "distinct and original" culture he proposed his peers co-create (Dunn 2001, 16).

Another problem confronted by the modernists was Europe's supposed racial and cultural superiority. In his "Cannibalist Manifesto" ("*Manifesto Antropófago*") (O. de Andrade 1991), also published in 1928, Oswald de Andrade claimed to have the solution: rather than imitate or reject European models, Brazilian artists should "devour" them to create an original national Brazilian culture (Dunn 2001, 18). Brazilian cultural cannibalism has endlessly fascinated generations of artists and cultural theorists ever since, some claiming it as a proto-decolonial move (L. F. Garcia 2020). However, celebratory readings overlook the racial politics. Andrade was a white elite intellectual from São Paulo who appropriated the concept of cannibalism from Brazilian Indigenous rituals, claiming them as already his own on the basis of his Brazilianness. Although Oswald's manifesto was aimed at cultures foreign to Brazil, it was premised on the assumption that Afro-Brazilian and Indigenous practices were already available for the modernists to incorporate at will. Thus I see in Brazilian cultural cannibalism an enduring tradition of white Brazilians "eating the other" (hooks 1992).[5]

Cultural cannibalism aligns with other articulations of white colonialist hunger. Dylan Robinson (2020) has written about white settler modes of perceiving Indigenous music and sound as "hungry listening," and though the objects of consumption may be different, his formulation opens up possibilities for exploring white colonialist sensory perception in relation to Black music, sound, and movement.[6] Saidiya Hartman also noted that white cannibalism of Black bodies "aptly described the devouring of life by the machinery of the slave trade" (Hartman 2008a, 113) and vividly underscores "the voracious and bestial character of power" (114). In contemporary Salvador, Danielle Hedegard (2013) observed a pattern of "omnivorous cultural consumption" in the ways that foreign white female tourists seek out experiences with male "dark skin-toned Brazilian bodies" in a capoeira school.

Interviewing white and non-Black Brazilian players about their attitudes toward Blackness and Black culture, I found that they expressed desires to consume Black culture that aligned with harmful yet commonsense understandings still dominant among the Brazilian population. Though "subtle and seemingly racially innocent" (Bonilla-Silva 2021, 522), these normative ways of thinking are what reproduce systemic racist-colonialist ideas and power relations. To be clear, these ways of thinking and acting are neither intentionally malicious nor innocent, nor do they go unnoticed. As this chapter shows, Black community members experience the violence of such subtle ideas in visceral ways. Even without the presence of "racists," the forces of colonialist racism permeate social relations in the group.[7]

White practitioners' attitudes and feelings toward Black ancestralidade are particularly revealing. Angoleiros of any racial identity can sense and transmit axé, and in similar ways, capoeira practitioners are understood to inherit, by virtue of their practice, the mestres and players of times past as their "ancestors." This may explain why many white and non-Black angoleiros claim to sense and access "Black ancestralidade" even while acknowledging not having African ancestry. Yet the ways they describe their relationships to ancestralidade contrast starkly with the embodied fabulations of Black community members. Most significantly, I found that white practitioners do not connect ancestralidade to historical or contemporary Black resistance movements, as their Black camaradas do. Instead, ancestralidade and, more generally, sensory experiences of Blackness become objects for white use and consumption. Thus, although white angoleiros use rhetoric like that of Black angoleiros, I suggest that individuals' racialized lived experience—how they are perceived racially and how they perceive others and the world through a racial lens—deeply inflects their understandings of ancestralidade and capoeira's politics, despite sharing in the same listening, moving, and sounding practices. When white and non-Black players sense, feel, and even embody Blackness through capoeira, but decline a place or say in antiracist politics, I argue that they reproduce racist-colonialist relations that render Blackness a resource for extraction. By considering how Black community members experience being "raw material" (A. do Nascimento 1989, 61), objects of white hunger and consumption, this chapter reveals some ways that "white supremacy and neocolonialism operate at the most intimate, visceral levels of social experience" (Berg and Ramos-Zayas 2015, 665).

Throughout the chapter I address a variety of attitudes and impacts that white and non-Black practitioners have in the capoeira community, from their hungering for ancestralidade, thingifying Black people, and appropriating capoeira's freedom discourse, to whitening capoeira spaces. However, the palpable sense of white people wanting to consume Blackness—or what Blackness can offer them—permeates these examples. White attraction to Blackness has been problematically framed as "love" (Lott 1993), also as when Gilberto Freyre valorized an irrepressible "sexual attraction between the races" (Freyre 2003, 66). However, white people's "pleasure" and "enjoyment" of Black expressions have historically converged with violence to reinforce "the mechanisms of racial subjection" not diminish them (Hartman 1997, 26). Attending to white people's desires for Black culture therefore requires questioning how these apparently positive valuations can harm Black people.

The chapter addresses primarily group members from São Paulo state and city (Paulistas and *Paulistanos*), who make up a large percentage of the Angoleiros do Sertão when including all of its núcleos. The first núcleo of the Angoleiros do Sertão was established in Bauru, in São Paulo's interior in the 1990s, and other núcleos followed as students advanced and began to teach their own students. During my research period there were at least six large, well-established núcleos in São Paulo state, mostly in the interior, echoing the sertão location of the original group. Thus, even though there were multiple núcleos in Bahia and other cities in Brazil, and a handful in Europe and the United States, a plurality of Angoleiros members lived in São Paulo state. Most of these members were white.

As the focus is on white Brazilian people, I tend to use "them," not including myself among the white subjects of the chapter. I use pseudonyms for most white and non-Black interviewees in this chapter as my intention is to critique persistent racist-colonialist ideologies and systems rather than call out individuals (Lipsitz 2011, 37). (In the list of cited interviews following the bibliography, I have also included only the state and year.) However, I do not exonerate other white non-Brazilians or myself from the critiques. Some of the ideologies expressed by white Paulistas may be specific to Brazil, or to São Paulo state in relation to Bahia, but I show that these ideas resonate broadly, too, both in history and across different geographies.[8] Long-enduring racial ideologies remain deeply entrenched among even the most progressive, well-intentioned actors, and despite their often veiled nature, these dynamics continue to harm Black community members.

White Brazilians Consuming Black Brazilian Music

Scholars have documented the long history of white cultural and political actors consuming, appropriating, emulating, and incorporating Black Brazilian expressive forms, as individuals and as part of broader nation-building projects. One of the most iconic instances is the white Portuguese-Brazilian singer Carmen Miranda, who sang samba and appropriated the costume of the Black *baiana*—who, with her white lace dress, turbaned head, and beaded necklaces (all from Candomblé), has become a near synecdoche of Bahia. In this way, Miranda essentially claimed Brazilian Blackness as her own through her performances in Brazil and the United States in the 1930s through the 1950s (Davis 2009; Bishop-Sanchez 2021). The tradition endures today, from white rapper Gabriel o Pensador "translating" Black peripheral perspectives for white audiences (Sovik 2009, 168) to Bahian axé music star Daniela Mercury appearing in blackface (darkened skin and afro wig) at Salvador's 2017 Carnaval (Travae 2017).

On the national scale, Getúlio Vargas's regime elevated samba—the Black music-dance form brought to Rio by Bahian migrants settling in its *favelas* (impoverished peripheral communities)—as Brazil's national music (McCann 2004). The brief but influential Tropicália movement of the late 1960s pushed back against "prescriptive formulas" demanding that artists incorporate Black and other traditional musics to produce "'authentic' national culture" (Dunn 2001, 73). Yet they did so by resuscitating Oswald de Andrade's anthropophagy and "cannibalizing" both Brazilian and foreign material (Dunn 2001, 74), fusing elements of bossa nova, samba, traditional regional styles, and "African things from Bahia" with rock-and-roll and the noisy sounds of electric guitars (Stroud 2008, 28–29; Treece 1997, 26). As música popular brasileira (MPB), Brazil's commercially popular urban music, emerged in this era, it consolidated previous conceptions of authenticity and continued to incorporate traditional musics of the Brazilian people—*o povo* (Stroud 2008, 4–5, 42; Sandroni 2011). More recently, in the twenty-first century, Rio's mostly white brass bands have re-embraced anthropophagy to justify freely cannibalizing Black North American musics (Snyder 2022, 100). I hear echoes of Brazil's national hunger for Blackness in the ways many white Paulista angoleiros speak of Bahia and capoeira Angola today.

Hungering for Ancestralidade

Mateu (pseudonym) is a white university-educated Paulista with fair skin and dirty-blond hair. He is a self-identified leftist who started playing capoeira because his friend from university was deeply involved in it. He described how at first he trained "without a lot of axé," without much commitment. Mateu said he first saw capoeira simply as physical exercise, good for strengthening his shoulder, which was weak from long hours of working at a computer. "But then," he said, "I went to Bahia, to the group's yearly event. I began to connect more with the ancestralidade, which isn't mine, but as every Brazilian has their Blackness, their relationship with all the Indigenous [peoples], the *Afro*, I began to [give more importance to] this ancestralidade, too. So Bahia awakened me to this."

I asked him to elaborate on how he had developed this connection with ancestralidade and Blackness. He reiterated that he was not claiming African ancestry. He was descended from Portuguese, Spanish, Italian, and even some German:

> I don't have any link through blood with this [Black/Afro] ancestralidade. But this is the thing: to be Brazilian brings with it this relationship. Really, my relationship with Afro ancestralidade, and even Indigenous, is this relation with difference, of what we really are. I think the Afro question awakens in me on the one hand a curiosity, and on the other hand, it's something that I am, but I never was, because I'm Brazilian, and I've had relationships with this big stew.

Mateu's claim to both be and not be African and Indigenous ("what we really are" and "something that I am, but I never was") reveals the tenacity of Brazil's foundational mestiçagem ideology, even among political progressives like Mateu. Unlike many white university-educated elites and MPB superstar Caetano Veloso, Mateu didn't deny his whiteness; he didn't go so far as to say, as Caetano has, "we are all mestiços and . . . we all have Black blood" (Sovik 2009, 148). Yet the ambiguity in Mateu's relationship to racial categories is possible only because of mestiçagem. Other group members spoke in this way, too, carefully acknowledging their whiteness but still claiming some connection to Black ancestralidade. One young white university student, Marmota (pseudonym), spoke about capoeira as a meaningful space for Black people to "understand themselves" and "feel recognized." Then she said, "There are lots of people in capoeira who are searching for this connection, this ancestralidade. I search for it too, but from another perspective. I'm white, but I think we feel this too in capoeira." Like Mateu, Marmota felt she could access the Black ancestralidade, echoing Beija-flor's epigraph to this chapter: "I don't have any Black genealogy. . . . But I *feel* the ancestralidade."[9]

When Mateu leverages mestiçagem to access ancestralidade, he also stakes his claim to the Brazilian nation. While at first it may seem contradictory for white people to claim to have "their Blackness," racial mixture as imagined under mestiçagem has not always conflated phenotype, biology, and culture (Munanga 2020). In Freyre's earliest iteration of the theory, Brazil's hybridity was intended solely for the white-European "Luso-tropical man" (W. Anderson, Roque, and Santos 2019), excluding both mixed-race and Black people from "Brazil's nonbiological African/European synthesis" (Isfahani-Hammond 2008, 121). When white Brazilians "perform" mixture, it allows them to get "(safely) closer to the national ideal by . . . bolstering a feeling of common subjectivity with black and brown Brazilians without necessitating that they relinquish white privilege or concretely challenge anti-black racism" (Costa 2016, 36). The nation's mixture has always also been metaphorical.

Mateu went on to describe how eagerly he sought to attain the ideal mixture in himself, expressing his desire in starkly binarized terms of both race and region:

> [Bahia] is a mirror. Going to Bahia as a Paulista brings me the ability to see the difference, the Other. It brings this question of the toughness of the body. We Paulistas are more rational, we say that we're more developed, in the sense of access to schools and literacy, compared to the Northeast, which has more regional inequality. This is not prejudice! It informs a lot of reparative policies in Brazil today. So there is this inequality, but because the Northeast doesn't have the tradition of education . . . they develop oral culture. They develop bodily expression. For me, this is a richness that I *want*! I *want to* develop this in myself. I *want to*! I want to develop my rational part, but I also search for the opposite, to have bodily expression, to have cultural expression, oral expression, which I didn't have access to at the university. So the ancestralidade comes from this question of orality and bodily expression.

In Mateu's mind, regional contrasts were a fact. Though he left out explicit references to race, Bahia with its majority Black population is coded as Black, and São Paulo, with its majority white population, is coded as white. Thus he saw the Northeast as the land of the Black expressive body and the Southeast as the land of the white rational mind. In this way, he collapsed centuries of systemic violence and targeted neglect into matters of so-called tradition and culture. In fact, Mateu's depiction of Bahia and São Paulo as mirror opposites—São Paulo modern and prosperous, Bahia backward and poor—draws on over a century of discourses espoused by white Paulista elites to justify and generate policies that would ensure São Paulo's economic flourishing and the Northeast's neglect and underdevelopment (Weinstein 2015). Interviewing white Paulistanos, Schucman similarly found that they associated whiteness with "intellectual superiority" as a matter of culture: whereas "Africans" (i.e., Black Brazilians) "give more value to music, entertainment," European immigrants to Brazil have always valued "working and studying" more (Schucman 2020, 128–32). Racialized regional difference, juxtaposing the Black North with the white South, also extends beyond São Paulo state, of course. Snyder cites a white musician from Rio who paints a similarly racialized picture, conflating Bahia's Blackness not only with the dancing body but also with stigmatized homosexuality:

> Brazil is huge, and the experience of people in the small [Afro-descendant] cities of Bahia is very different from our middle-class experience in Rio de Janeiro. Here the South Zone is very much the culture of the White man. Men don't dance here. Brazil has prejudices against homosexuality. We have all the problems of a Eurocentric society. We don't know how to dance like Afro-Brazilians. (Snyder 2022, 17; bracketed text in original)

Thus, while Mateu's claim that his views were "not prejudice" may not convince, his confidence likely stemmed from the fact that he was expressing widely held, commonsense views.

Mateu's conception of Bahia as a (re)source for learning authentic Black practices—capoeira, orality, bodily expression—also echoes decades of Bahia's self-marketing for tourists as a place to touch, feel, and possess Blackness.[10] In the early 1950s, white Bahian elites began to market Bahia as an enchantingly exotic Black (African and Afro-Bahian) destination for Brazilian tourists (Romo 2022), and live stage performances of capoeira, samba, and Candomblé were promoted as tourism programming (Höfling 2019, 100). By the 1970s, white leftist counterculturalists from Rio de Janeiro and São Paulo, having grown disenchanted under the dictatorship (1964–1985), discovered in Bahia's cultural "others" an ideal source for the authenticity they felt they lacked, and they traveled to Bahia in great numbers (Dunn 2016, 108–145). Although Black cultural actors in this period also derived genuine political empowerment from their "re-Africanized" expressions, such as the blocos afro carnival groups (Crook and Johnson 1999), Salvador's tourism agency soon incorporated this renewed Africanness into its marketing strategies (Paschel 2009).[11] The image of Bahia endures as a Black Mecca (Ickes and Reiter 2018) and Afro-paradise (Smith 2016) offering its magical resources—Black bodies among them (Hedegard 2013; Williams 2013)—to tourists, both Brazilian and foreign (P. Pinho 2018). Mateu was therefore expressing how many white Brazilians see Bahia and, indeed, how many white and Black Bahian cultural actors, politicians, and tourism officials market Black Bahian culture to attract paying visitors.

White Paulista scholar and capoeira practitioner Pedro Abib (2004) also characterizes Brazil's Black culture as wholly "other" in his book on capoeira Angola's unique knowledge system, which he argues has its own concepts of time, memory, orality, and ritual that contrast with Western ways of knowing. Abib ultimately proposes integrating (white European-derived) "modern rationality" with Black popular culture's completely "other logic" to improve Brazil's educational system (Abib 2004, 21–26). To this end, he concludes his monograph with a lament:

> Unfortunately, this universe [of Black cultura popular] still remains practically unexploited [*inexplorado*], like a virgin forest that guards riches, secrets and enigmas, which appear alive and dynamic, but still invisible to the eyes of those responsible for most of the programs involving formal education in this country. (215)

Abib advocates approaching Black popular culture, which contains the "strength and wisdom of the simple people of our country" (216) as an untapped resource, ready to be mined and consumed by the powerholders and policymakers of Brazil.

Other white group members I spoke with similarly valued capoeira Angola because it provided them access to otherwise inaccessible—and wholly "other"—knowledge. A white Paulista who had moved to Bahia to be closer to Mestre Cláudio found that capoeira offered him "an education in behavior." Then he qualified the knowledge that capoeira transmitted: "Popular culture, especially when it's from the interior, is very simple, very, very, very simple. And you learn it through observing the behavior of the people and seeing how they act in a very simple way, but very intelligent, very cunning [*esperto*]." A white Bahian group member similarly said that capoeira had taught him "the language you need to use to talk to the people, a simpler language that can touch them [so that you can] communicate more easily." Encountering and incorporating alternative knowledge systems is one way to understand Mestre Cláudio's claim that capoeira "Africanizes white minds." Yet this still renders capoeira Angola as a resource for white players' individual edification.

The ways in which white practitioners position capoeira and Bahia as desirable resources reveal the coloniality of their thinking and how they view themselves in relation to Black Brazilian culture. In Mateu's repeated "I want . . . I want . . . !" (*Eu quero . . . Eu quero*!), his impassioned desire for everything the Black Northeast can provide him, I hear "the starving attitude of settler colonial perception" (Robinson 2020, 53). By positioning Black popular culture as a resource to be exploited, these white Paulistas render capoeira another raw material. Black Brazilian people—along with their hopes, dreams, and desires—are absented from consideration. This colonialist hunger "consumes without awareness of how the consumption acts in relationship with those people . . . who provide sustenance" (53).

Mateu spoke knowledgeably about Brazil's intersecting racial and wealth disparities and injustices, so I asked how he had formed his racial-political consciousness, curious if participating in capoeira had shifted his thinking. No, he explained, he had "always been on the left" politically and always sought to experience something beyond his "white, middle class, bourgeois bubble." Mateu declared that Brazilians denied how racist they were, but they were racist nonetheless: "We're raised naturalizing an absurd violence! . . . Because there is no subtlety in the racism of Brazil; there's no subtlety in the police violence of Brazil!"

Mateu understood his position as a white bourgeois elite and his responsibility to confront his own racism. Yet by gesturing to Brazil's "absurd violence" against Black people, he seemed to restrict racism to blatant acts of anti-Black violence. Meanwhile, despite Mateu's close embodied encounters with Bahia and Black Bahian people, his ideas about Blackness and Bahia remain intact. Mateu said the right things—acknowledging his whiteness, privilege, even his racism—but his declarations were "nonperformative," preserving that which they attempted to undo (Ahmed 2004).

Instead of shifting his consciousness, Mateu's experiences in Bahia seem to have reinforced his understanding of the region as totally "other," as embodying everything he lacks but wants (Ahmed 2000, 123). By imagining Bahia as a mirror, Mateu projects himself onto its image. His desire to incorporate Black Bahian corporeality into his own body is therefore not a desire to *become* Black or Bahian; rather it is a hunger for hybridity (121–23)—for mestiçagem. Mateu wants to integrate Black orality and bodily expression into his white rationality, just as Abib wants to integrate popular culture's "other logic" into Brazil's mainstream educational system. Whiteness, with its supremacist logics, remains intact.

Writing about white people's relationship to their whiteness as possessive investments, George Lipsitz writes, "While one can *possess* one's investments, one can also *be possessed* by them" (Lipsitz 2006, viii). The double meaning of possession eloquently expresses how habituated racialized thinking and behavior perpetuates systems of racial domination (Bonilla-Silva 2021). When white Brazilians seek to possess Blackness or Black things, they reinforce the ways in which they are also possessed by whiteness. This reveals that for white people to relinquish their investments in whiteness will take more than letting go of supposed possessions, of the "things"; it also requires actively divesting from white supremacy (Lipsitz 2006, viii) and from the whitening ideology of mestiçagem.

Experiencing Thingification

Although Mateu expressed racist and colonialist attitudes toward Bahia and Blackness, he did so with words of praise. Many white practitioners in the Angoleiros do Sertão voiced similar positive valuations of Black popular culture, and they expressed these opinions openly, in the presence of Black people. Yet rather than feeling assured of their white camaradas' antiracism, some Black community members reported experiencing this "hypervalorization" (Balaguer 2017, 125) as objectification. When white Brazilians and foreign practitioners come to Bahia, "enchanted" by Bahian Blackness, Black Bahians often experience being seen as "things" for these visitors to study and consume.

Iaiá is Dona Ivannide's daughter and a Black movement militant like her mother. Iaiá trained with the Angoleiros do Sertão when she was younger and remains close to Mestre Cláudio and the group, regularly attending the Saturday roda and dancing samba in the years I was conducting fieldwork. Before our interview, I told Iaiá how I had witnessed Maximus (pseudonym), a white European male group member, talk greedily about his lust for negras, Black women. I was on a public bus in Feira de Santana with Maximus and other group members. We were both standing in the aisle, and he was talking loudly, in Portuguese, about how much he loves negras, wondering where he could find some negras. I watched as a seated Black woman passenger, not a group member, stared blankly, through and past us. On other occasions I had heard Maximus talk about Black women in the group he wanted to have sex with. Maximus's public declarations of his sexual desires disturbingly reminded me of bell hooks's essay "Eating the Other," in which she describes overhearing white male Ivy League students casually discuss "their plans to fuck as many girls from other racial/ethnic groups as they could 'catch'" with "Black girls . . . high on the list" (hooks 1992, 23).

In our interview, I asked Iaiá what she thought about all the white people entering and visiting the Angoleiros do Sertão. I asked if she thought they exoticized capoeira and Black culture, as if to say, "Ah, how beautiful! Black people have such a spiritual culture, I want to feel it, too!" She responded:

> Yes, exactly. It's this: [They want] to see the thing [*a coisa*]—the *thing*—from close by, that thing, the object. As if you are always an object of study. . . . I think it's really a way of getting to know us, to understand us, but not in a healthy way. To take advantage of it, too, to know what's behind it, how Maximus says, "Oh, negra!" Like it's something exotic—it's not a human being like he is. It's a *thing*. It's not the same. You and me, we are not the same. He's a human being, I'm a thing, to be discovered: "A-ha!" Like Darwin, who treated people like things not like human beings. The thing, the animal, the brain is different. "I'm going to go study that thing, that being, that's not the same as me, it's other." It's always other.

Because she had used the example of Maximus, who is not Brazilian, I asked her if she thought white Brazilians also saw Black Bahians in this way. She responded, "Certainly, I am absolutely certain they do."

Iaiá's emphatic repetition of "thing" evoked the dehumanizing violence of colonization, which Aimé Césaire equates with "thingification" (2016, 202). In terms that echo Iaiá's, he wrote, "The colonizer, who in order to ease his conscience gets into the habit of seeing the other man as *an animal*, accustoms himself to treating him like an animal" (201; original emphasis).[12] While referring to the process of studying Bahian people as "things" and referencing the racist pseudoscience of phrenology, Iaiá also gestured to the scene of our interview. In that moment, I was also studying her, trying to understand her community. Clearly, she included me with the other whites who came to Bahia to study Black "objects" from close by.

Iaiá's experience of feeling thingified powerfully illustrates how positive feelings about Black people can also harm them. White Brazilian group members regularly spoke about Bahia as a place of *encantamento* (enchantment), where they went to "recharge" (*recarregar*) their batteries, as if literally plugging into the axé. Yet Black Bahian members also spoke of enchantment and (re)charging energy in the roda. Indeed, capoeira scholar-practitioners Machado and Araújo assert that "capoeira Angola operates in the world through enchantment" (2015, 110). Are white practitioners simply echoing accepted capoeira discourse? Perhaps. Yet when white practitioners reinforce the view of Bahia as an enchanted Afro-paradise (Smith 2016), a space for encountering a wholly other Bahian Blackness or Africanness and incorporating it into their bodies and blood (Abib 2004, 22), they also reinscribe the slavocratic-colonialist production of Black Bahian bodies as raw materials—things—thereby denying Black Bahian people's humanity. White players' hunger to consume Blackness thus undermines claims that participating in capoeira Angola causes white practitioners to shift their racial attitudes—or, as Mestre Cláudio put it, to "Africanize" their minds.

Foreclosing Freedom

Carlão (pseudonym) is another politically progressive group member from São Paulo, who was actively engaged in left-wing activism and protests at the time of our interview.[13] Carlão graciously hosted me for a few days in his apartment in a middle-class neighborhood, in a building I believe was owned by his parents. He had long dark locks, a wide nose, and easily tanned skin, so I asked if people ever thought he was Black, even if light-skinned. He said, "Yes, many times! Because of my hair. . . . It's funny, sometimes in Bahia, I get really sunburned and the boys in Mantiba [Mestre Cláudio's neighborhood] say I look like the mestre." At the time of our interview, he told me that he had no "connection" with Blackness in his family. (However, years later when I asked how he self-identified, he told me he was a "pardo," with a father who was "white mixed with índio" and a mother who was "negra mixed with índio.")

In our interview, Carlão spoke at length about capoeira as a practice of freedom (*liberdade*) and liberation (*libertação*) and how he experienced freedom personally through his practice.[14] For example, he said that wearing "dreads" meant that he faced prejudice (an employer had fired him once when he refused to cut his hair), but liberating himself meant not caring what other people thought about him. Believing in a "liberatory capoeira," he said, meant knowing that when one door closes, you're able to see the full range of your capacities, and another door will open. Though he didn't reference the capoeira game, this way of thinking about choices, obstacles, and actions aligns with strategies of capoeira play: when an opponent attacks you or prevents you from completing a movement, the art is to transition without hesitation, find a new way, shift your movement, and improvise a split-second change of plans that opens a new "door" of the game. He went on to say, "As long as you keep putting yourself in a super comfortable place . . . then it loses its sense for me." For Carlão, freedom included a willingness to experience discomfort, be challenged, and have the wisdom to see beyond the situation and act advantageously.

Seeking to understand better if and how Carlão felt capoeira training related to a more collective sense of political freedom, beyond the individual, I added, "Capoeira Angola is a school, a place for learning about freedom, but just practicing capoeira isn't enough. Because at a given moment, you're going to have to organize yourself in other ways, too. Just staying inside capoeira isn't enough to arrive at freedom, to fight—"

Carlão jumped in and said, "I think this is something very significant: Capoeira is a tool [*ferramenta*, also instrument], a tool of liberation. Only, the one who frees themself, who picks up the tool and grasps it, is you! And so [capoeira] shows you that freedom exists, but to *be free* is different for everyone. It shows you the path, but you are the one who must cross that path!"

Carlão's concise assessment touches on the heart of this book's argument: capoeira may be a symbol and even a practice of antiracism (Machado 2016; Griffith 2023) but only if practitioners intentionally use the tool to reach such ends. Capoeira provides practitioners with strategies, wisdom, and ways of thinking and doing, but it is up to each player how to wield capoeira's instrument in their lives. As we continued to discuss freedom and capoeira, I wondered if he would address how capoeira could serve as a tool in Black people's freedom struggles. Finally, I asked him directly, "How can capoeira contribute to Black people's liberation? To a more collective liberation?"

Carlão responded, "It's very hard for me to talk about this because I'm a boy of the middle class. I have friends from the periphery, and I work in the periphery, but then I go away again. You should ask someone from the periphery." Carlão's answer reveals how deeply race and class are entwined in the Brazilian racial imaginary: the middle class signifies whiteness and non-Blackness and the periphery signifies Blackness. Like many white group members, Carlão was reluctant to comment on Black movement politics, despite his profound involvement with the Black movement of capoeira Angola. For instance, Marmota also declined to comment about capoeira's contribution to the Black movement, saying, "I think it's a complicated question because I'm not even Black. . . . I don't feel I have the right to talk about the Black movement." When white and non-Black members decline to discuss Black politics, I see this as a way of absolving themselves from responsibility.

Carlão elaborated his perspective: "As I see it, from the outside, I wonder if people [in the periphery] really search for freedom. . . . Freedom for them is very different than for us. Liberation for them is to survive, to live well. They aren't interested in the social context that surrounds them. . . . The idea of being free for [Mestre Cláudio] is much simpler than [it is] for us!"

It was clear to me that Carlão had thought extensively about some of these questions. However, like Mateu, he still saw Black communities as diametrically opposed to his. In his mind, people in the periphery had totally other ways of thinking about freedom, if they thought about it at all, and wholly other ways of accomplishing their political goals. To some degree, this reflects Mestre Cláudio's own philosophy of political action. With the Saturday roda, Mestre Cláudio enacts his politics in ways otherwise to mainstream political modes, proclaiming the value of Black culture through movement, sound, and presence on the city's streets. Yet the "universe of cultura popular" with its "most significant knowledges" generated by subjugated people (Abib 2004, 215) is not differentiable from so-called modern rationality but rather entangled with, and co-constitutive of, modernity (Höfling 2019). In other words, while capoeira and other African matrix practices do generate their own theories and concepts, they do not represent perfect mirrors or inversions of European-derived values, as many capoeira scholars, practitioners, and philosophers claim.[15]

It must be possible to valorize peripheral knowledges without characterizing them as utterly different and so "much simpler" than "ours." After all, Dona Ivannide has generated knowledge from her lived experiences, both inside and outside of formal education systems. She inserted her "organic" Black Marxist feminism into the organized party system while she led the local Workers' Party chapter in Feira. Mestre Cláudio has kept his Saturday morning street roda running for over twenty years. Creating, enacting, and sustaining alternative forms of politics, sometimes within more formalized political systems, is extremely complex work. Perhaps Carlão's view of the periphery reveals the illegibility of peripheral politics to elites more than it exposes their supposed simplicity or lack. Indeed, Black movement activism, especially when led by Black women, is often ignored, misrecognized, and invisibilized (Perry 2013).

Black community members do, of course, think, theorize, and philosophize about freedom and the role of Black popular culture in politics. In my interview with Bolinha, I asked him point-blank, "What is liberdade? What is the liberation that capoeira brings?"

He responded, "Liberation for me is consciousness. Consciousness of being Black, of suffering racism." He explained how often when Black people in Brazil are "racially violated . . . they don't understand that the violence is racial," so powerful is the national denial of the racism pervading Brazilian society. He went on:

> Liberation is consciousness. Liberation comes when you determine for yourself the way that you want to live. . . . You have to have a discourse, to say all the time to the racist society that you are Black [preto], that you accept yourself as preto, that your religion is Candomblé. Because capoeira and Candomblé have a connection that brings me freedom; the freedom of no longer suffering inside your head psychologically, because we die psychologically almost every day. When we are violated, we have to say, "No, I have the force [força] of capoeira. I have an ancestral manifestation that the Blacks created back then, to free themselves from another [form of] oppression." So I have this in me, I will live this, because I understand this as an instrument *of freedom.*

When I pressed Bolinha further, he conceded that there was a broader concept of freedom, "this liberty that we always dream about." This freedom would see the end of oppressive systems, not just their reform:

> Today I believe that I will die without experiencing this liberty: the freedom of being certain that the Black people will be able to know spaces, have access, have quality education, have access to leisure, to be able to know their history. . . . We know that it is very difficult to achieve this freedom, and it will take a long time for it to happen, and capoeira Angola does not fulfill this role totally . . . because it won't reach everyone.

"But even so, it's worth it?" I asked.

"It's very much worth it! This is nothing illusory, it's not in my head! When you play berimbau, when you play samba, it's as if the force is internalized as part of you. As if an ancestral energy, something from your past, becomes internal, and calls me to it."

This brings full circle the discussion of ancestralidade begun in the previous chapter as both a spiritual energy that empowers many Black community members' politics and an object of white players' desire and consumption. I have cited Bolinha to juxtapose his thinking with Carlão's deracialized conception of freedom and mischaracterization of Black peripheral thought as simple and unconcerned with freedom or social context. To the contrary, Bolinha's responses reveal a complex theorization of Black freedom that extends from individual racial consciousness to a collective freedom, foreseeing a different world where Black people are fully human.

Bolinha's vision also refutes Carlão's view that freedom was primarily a concern for white and non-Black (upper) middle-class people like "us." Indeed, Carlão's exclusive claim to seeking and possessing liberty reproduces the Western hegemonic "colonial-racial foreclosure" of Black political thought (Hesse 2014). As political theorist Barnor Hesse has argued, the "Western political formulation" of freedom "has perpetuated a conceptual inheritance that has largely subordinated the meaning of freedom for the colonized and the enslaved to the meaning of freedom for the colonizers/enslavers as the citizens" (2014, 300). Dominant political thought on liberty/freedom deracializes freedom by foreclosing the possibility that peripheral people could contribute to thinking about freedom (290).[16] This renders freedom the exclusive property of elite white liberal subjects and those that align with them, disavowing centuries of Black people's political theorizing and freedom dreams (C. Robinson 2000; Kelley 2002).

Not every Black person in Feira's peripheries thinks about politics, nor does every white person in São Paulo. Yet radical political thinking clearly does originate in marginalized communities. As Sylvia Wynter argues, it is precisely in these "liminal" spaces that the necessary new descriptive statements of the human must emerge (D. Scott 2000, 149). Despite Carlão's leftist politics, Black hairstyle, Black friends, profound involvement with Black cultural practices, and his work in the periphery, he declined to speak about the Black movement. Despite devoting himself to an Afro-Brazilian expression that he and many others consider a practice of freedom, Carlão did not see how freedom could also concern Black peripheral residents. If many white practitioners hold similar views, then capoeira Angola appears more as an instrument for individual (white) freedom than a tool for redressing racial injustice.

Whitening Black Spaces

At the time of our interview, Marmota was an undergraduate at a prestigious public university in the interior of São Paulo. A young, white Paulista woman with wispy, dirty-blonde hair, she was relatively new to capoeira Angola, having trained for several years with a small group of fellow students at her university, but very dedicated. I had heard about an incident involving her capoeira group, and I wanted to hear her perspective. When I asked if she would talk about what had happened, I could sense her discomfort, but she agreed to talk about it and gamely responded to my questions.

Marmota began with a disclaimer, reminding me that she still knew very little about these debates and issues. Then she recounted how a *coletivo negro*, a Black student collective on her campus, was holding a private discussion for Black students only. After the meeting they had planned a film screening, which was open to the public. The film was about Zumbi, the rebel leader of the Quilombo of Palmares and a significant figure both for Black movement activism and in capoeira's folklore and song repertoire.[17] Marmota and other members of her capoeira group decided to attend the screening. They arrived when the film was supposed to start, but the meeting was running late and the Black students were still in discussion. The Black students invited the capoeira students to join them, and soon the conversation turned to address the whiteness of the capoeira group. Marmota recounted:

> The critique was that there are only white people in our capoeira group. This is really significant. We talk about it all the time. For some people [in the group] it's not a problem, but for me it has weighed heavily. . . . At the meeting, one guy said, "It's very difficult to hear our songs being sung by whites." It must be awful. I can't imagine what it must feel like! I can't judge him. And yet, how should we act? Because stopping capoeira—! Right?

Marmota's self-interruption implied that she could not imagine giving up capoeira as a solution to this problem. It also seemed that no one (not even the Black students, from what I gathered) was suggesting that white people shouldn't participate in capoeira at all.[18] Abusada, for instance, expressed her frustration with being one of few Black people in a group "without a role model [*referência*]. . . . Because there are lots of capoeira groups today where you don't see even one Black person! You only see white people!" She said, "This affects me a lot. . . . Because Black culture brings people together [*agrega*], it calls [chama] everyone!" However, she insisted, "It isn't a problem for me to have whites in capoeira. The problem is their domination, without a *single* Black person!"

The overwhelming presence of white members is a core concern for many

Black group members I spoke with, but they also voiced their reluctance to speak openly about the issue with the group. This is why the Black collective's perspective is so valuable: as nonmembers of the capoeira group, they were not beholden to its norms of cordiality and could freely voice the critique. Yet as someone inside the capoeira group, Marmota struggled to understand them:

> I think it's complicated. Because we perceive that these critiques—we think, "Goodness! [*Nossa!*] But what is at the bottom of this?" I think the person [who made the critique] didn't know the culture, really. I don't judge them. I understand their critiques, about certain points, but these are critiques coming from people who are outside of the culture.

I was confused by Marmota's last statement that the Black students were "outside of the culture," so I asked, "Outside of—the culture of capoeira Angola?"

"Outside of these spaces where we exchange this tradition that we are learning," Marmota confirmed.

"But maybe they think that they are *inside* of it because it's Black culture?"

"Yeah, because it's Black culture! And I don't dispute this at all! I don't question it!"

Marmota understood that capoeira Angola was Black culture, but by seeing the Black students as "outside" of capoeira spaces, she seemed to imagine Black people and Black culture as mutually exclusive (Smith 2016, 13). Marmota was still "young in capoeira," but she knew that participating in capoeira Angola requires enormous dedication to learning movements, song repertoire, and instruments. Perhaps she was starting to understand that capoeira also demanded other long-term commitments. When she saw the members of the Black student collective as "outside" of capoeira spaces, maybe she meant they had not assumed a compromisso with capoeira Angola. Yet this reveals the limits of her understanding of compromisso, as something restricted to capoeira. In contrast, many Black capoeira players, like Bolinha, felt that their commitment to capoeira extended to Black communities in Brazil and beyond. Likewise, many Black community members, like Iaiá, Karine, Dona Ivannide, and others, felt they belonged to the capoeira community even if they didn't play capoeira. They regularly attended the Saturday rodas in Feira to dance samba and show their support.

Marmota's insider status in capoeira is comparable not only to that of ethnomusicologists (see note 18) but also to that of white initiates in Candomblé. White people have participated in Candomblé at least since the late nineteenth century, often as *ogãs*, a position of sponsor and protector: white people in positions of power or influence, such as "police, politicians, artists and intellectuals," helped legitimize the religion among broader society and shield it from persecution (Amaral and da Silva 1993, 107). In this first stage of white participation, Amaral and da Silva contended that neither the "presence of whites in the religion" nor their "capacity to possess and transmit axé" were questioned (107). From the 1960s onward, more widespread white influx into the religion was surely influenced by MPB stars like Baden Powell, Clara Nunes, Vinicius de Moraes, Caetano Veloso, and Maria Bethânia, who openly participated in Candomblé (Amaral and da Silva 1993; Prandi 2004; França 2018) and incorporated Candomblé themes and rhythms into their music (Henry 2008). Great numbers of white people have now become initiated into the religion and many have become mães- and pais-de-santo (França 2018). As white practitioners rose in rank and power in Candomblé, tensions increased among white and Black members (Amaral and da Silva 1993), and today the "whitening" (*embranquecimento* or *branqueamento*) of Candomblé remains an issue of concern in popular and scholarly media (e.g., Rodrigues 2017; William 2019).

Within the Angoleiros do Sertão, Mestre Cláudio has likewise conferred the titles of mestre, contramestre, and *treinel* (advanced student) to numerous white practitioners, thereby entrusting them with the responsibility of teaching capoeira. In the circles I have frequented, it is a given that white players can also gain fluency in the movements and musicality necessary to carry on the tradition. As Abusada stated above, however, the problem is not that white people are practicing capoeira, but it is their domination. França suggests that white people "inserting" themselves in Black spaces such as terreiros should assume certain responsibilities, one being that they should recognize that these are spaces where Black people connect with their ancestralidade and build emotional bonds with one another (2018, 73–74). França contends that even with a large presence of white people, these spaces can continue to combat racialized violence (74). The questions remain if Black spaces like capoeira can confront racism even in the absence of Black practitioners and how they would do so.

Since her difficult encounter with Black students at her university, Marmota told me, she had entered a process of "putting together little bits and pieces." She was "thinking about this thing of appropriation, this question of inserting [whites] into capoeira," and continuing to talk about these questions with friends in the Black collective. She had also enrolled in courses on Afro-Brazilian and African Populations and Oral Memory and History, which, she said, she otherwise might never have taken. Though her thinking still reflected entrenched ideologies, she was clearly unsettled and therefore perhaps starting to unsettle her habituated ways of thinking, thanks in no small part to the Black militants she continued to dialogue with.

Africanizing White Minds?

Returning to the scene that opened this chapter, when Raul voiced his desire to "buy ten Black women" just like Dona Ivannide, he invoked slavery, as if calling it back from the past. Dona Ivannide lay his fantasy firmly to rest, declaring, "You cannot!" But the specter of slavery had been summoned, easily and casually, clothed in an expression of affection. This reveals how closely racial violence hovers beneath the surface of the group's affective interracial relationships. The previous chapter described how Black practitioners drew on their spiritual memory to summon their past in slavery through what I called "embodied fabulation": they called on the past to recover the full humanity of their enslaved ancestors and counter racism in the present. In a way, Raul's re-embodiment of a "white, macho, rich" slave owner performed a similar summoning of ancestralidade, only with the opposite effect: calling forth his slave-owning ancestors into the present, he reenacted the dehumanization of Black women, imagining the beloved figure of Dona Ivannide as human chattel. However, in that moment, at least within the space of the bate-papo of the Angoleiros do Sertão in November 2020, Dona Ivannide demonstrated that the subaltern could indeed speak (Spivak 2010). After more greetings and professings of love among group members, it seemed as if the talk might move beyond Raul's abhorrent interruption, but Dona Ivannide brought it back, saying she wanted to address Raul directly. She said:

> How good that you have been in the Angoleiros do Sertão all this time . . . [and] contributed in various ways. . . . But for me, it's not enough for you just to be allied, caring for the mestre, loving capoeira. This is not enough. I need you allied in the Black struggle [*a luta negra*]. I *need* you as an ally in the Black struggle. . . . You don't need to be just a guy who is not racist. You need to assume the fight of antiracism. . . . This is your task! . . .
>
> Today I am [here] in Black November, so I allowed myself [to address Raul this way] because he dares *during Black November* to come

> here and say that he would buy ten Black women like me! There is not enough money in the entire world, Raul! This doesn't happen anymore, it is over! But I want to say that in Black November, I am honored to see these young Black women speaking in such a focused manner.

Dona Ivannide allowed her speech to be diverted to address Raul directly, and via Raul she spoke to all white people similarly deeply involved in capoeira. Yet she made sure to end by acknowledging the featured speakers and interlocutors of the day, recentering their contributions. One of the women who spoke earlier in the bate-papo had similarly addressed Raul, who was being disruptive throughout the session. When he had introduced himself as "male, white, rich," Raul had added, "everything that doesn't belong in this session today." Later, Lúcia (pseudonym) addressed Raul directly, saying, "No, you're exactly who *must* be here! Racism isn't Black people's problem, it's white people's! . . . Many more people like you need to hear [these perspectives]. As the mestre says, whites have to do capoeira—cool! . . . But capoeira must change your way of being, because there's no point in our doing capoeira and continuing with racist attitudes." Karine, Lúcia, Dona Ivannide, and other Black women who spoke that day made a clear demand: white community members must do more than love capoeira and love Black women. White practitioners must allow capoeira to change them. They have mastered the discourse; now they must act.

As Lúcia noted, white members' refusal to take action fundamentally denies the root of the problems—white people's perpetuation of coloniality and white supremacy—and leaves it to Black people to fight racism. Speaking with friends and colleagues in the Black movement, I found a consensus that white people were welcome as allies in the struggle, as Dona Ivannide had indicated. Yet judging by the ways many white group members spoke about the Black movement, it seems they either feel it is not their responsibility to contribute to the antiracism struggle or they simply do not want to. When I asked Iaiá why she thought white people felt they couldn't join the Black movement, she immediately replied, "Did they try?"[19]

Thus far I have focused on white Paulista angoleiros whose racial ideologies seem to remain unshaken despite their capoeira practice. However, several white group members reported experiencing profound transformations in their thinking about race and racism. Rita grew up in the interior of Bahia and has trained with the Angoleiros do Sertão in Feira for many years. She felt strongly that both Mestre Cláudio and Dona Ivannide had raised her consciousness about racism, helping her understand the systemic nature of disproportionate racial representation in jobs and careers. She explained that Dona Ivannide "recharged people's energies that had been lost over time because of racism. . . . She made us believe that we *could* do it! . . . She believes more in me than I believe in myself. How important she's been in my development, my consciousness! How much I have changed since I started capoeira Angola and met her—*especially her*!"

I knew that Dona Ivannide was an ardent feminist who sought to empower the women in the capoeira group. Yet as Rita spoke in the first person, I wondered how she identified racially. She would not be considered white in the United States, with her shiny, curly dark brown hair, full lips and nose, but paler skin, so I asked how she identified. She was silent at first, and then lowered her voice:

> It's difficult. And I can't be hypocritical. Because I never will have the history, nor will I have experienced half of what a Black person has experienced "in the skin" [*na pele*]. [She tapped her arm several times.] Because I am white. I learned this with Ivannide. I can be a militant, conscious, but I will never be capable of explaining the pain of prejudice. As much as I know about it, I've heard it spoken about, I have never been a victim. . . . [But] I can say that I'm a militant in the Black movement because I am at the roda every Saturday; that we make it stronger, in the samba.

In contrast to nearly all the other white people I spoke with, Rita identified explicitly as a Black movement militant despite her whiteness. She acknowledged that it was difficult, gesturing to the challenge of fighting racism from the position of someone who doesn't experience racism firsthand. She also identified her activism as primarily taking place through the Saturday roda, which leaves aside other possible actions white people could take in combating racism in Brazilian society. However, at the very least, empowered by Dona Ivannide's mentorship, Rita acknowledged her whiteness yet still declared her political commitment to antiracism movements.

Finally, there was one white Paulista man, Afonso Mesquita, who had profoundly shifted his ways of thinking about Blackness and Black culture since moving to Bahia, and this had in turn changed how he spoke and acted.[20] In our interview in 2017, he had told me that he saw capoeira as the "riposte to racism . . . because of its affirmation of Black people, of the strength, beauty, aesthetic, the art, the dignity [of Black people]." Yet he also explained that capoeira was most meaningful to him because it had raised his self-confidence. When we spoke again in 2022, he had been living in Bahia for four years and said he had been confronted with his whiteness in new ways. He had undertaken a process of radically reexamining his relationship to Blackness, unlearning what he thought he knew. He said, "I have a role, to talk with other white people, to admit our privileges. . . . Racial relations are white people's problems." He also spoke about the importance of being in relation, connecting with Black people in the community with respect and attention. He was describing moving beyond Brazil's cordial, "affectionate" interracial relations. (In contrast, Mateu had said that he had always had "close relations" with Black people but gave as an example the people who cleaned the pool at his country club.) Schucman made a similar point "that the key is not in [white people's] convivência with Black people, nor in the peaceful convivência, but it is in the non-hierarchized convivência with them" (2020, 191). I return to Afonso's story in the epilogue, but for now let it illustrate that it is possible for white practitioners to allow capoeira to change them. Indeed, this suggests that the decision to change or not to change, to act or not to act, is entirely up to them.

Conclusion

White participation in capoeira neither "whitens" capoeira nor "Africanizes" white minds. The harm comes from great numbers of white and non-Black people not only dominating capoeira spaces but also bringing with them racist-colonialist ideas about capoeira, Blackness, Black people and culture, and Bahia. In often hidden, subtle ways, white practitioners collectively hunger for ancestralidade, thingify Black people, foreclose capoeira's freedom potentials, and whiten capoeira spaces. Although they are welcome in capoeira's alternative Black spaces, white players generally decline to align their participation in capoeira Angola with political participation in Brazil's antiracism movements. Yet the potential to practice ancestralidade—to do the work of retrieving the past in order to create a better future—does not lie with Black people alone. White people must also have this capacity. When white practitioners sense axé, feel the ancestralidade, and take on a great compromisso with capoeira yet fail to translate their involvement with capoeira into action aimed at combating racial injustice, it is therefore a choice. Black practitioners do not possess an inherent capacity to be more politicized than white people. Indeed, many of the group's white members are politically active in some of the most radical sectors of Brazilian society. Choosing not to engage with Black movement politics is therefore just as much a decision as choosing to devote one's life to fighting for racial liberation.

As Dylan Robinson warns, "To be starving is to be overcome with hunger in such a way that one loses the sense of relationality and reflexivity in the drive to satisfy hunger" (2020, 53). To retrieve a more reflexive way of being in relation, to move "toward anticolonial listening [and perceiving] practices requires that the 'fevered' pace of consumption for knowledge resources be placed aside in favor of new temporalities of wonder disoriented from anti-relational and nonsituated settler colonial positions of certainty" (53). What would it mean for white practitioners' perception of Blackness to become both relational and situated? At the very least, this would suggest that white capoeira practitioners interrogate their relationships not only with Black Bahian culture but also, more crucially, with Black Bahian (and other Black Brazilian) people. It would mean opening their eyes, hearts, and minds to the ways in which their historical and geographical situations have shaped their received notions of Bahia, capoeira, and Blackness. Perhaps these could be first steps toward imagining, along with Shana Redmond, "an alternative model of identification that does not sacrifice difference for the sake of rhetorical or political clarity or consumption" (2016, 37).

There must be ways to recognize difference without collapsing or reifying it, without "othering" or "thingifying" Black people. Instead of interpreting capoeira Angola through a lens of oppositional categories and inverted hierarchies (body versus mind, simplicity versus complexity, orality versus rationality), could we accept that bodies also think through movement (Browning 1995, 13) and that capoeira simultaneously incorporates rationality, intellect, affect, emotion, discourse, (corp)orality, spirituality, and body-spirit-mind? The ways of knowing, thinking, being, and doing cultivated in capoeira Angola involve theorizing with a sensing, musicking, moving body—philosophizing through sound, energy, discourse, and corporeality all in convivência rooted in Black Brazilians' various understandings of their culture(s) and their Blackness. There can be time and space for "wonder" if white practitioners allow themselves to embrace disorientation (Hahn 2007), to lose balance and unlearn what we thought we knew. But much of this work is yet to be undertaken.

The following chapter complicates this chapter's critique of white participation by examining how the capoeira group's economic structure depends on the ways that visiting white practitioners and group members contribute to sustaining Mestre Cláudio's capoeira enterprise.

Four

Playing with Money and *Mandinga*

Capoeira gives, but it demands payment. (*Capoeira, ela dá, mas ela cobra.*)
—Mestre Cláudio

A quick corrido sets the pace. Mestre Cláudio's leg swoops in a swift arc, his hands on the ground, head down peering between his arms. His son Onirê bends deep at the waist to dodge the kick, puts his hands on the ground, and lowers his torso sideways onto his bent elbow, the side of his rasta tam brushing the ground. They shift their weight easily from hands to feet, side to side, bending deeply in the joints, playing with the agile and angular movements of the Angoleiros do Sertão's signature style. Mestre Cláudio and his son exchange corporeal calls and responses—answers blending seamlessly into questions and back again. Arms support body weight, heads and balls of feet are pivot points as their bodies twist and invert, only to land again in a wide-spaced stance. It's a beautiful game, um jogo bonito, full of wit and grace, at a Saturday roda in February 2016.

Then Mestre Cláudio initiates a counterclockwise walk around the edge of the roda—*volta ao mundo*—and Onirê follows at the opposite side of the roda. But before they complete the circle, Mestre Cláudio stops and steps back: a blue two *real* bill, loosely folded, lies on the ground beside his feet. He picks it up and starts unfolding the bill as he continues to walk the volta ao mundo. The money game begins.

Both players return to the foot of the berimbaus, the starting position, and Mestre Cláudio gently tosses the bill to the ground between them. Mestre Cláudio begins to lightly stomp his feet and shimmy his shoulders—a kind of *sapateio*—and then releases a kick, the back of his heel careening at Onirê's face. Onirê falls back on his hands to avoid getting kicked in the face, then pushes himself back up to clasp hands with the mestre to commence play. But before they can start, the mestre begins meticulously retying his shoelaces, delaying the game, and building anticipation. Eager to begin, Onirê maneuvers into a handstand above the bills, but his father soon calls him back to properly start the game.

Moments later, the game is under way, more bills have been thrown into the ring and added to the crumpled wad, and the song has shifted:

[*coro*] *Ô me dá meu dinheiro*	[chorus] Oh give me my money
Ô me dá meu dinheiro, valentão	Oh give me my money, tough guy
[*solo*] *Ô me dá meu dinheiro, valentão*	[call] Oh give me my money, tough guy
Que lhe dou uma rasteira e lhe ponho no chão	[Or] I'll give you a *rasteira* [leg sweep] and put you on the ground

Mestre Cláudio and Onirê move freely and quickly, but they keep close to the bills, spinning on the balls of their feet, lifting onto their hands, never far from the money, which becomes like a third opponent, to be kept close and guarded (from) (see fig. 10). At one point, the mestre cartwheels above the money, spreading his legs wide (see fig. 11), and Onirê sees his chance. He dives his face toward the bills, but the mestre's hand is already there to scoop Onirê's chin away from the money, causing him to roll sloppily on his back to the ground. He recovers just in time to see the mestre dip his head down to the ground and bite the bills in his teeth (see fig. 12). "Aiii!" someone screams. Onirê pats his neck tenderly, looking to the mestre as if in injured disbelief, and the mestre walks victoriously in volta ao mundo.

As the game goes on, Mestre Cláudio continues to thwart Onirê's attempts to secure the money (see figs. 13 and 14). Yet after a final intercepted dive, as they walk again in volta ao mundo, Mestre Cláudio hands Onirê the bills and claps, ending the game. Mestre Cláudio refused to let Onirê "win" the game, yet by giving him the money anyway, perhaps he acknowledged his son's contributions to entertaining the roda (see video 4 at https://doi.org/10.3998/mpub.12771665.cmp.29 and https://doi.org/10.3998/mpub.12771665.cmp.30).

• • •

Capoeira's money game, or "Tico-Tico" as group members call it after one of its songs, dates back at least to the early twentieth century. Greg Downey

Figure 10. Mestre Cláudio (right) and Onirê (left) playing a money game. See the crumpled blue bill near Mestre Cláudio's left hand. Video still by the author, 2016.

Figure 11. Mestre Cláudio (right) performs a bananeira (handstand) during a money game with Onirê. See the crumpled blue bill now near Mestre Cláudio's right hand. Video still by the author, 2016.

Figure 12. Mestre Cláudio grabs the bills in his mouth as Onirê, recently fallen to the ground, turns to see it. Video still by the author, 2016.

Figure 13. Onirê dives toward the money with open mouth—

Figure 14. —only to have Mestre Cláudio snatch the money from his mouth before he can right himself again. Video still by the author, 2016.

reports that Mestre Bimba, who innovated capoeira Regional in the 1930s and onward, "was disgusted by what he viewed as the impoverished capoeira seen at public festivals [on the streets], in which participants competed to pick up with their mouths money thrown into the roda by spectators" (Downey 2005, 61). Yet while the money game was discouraged in indoor academies, the game seems to have endured on the street. By the mid-twentieth century, it was apparently still common "for the audience to throw several banknotes on the ground, for the capoeiristas, in strategic leaps, to grab with their mouths" (Rego 1968, 54). After the game, Rego observed, the mestre would split the earnings between his students, thus ensuring they could afford transportation home. The money game persisted, for J. Lowell Lewis opens his monograph (1992) with a description of a money game he observed in a street roda in early 1980s Salvador, though he called it "mostly a thing of the past" (126). When Downey conducted his research in Salvador with GCAP (Mestre Moraes's *Grupo de Capoeira Angola Pelourinho*) in the 1990s, the money game was "rare" in academies (Downey 2005, 93). However, among the Angoleiros do Sertão, the money game is alive and well.

Rarely does a Saturday roda of the Angoleiros do Sertão go by without multiple iterations of the money game. Yet in contrast to the games Rego describes, the Angoleiros do not play the game to earn bus fare. What is it about the money game that makes it so popular with the group? The money game demands not only physical virtuosity but also a special form of mandinga, capoeira's foundational trickery. Also, in contrast to regular games, someone can win a money game. The heightened stakes enliven and entertain the roda. However, there is more to the game than money and fun. In this chapter, I explore the ways in which Mestre Cláudio's partiality for the money game and his way of playing it provide insight into his relationships with money and capoeira group economics more broadly. Considering capoeira's economy, I show how it extends longer histories of socioeconomic relations of power. This reveals that capoeira mestres work both against and within enduring racialized political-economic systems that are deeply relational in nature. In other words, capoeira mestres play with the "rules" of racist-colonialist systems as they play with their students, both in and out of the roda.

As I didn't anticipate writing about money, I rarely asked about it in my interviews. Yet I observed numerous conversations, occurrences, and conflicts around money and heard multiple stories about both money and mandinga. I take the stories seriously in part because Mestre Cláudio uses storytelling didactically, treating tales like parables that advise with varying degrees of directness how the listener should alter their behavior or be prepared to confront "life's traps" (U. Santa Barbara 2019, 5). Perhaps, as a *gringa*, a foreign white woman, I heard more stories about money than Brazilian students did. Gleaning lessons from these tales and placing them within larger interlocking forces of history, coloniality, and economics, I argue that money and mandinga intertwine and operate as powerful, interconnected forces in the capoeira community.

While mandinga has received ample attention in capoeira literature, money has not.[1] Considering the power of money in capoeira reveals that multiple overlapping types of exchange keep money, gifts, services—and axé—flowing in capoeira communities. Understanding the capoeira economy thus requires a "more flexible reading" of the relationship between gift exchanges and capitalist economics, as Baptista proposed when studying Candomblé's economy (2007, 12). Baptista found that Candomblé's economy establishes perpetual relations of exchange because the "sacred link between man and divinity has to be continually renewed, maintaining the circuit in constant movement through the celebration of diverse rituals and *obligations*" (13; original emphasis). In capoeira communities, ongoing cycles of exchange likewise maintain and strengthen bonds among group members and between students and mestre. In both economies, exchanges of money are directly related to the propagation and exchange of axé.

In contrast to studies emphasizing the newness of neoliberal labor practices in contemporary arts economies (Robitaille 2013; Foster 2019; Enriquez 2022), I draw out the historical continuities between mestres' labor practices today and those of informal cultural workers of the past. Today as in the past, capoeira mestres face precarious conditions similar to those faced by music and dance professionals (Packman 2021, 8), such as the lack of job security and safety nets including social security, pensions, and workers' compensation insurance. As such, I argue that mestres mobilize and adapt tactics developed in the past to address current conditions of economic precarity.

Examining the capoeira group's economic structure, I also complicate some common characterizations of relations among mestres and students. If on the one hand capoeira groups idealize or romanticize themselves as "families," I show that maintaining these familial relations also depends on monetary payments. On the other hand, where white foreigners often distrust "commodified experiences" (Griffith 2016, 69) and can feel exploited by capoeira mestres who charge them "exorbitant rates" for trainings or rodas (68), I challenge reductive portrayals of capoeira mestres as hustlers. Moving beyond stereotypes and the overemphasis on "deception" in capoeira literature, I propose a revalorization of trickery in capoeira. After all, across the African diaspora, tales of tricksters like Brer Rabbit and Anansi the spider "document how the weak fight back against the strong" (Lussana 2018, 124).[2] These tales have much in common with capoeira strategies of using wit to fight against a stronger foe. Yet delving into the ambiguities of the mestre-as-trickster or *mandingueiro* (sorcerer, or one who possesses mandinga), I find more than tactics for bettering a powerful opponent. I argue that embedded within acts of dissimulation can also be found an ethic of care, which extends to community members, as the following tale shows.[3]

Tales of Meat and Money

Sofie is tall and lanky, in her early thirties, with ruddy cheeks and short-cropped, wispy blonde hair.[4] A seasoned apprentice-pilgrim (Griffith 2016), she has trained capoeira for many years and traveled to Brazil numerous times, often for extended stays of months on end, as is more common for European visitors. On one of her trips, she visited a mestre she had met in her home country, the Netherlands. The mestre, whom I will call Mestre Brabo, had stayed there for several months, guest teaching with local groups and traveling to teach at events throughout Europe. During that time, she felt she had gotten to know him well, and she looked forward to visiting him in Brazil.

The opportunity arose when she returned to Brazil, this time traveling with two other Dutch capoeira friends. She contacted Mestre Brabo, and he offered to have them stay with him for several weeks. She eagerly anticipated spending time with him again. Yet almost immediately, on the first morning after their arrival, Sofie sensed a shift. She accompanied the mestre to the market to buy food for the week, including meat for the substantial midday meals: two large cuts of beef and a whole chicken cut into parts. While on the shopping trip, Sofie noticed that Mestre Brabo no longer seemed like the laid-back, gregarious person she had hung out with in Amsterdam. He seemed preoccupied and stressed out. He grumbled to her about visiting "gringos," which in Brazil refers to all foreigners, who interrupted his routine. Sofie felt bad but also confused. After all, the mestre had invited them to stay at his house, and they had agreed to pay him an all-inclusive fee that would cover meals and trainings and should also leave him with a nice profit. She was also unsure if he was including her in the "gringo" category: Did he resent her presence, too?

Sofie had spent a lot of time in Brazil, and she was used to having the main meal of the day at midday. Yet over the next several days, she started to feel hungry. Without eggs or other protein at breakfast, she found herself lingering in the kitchen with the other woman on the trip, making more coffee, eating more crackers, attempting to stave off their hunger until lunchtime. Seeing them in the kitchen, Mestre Brabo complained, "All gringos do is eat!" Yet the midday meals were meager, too. Sofie realized that the mestre had cooked the chicken at the start of the week and was reheating it, doling out little pieces every day—several knuckles of a chicken foot one day, a neck bone the next. In this way, he fed five people with one chicken for a whole week. Meanwhile, she realized that her companions knew nothing of the large chunks of beef stored away in the freezer.

One night, Mestre Brabo went out and returned with a large take-out container of stewed meat. The next day, Sofie saw that he heated up the meat in the pot of beans but then scooped it out and hid it under a pile of rice and beans, which he served to himself and his student, who was living with the mestre at the time. She and the other gringos got only rice and beans. Sofie suspected that the mestre was feeding his visitors as little as possible to maximize his profits. Clearly, the less food he served them, the more money—and meat—he would have left over at the end of the week. Sofie considered saying something to the mestre, but she felt embarrassed and realized this would only confirm his accusations about gringos' insatiability. At the end of the visit, she was left with a lingering sense of sadness and regret. The good rapport she had cultivated with Mestre Brabo in Amsterdam seemed to have been replaced with mutual resentment.

• • •

Sofie's tale of meat and money recalls other tales I heard or experienced. On my first fieldwork trip, Mestre Cláudio's mother, Dona Antônia, was living with him at the roça. Whenever she caught me alone, she'd whisper, "Give me twenty *reais*!" But she told me not to tell Cláudio. She was hungry, she'd say. Or she would see my sweatshirt and say it was just what she needed: She was cold. I felt conflicted. I didn't want to be stingy, but I also felt I was already paying for my visit. Not sure what to do, I confided in Rita, Mestre Cláudio's wife. She told me how once, earlier in her relationship with Cláudio, she had asked Dona Antônia to purchase meat for her at the market. When Dona Antônia returned with the meat, Rita noticed it was a smaller amount than she had requested. When she asked about it, Dona Antônia admitted she had cut off a piece for herself, explaining this was what she used to do when she worked in wealthy white people's homes. Rita told me that this had shifted her thinking. Dona Antônia was not "stealing" from her, she realized, but rather behaving as she had done out of necessity to feed her children. When Mestre Cláudio was growing up, there were days when Dona Antônia had no food at all. Mestre Cláudio and some of his friends, other hungry children, would rummage through the dumpsters for scraps of food. Cutting off a piece of meat was a kind of habit, indeed part of an "economic habitus"—that is, a set of "economic dispositions" and "embodied beliefs" formed under previous economic conditions that endure even when those conditions have changed (Bourdieu 2000, 17). Dona Antônia was behaving how she had to when she was feeding three children on insufficient wages, even though Rita might soon be serving her from the same piece of meat. Dona Antônia was not stealing meat, therefore, but rather practicing a "morality that hunger teaches" (37). Mestre Cláudio took good care of his mother. She had enough to eat and enough colorful cardigans to ward off the chill. But my presence seemed to summon familiar patterns of relation and behavior.

Mestre Brabo, in Sofie's story, demonstrated related skills of reserving meat and stretching limited food resources, as when he fed five people from one chicken for a week.[5] Sofie experienced this as deprivation, but the practice also recalls the familiar Brazilian expression "*bota água no feijão.*" The spirit of this expression, "put water in the beans," is not one of withholding but of generosity, hospitality, and care. Extending the simple dish, the host can feed more people, leaving no one (truly) hungry. (Sofie readily acknowledged that her hunger was nothing compared to someone who had no food.) I saw Mestre Cláudio stretch meals, too. On one occasion, he had just finished preparing a beef stew for lunch, when one of his cousins showed up at the roça unannounced. Mestre Cláudio was annoyed that he now had to further divide a meal prepared for three (himself, his son, and me). Yet rather than turn his cousin away, he retreated to the kitchen. He took out one chunk of tender beef, shredded it with a fork in a bowl, ladled broth on top, and poured in a generous heap of *farinha*, manioc flour. Mixing it together he formed a tasty-looking paste, which would certainly fill the stomach of his relative. Though Mestre Cláudio would have preferred not to share the costly meat, by stretching the stew he still fulfilled his kinship obligations. In Sofie's story, Mestre Brabo had taken in a student in need of housing, and he had hidden meat under the student's rice and beans in addition to his own, treating the student as family. In these ways, the mestres were caring and providing for their family and adopted kin relations.[6] As when Dona Antônia reserved a slice of meat to feed her children, these practices are not so much acts of deception or thievery, but rather acts of care and love. It made sense that gringos were not included among those community members most in need of the mestres' care.

Dona Antônia's behavior aligns with "a whole array of creative strategies" employed by Black domestic workers, including the bringing home of leftover or excess foodstuffs, or "pan-toting" (Kelley 1994, 18–19). In a nostalgic opening passage, Kelley recalls employing these strategies alongside other Black teenagers working at McDonald's, "accidentally" cooking too many hamburgers (more meat) close to closing time because they could take home leftovers (1).[7] Where white employers saw "theft," Black employees asserted their moral right to a portion of the goods whose production and distribution depended on their labor (19).[8] I understand capoeira mestres as operating under similar conditions. While we cannot know what became of the meat stashed in Mestre Brabo's freezer, he clearly took advantage of the gringos' visit to maximize his earnings, thereby increasing his ability to provide for his dependents.

In these stories, then, meat is more than simply food. Perhaps as in African American trickster tales, so many of which involve Brer Rabbit tricking another animal out of food, the meat can be seen as a "symbol of enhanced status and power" (Levine 1977, 108). Levine even recounts a tale in which Rabbit hides meat, though he is tricked back by weaker Partridge to reveal where he had hidden it (110). The stories told above likewise reveal something about meat's power. Nourishing as it satiates, providing protein and nutrients, building muscle and strength, meat is the embodiment of sustenance. As the most expensive and nutrient-dense food, meat is the antithesis of hunger and poverty and a potent symbol of wealth. Ultimately, like money and axé, meat both symbolizes and contains energy: not only calories that transform into physical energy but also the nurturing energy of love. As with the axé-infused meats offered in Candomblé rituals, meat has and is power.[9] Meat, like axé, sustains life.

The tales of meat and money thus reveal the inaccuracies of narratives portraying mestres and other (previously) impoverished people as "deceiving" or "stealing." If meat and money are forms of energy, then these stories reveal how people in peripheral communities leverage energies, conserving, stretching, or tapping into resources as needed—like the power-tapping in Brazil's peripheries, the only means for some communities to access the electric grid. Yes, these are tactics of survival, weapons of the weak (J. Scott 1987), and perhaps "justice is only possible through trickery" (Lussana 2018, 131). Sequestering and providing food is also a form of love—sustaining family, community, and community-that-becomes-family.

The Money Game: "Rules" and Rule Breaking

In capoeira's money game, tactics of trickery may steal the show, but they also rely upon other more positively valenced skills that are equally fundamental but receive less attention in English-language capoeira literature. Far more often than he talks about mandinga, *malícia*, or *malandragem* (all words for trickery), when teaching how to play a jogo bonito, Mestre Cláudio emphasizes playing with "intelligence," "spirit," and "expression." When playing on the streets every Saturday, he also insists that his students play to "entertain the roda," bringing joy to the roda's spectators—as their focused attention, laughter, and exclamations attest. Producing beautiful, entertaining games requires relations of camaraderie, collaboration, communication, trust, and care between players and with the audience. Could playing with these qualities be just as essential to capoeira as the ability to deceive, or even integral to it? Is to mistrust the most fundamental wisdom learned in capoeira, or is it impossible without trust? Indeed, if the deception fundamental to capoeira is often explained as having roots in the survival strategies of early enslaved capoeiristas, then reevaluating mandinga in capoeira today can shed light on capoeira mestres' tactics to survive and help their communities thrive in the broader game of capitalist economics in the afterlife of slavery (Hartman 2008a).

The money game fundamentally shifts some key parameters of "regular" capoeira play. Whereas there are usually no winners or losers in capoeira, in a money game the player who gets the money clearly seems to win. Whereas trickery, cunning, and bending or breaking "rules" are always part of capoeira (Varela 2017, 113–15), the money game delightfully intensifies these elements, exaggerating so much of what makes capoeira difficult to play and entertaining to watch. For instance, while the use of hands is always restricted, the money game adds the proscription that the money cannot be grabbed with hands, only with the mouth. Indeed, two of the most common songs sung for money games make this "rule" explicit. The song cited above, "*Me dá meu dinheiro*," has another line with a double meaning:

Que no meu dinheiro ninguém põe a mão	For no one lays a hand on my money

The lyrics of the "Tico-Tico" song likewise play with the idea of not using one's hands, for a bird, of course, has no hands:[10]

[*coro*] *Apanha a Laranja no chão tico-tico*	[chorus] Grab the orange on the ground Tico-Tico [Rufous-collared Sparrow]
[*solo*] *não é com a mão que se apanha é com o bico*	[call] It's not with the hand that you grab but with the beak

Yet perhaps because of the explicit nature of this rule, it is even more tempting to break. At least in the Angoleiros do Sertão, such a hard and fast rule seems to call out to players to mess with it.

Even though breaking rules can be expected, and is extremely entertaining to watch, it still often feels unfair to the players involved. After all, if players accepted rule breaking, what force would the rules hold? For example, restrictions on using hands surely also prohibit grabbing an opponent's face or snatching the money out of their mouth! Yet this is often how Mestre Cláudio "wins" money games. Mestre Cláudio's defiance of the rules does provoke complaint, if muted—Onirê gestured his protest each time the mestre grabbed his chin or neck—but there is little one can do to challenge the mestre. Who gets to bend or break the "rules" thus depends largely on the player's power and authority (Varela 2017, 115)—and in Onirê's case, Mestre Cláudio has perhaps double the authority as both mestre and father. Yet as their game also revealed, Mestre Cláudio does not necessarily wield his power simply to win. In the end, he gave Onirê the money anyway, perhaps rewarding a game well played, or perhaps reminding everyone present that the point is not who "wins" but rather that playing with the rules must be done artfully, with care, and with mandinga.

Terms of Deception

The fundamental concepts of malícia, mandinga, and malandragem, often used interchangeably, all refer to capoeira's trickery, outsmarting one's opponent rather than using brute force. Yet none of the terms has a simple definition and each has different connotations. Scholar-practitioner Christine Zonzon calls malícia "the art of disguise or 'make-believe'" (2014, 46) and lists a host of definitions: "*traição* [betrayal], *brincadeira* [playful joking], *esperteza* [cunning], *manha* [trickery], *maldade* [cruelty], malandragem, mandinga" (156). Greg Downey translates malícia as "cunning," also in the subtitle of his book (*Lessons in Cunning*), and explains that malícia means "a combination of wariness, quick wit, savvy, unpredictability, playfulness, viciousness, aesthetic flare, and a talent for deception" (2005, 123).[11] Malícia's English cognate may be "malice," but clearly it exceeds this negative sense.

Historian Adriana Dias instead privileges mandinga as the "essential characteristic of capoeira," noting that the term served as a synonym of capoeira at the end of the nineteenth century in Salvador (Dias 2006, 17–20). Mandinga also meant "fetish" (*feitiço*), referring to "the magic practices" of the enslaved (17), and was also synonymous with Candomblé and used to target religious practitioners (*adeptos da mandinga*) for persecution, violence, and formal punishment (J. Oliveira 2010).[12] Finally, when discussing malandragem, many cite the seminal texts of anthropologist Roberto DaMatta (1992 [1979]) and ethnomusicologist Carlos Sandroni (2021 [2001]), noting the term's "broader significance in Brazilian culture, [referring] to the character of the malandro, an archetypal 'rogue' or 'hustler'" (Downey 2005, 118; see also Varela 2017, 122; Lewis 1992, 47). As Downey put it, "Malícia guides both the malandro and the capoeirista" (2005, 119), and according to Varela, "Deception . . . creates malandros out of capoeira practitioners" (2017, 122).[13]

While the authors all acknowledge the complexity of these terms, I find that English-language texts by non-Brazilians collectively, if unintentionally, collapse the nuance and ambiguity of these concepts, reducing capoeira's essence to deception.[14] For instance, Varela defines mandinga as a power specific to capoeira, founded upon capoeira's "ontology of deception" (2017, 94–109). Even Downey, whose exploration of cunning is more nuanced, still argues that capoeira players ultimately learn to "walk in evil," in the game as in their lives, trusting no one and suspecting everyone of potential betrayal

(153–68).[15] It seems as though ever since Lewis (1992) argued for understanding capoeira play as "deceptive discourse," the mandinga of deception has enchanted capoeira scholars.

Brazil-based scholars, as cited above, offer more multivalent explanations, which are also more in line with how Mestre Cláudio used the terms. Scholar-practitioner Rosângela Araújo (Mestra Janja, Zonzon's mestra) deemphasizes deception in her definitions, understanding mandinga and malícia as "enchanting" forms of play (*brincar*) responsible for the joking around (brincadeira) in the roda, which emerges through "theatricality, improvisation, and simulation" (Araújo 2015, 85).[16] Araújo understands play broadly as "a process of metacommunication in which ludic pseudo-conflict becomes an expression of agreement" (84), thus emphasizing its unifying potential.

Understanding mandinga and related concepts as play also relates them to other African and African diasporic performance practices, with their "dynamic amalgamation of pleasure and critique" (DeFrantz 2004, 65). In the context of Yoruba expressive practices, Margaret Drewal (1992) theorized play as serious work that was also improvisatory and deeply enjoyable. Drewal also discusses trickster figures but makes clear that the aim of play is not simply to deceive. (This would be like arguing that the purpose of theater is to convince the audience they are witnessing real life, not actors on stage.) Emphasizing play, theatricality, and make-believe as essential to definitions of mandinga thus makes room for the ambiguous multivalences of capoeira's aesthetics without characterizing capoeira players as suspicious and superstitious, distrusting and untrustworthy, lying and cheating.

A more holistic, multivalent understanding of mandinga thus allows a reevaluation of mestres' dealings with money in their lives. Rather than feed racist tropes and stereotypes of capoeira mestres as untrustworthy malandros, I seek to place their economic tactics in the context of their lived experiences and histories. Instead of seeing the capoeira world as one where no one can be trusted, I find it more like Candomblé, a world "in which there is a high degree of intimacy and trust" (Baptista 2007, 4). Indeed, as another prominent Black activist mestre in Salvador, Mestre René, said in a workshop I attended, "In order to distrust, first you have to trust!" He explained that our enemies were not here in this room, referring to the capoeira community, but rather out there, referring to the "system." We needed to strengthen one another to fight the system together. I am not proposing a simple inversion—that the foundation of capoeira is trust rather than distrust—but rather suggesting that capoeira holds both trust and distrust in tension. Capoeira cultivates the wisdom to determine when to trust and when not to. In the capoeira communities I know, students are not taught to suspect everyone as a potential enemy. Rather, these communities are based on shared commitments, loyalty, and love—which does not mean they are without disagreement, betrayal, and conflict.

My First Installment

My field journal from my first visit to Mestre Cláudio's roça in 2013 is filled with notes about money. While this speaks to my own anxieties, these notes also reveal broader themes that arise in relationships between mestres and students, especially foreigners. Almost from day one, I grappled with strong emotions provoked by our frequent discussions about money, but my emotions are not the focus here. Rather, they reflect the broader fact that money often evokes intense feelings and causes interpersonal conflicts, in part because money is so closely linked to our survival and security.

Though I only stayed at the roça for two weeks in 2013, I experienced an intense whirlwind of highs, lows, insights, and revelations, which would come to typify my time spent with Mestre Cláudio. The highs came from being swept up in his charisma, sharing jokes and stories, feeling euphoric after training, emulating the beauty of his playing style, and drinking beer with the group after the Saturday roda. During my first visit, Mestre Cláudio told me numerous stories about other foreigners who had stayed at the roça, some for many months, and he constantly compared me to other gringos. For instance, he approved of my bathing habits compared to some Europeans who never showered after training. (We laughed.) He also spoke of gringos who treated him to lavish meals and bought him expensive gifts. Soon I found myself writing field notes about the special running shoes I wanted to send him when I returned home.

The lows mainly resulted from our interactions around money. Several days into my visit, Mestre Cláudio initiated our first conversation about money. He framed it as a negotiation, proposing an amount that would cover food, lodging, and capoeira lessons and asking if I found it fair. The amount he proposed was only slightly more than what I had estimated, so I agreed. I was relieved that we had settled the money issue so smoothly—or so I thought. A few days later, Mestre Cláudio said he had to go to Salvador to pick up a friend from the airport and asked if I wanted to come along. He described how we could have a fresh fish dinner at a beachside place he knew. I envisioned a mini road trip, the two-hour drive filled with conversation, and I accepted the invitation. (And Mestre Cláudio agreed to be interviewed during the car trip, one of only two recorded interviews he has granted me.) When we stopped for gas, Mestre Cláudio informed me I had to pay for it. I proposed splitting the costs, reminding him that he had invited me on a trip he already had to take. No, he told me, he no longer needed to go to Salvador. We were only going because I had seemed so enthusiastic, and he didn't want to disappoint me. (We still picked up his friend.) I paid for everything on our two-day trip: the expensive fish dinner, gas, meals, snacks, and water. I was in graduate school, on an unfunded research trip, paying out of pocket at a time when the exchange rate was not so favorable. In one day I spent nearly three times what I had allotted as a daily budget. However, what left me feeling "awful," as I wrote in my notes, wasn't spending the money—I could still afford it—it was the feeling of being coerced. I wrote, "I couldn't even have the pleasure of offering to treat him to dinner."

I do not wish to overemphasize this minor anecdote, which I'm sure Mestre Cláudio has long forgotten. I have since learned what Mestre Cláudio expects of me financially, and I am far more accepting of my role to play in these games. Rereading these notes, I cringe at my lack of generosity and how green I was, new to seeing myself as a researcher and new to navigating a relationship with a renowned mestre. Yet I also see how Mestre Cláudio was trying to run his business. On subsequent visits, Mestre Cláudio spoke about how he understands his capoeira group as a business (*empresa*), even as it operates in an informal economy constrained by discriminatory policies beyond his control. Like many mestres, Mestre Cláudio has structured his business to earn income from a variety of sources and using multiple tactics. Taking these tactics seriously as business practices, I place them in the context of Brazil's cultural systems and the longer histories of Black entrepreneurship in Bahia.

Brazilian Cultural Policy

Brazil's young democracy already has a strong legacy of supporting the arts, but state sponsorship has not been distributed equally throughout the country, rendering public support difficult to access for many practitioners of Black cultura popular.[17] President Lula da Silva's first administration (2003–2010) ushered in a new era of ideology-driven cultural policy in Brazil, most notably through its Cultura Viva (Living Culture) program, which established cultural centers (*pontos de cultura*) throughout Brazil and abroad, with the aim of increasing both support for and access to diverse cultural manifestations (Moreira 2023). Although under right-wing President Jair Bolsonaro (2019–2022) public commitments to culture (along with democracy, diversity, and basic human rights) came under attack, when the COVID-19 pandemic halted most cultural activity, the Brazilian state instituted the Aldir Blanc Law in 2020, in an emergency effort to keep cultural institutions and workers afloat.

Brazil's public cultural system has also produced policies specifically aimed at supporting capoeira. In addition to Brazilian recognition of capoeira as intangible cultural heritage in 2008, leading to UNESCO's recognition in 2014, the Ministry of Culture established the Projeto Capoeira Viva (Living Capoeira Project), which ran competitive selection processes to fund capoeira-related projects from 2006 to 2015 (Lacerda 2021, 17). However, as I have observed firsthand, and Lacerda also found, such funding mechanisms tend to exclude the very people they are aimed to support. Applying for funds requires literacy in bureaucratic language and financial management (Lacerda 2021). While some capoeira mestres have now earned PhDs, there are still many mestres who never completed a high school education. Mestres interviewed by Lacerda also complained of the absence of institutional support for mestres navigating the bureaucratic requirements and, finally, the lack of continuity: when administrators changed, Capoeira Viva abruptly ended, without any official conclusion (Lacerda 2021).

As far as I'm aware, Mestre Cláudio did not participate in the Capoeira Viva project, but he had formed his opinion about public policies long before it was over. Mestre Cláudio is deeply cynical about public support for cultura popular. Some of his students have successfully applied for funding in other states—to support annual events, for instance—and he applauds these efforts, but Mestre Cláudio does not seek public funding for his own projects. He has explained to me that the instability of political favor is a main concern: even if he received support one year, when someone else came into power the next, the funding would be canceled. Project-based funding models, even if one possesses the skills to write successful applications, simply cannot sustain the life-long project of running a capoeira school.

Capoeira Economies and Their Precedents

In this context, Mestre Cláudio runs his capoeira school as a business. He prizes his independence as a sole proprietor, in full control of his enterprise, and is proud of his self-reliance—with the assistance of Rita, his wife, who is an accountant and handles his finances. As he sings in a ladainha (see the introduction for full lyrics), he was raised by a single mother in the rural outskirts of town and traveled "by horse or on foot." However, "Today I go by plane / I go wherever I want." All of this, he sings, is due to capoeira: "Capoeira gave me everything." Living by a bootstraps philosophy of hard work and a single-minded compromisso to capoeira, he has pulled himself out of poverty and built a multinational capoeira enterprise that sustains his livelihood and that of multiple dependents. Living on the outskirts of Feira de Santana, in Mantiba, he has positioned himself to give back to his community, such as by hiring them as workers or lending them money. He also serves as a role model, showing that it is possible to evade the snares of peripheral life. The influx of wealthier white Brazilians and foreigners visiting the roça to learn from him further signals to the community Mestre Cláudio's international prominence and success.

Mestre Cláudio derives his income from several main sources: students' membership fees, instrument sales, and giving guest workshops. His students in Feira de Santana pay a modest monthly membership fee (*mensalidade*), as do those who lead the group's many núcleos, located throughout Brazil and abroad. Yet by my estimates, student fees and instrument sales make up only a fraction of the mestre's income and alone could not sustain him. The mestre seems to earn the bulk of his income from teaching at annual events, including those held by the núcleos. Like many mestres, Mestre Cláudio travels throughout Brazil and the world at the invitation of other capoeira groups, and he likely earns thousands of reais, Euros, or dollars for each engagement. On a well-organized trip, the mestre participates in multiple events in different cities, timed closely together, with all lodging, meals, and travel covered.[18]

Mestre Cláudio, like other mestres, also deploys more informal tactics for supplementing his income. As I learned in 2013, my role as a foreign visitor was to pay for meals, gas, and beer. Often the visiting gringos and higher-earning students shoulder more of the bill at a post-roda Saturday drinking session. These practices have earned mestres the reputation of hustling for their money. Yet portraying mestres as hustlers overlooks the context in which they work, in a system not designed for their success. I see the roots of mestres' creative tactics and entrepreneurial spirit in the labor practices of enterprising Black workers in Bahia—enslaved, free, and liberated—working within the slavery economy and its aftermath.

Historical Black Entrepreneurship in Bahia

[*coro*] *Ô, nega que vende aí*	[chorus] Oh, Black woman who sells there
[*solo*] *Vende aí, vende aí*	[call] Sells there, sells there

[*coro*] *Ô, nega que vende aí*	[chorus] Oh, Black woman who sells there
[*solo*] *Vende pipoca que vem da Bahia*	[call] Sells popcorn that comes from Bahia

This capoeira corrido, which appears on Mestre Cláudio's CD (Santo Amaro and Costa 2003), valorizes the Black women who worked and continue to work by selling food and other products on the streets of Bahia. During the nineteenth century, enslaved Africans and Afro-Brazilians carved out opportunities to earn money through the system of *ganho* (earning). These *ganhadores* (earners), or *negros de ganho*, worked outside of their owners' homes, sometimes even living separately, under the agreement that they would deliver a predetermined amount of their earnings to their masters (A. de L. Costa 1991).[19] In Salvador, ganhadores, who also included free and freed workers, organized themselves into groups called *cantos*, each occupying a fixed street corner or crossroads in the city (22). They mainly worked as porters, carrying and transporting goods and people (in carried chairs) across the urban terrain. In their downtime, they also produced goods such as bird cages or woven straw hats (22). Ambulant barbers offered their services, too, at these corners, and enslaved and free women would cook and sell food (23). Thus a thriving informal economy arose on the streets of Bahia, echoes of which can be seen today in ambulatory street vendors and food stands. While the "freedom" of these workers was only "relative" (27), Africans and Afro-Brazilians took advantage of the small cracks they pried open in the slavery system, responding to constraints with truly entrepreneurial tactics.

Capoeira emerged out of these same communities, as many early capoeiras were also porters or stevedores, working in Salvador's port (Abreu 2005). Mestre Cláudio, like many mestres, also has a direct connection to this informal economy through his mother, who used to sell *acarajé* (black-eyed pea fritters) on the streets of Salvador. By recognizing these precedents, I underscore the historical continuities both of Black entrepreneurship and the precarious labor conditions that mestres face today. As with other "informal" laborers (Coletto 2010) today and in the past, capoeira mestres often make financial transactions outside of formal channels of payment, agree to work without contracts, and labor without benefits such as pensions, unemployment, workers' compensation insurance, or paid sick days. For just one example, Mestre Cláudio told me about a time he traveled to a capoeira event abroad, having been promised a certain amount in payment, but was told on arrival that they didn't have the money to pay him. He had no recourse. There are also no accredited degree programs to certify someone as a capoeira mestre and very few opportunities for permanent, salaried employment.[20]

Mestre Cláudio secures his living in yet another, less overt way, through the financial support he receives from several wealthy, white group members. Perhaps the most notable member is Fabio Sadan, one of the mestre's oldest students in terms of years of involvement. Sadan runs a profitable construction company in São Paulo state, and it is known among the group that he supports the mestre far beyond paying membership dues. As Sadan himself put it in our interview, for a long time he has earned more money than he needs, and he decided years ago that he would support the mestre in any way he could. Indeed, it is possible that Mestre Cláudio has learned some of his business sense from Sadan, for it seems Sadan serves as a financial advisor to the mestre, if informally. These relationships reveal that capoeira businesses also give continuity to historical economic systems of patronage.

Patronage, Candomblé, and Economies of Axé

Powerful and wealthy white capoeira students who support capoeira groups play a similar role to that of ogã in Candomblé communities. Broadly, ogãs are non-initiated male members who support the functioning of the terreiro. However, there are two kinds of ogã. One is responsible for "ritual functions in the terreiros," such as drumming or performing sacrifices, whereas the other refers to wealthy, usually white, and often politically powerful patrons who not only provide financial support but also leverage their political connections to protect and aid the religious organizations (Baptista 2007, 14). In the latter role, ogãs historically leveraged their power and positions to protect Candomblé while it was still outlawed.[21] However, Baptista demonstrates that wealthy white ogãs continue to provide "financial and political resources" for their terreiros—for instance, by negotiating with government officials on their behalf and "working to obtain public benefits and jobs for members of the community" (Baptista 2007, 14).

I see parallels with the role some wealthier white members play in Mestre Cláudio's group. The mestre made this role official at the event in 2023 by creating a new title of *conselheiro* (advisor).[22] Mestre Cláudio bestowed the title on several older white male group members, including Fabio Sadan, explaining during the ceremony that he wanted to recognize that these members contributed to the group in ways that were different from, but equally valuable to, those of younger students teaching their own satellite groups. The conselheiros have since established a fund to finance Mestre Cláudio's health care. Sadan has also contributed in many other ways over the years to Mestre Cláudio's present and future well-being. As he told me, he often declares to the mestre, "We will grow old together!" His commitment to Mestre Cláudio is life-long.

The role of white advisors to the capoeira group, like that of ogã, also relates to broader patterns of patronage in Brazilian society. As historian Kim Butler has argued, from the colonial era onward, patronage has remained the "principle underlying all social relationships" in Brazil (1998, 18), constituting an "unspoken bargain" (Graham 1990, 24) whereby parties agree that "social relationships are based upon an exchange of fealty and services for protection and economic support, and that disloyalty to one's patron merits punishment" (Butler 1998, 18). At the heart of the historical system was the (white) family unit, with the authoritarian father at its head, though the "familial" connections extended beyond the nuclear family to include any number of "ritual kinship" relations, such as godparents/godchildren and other dependents (*agregados*) (Graham 1990, 20–21). The latter included "poverty-stricken" and "free but likely black or mulatto" workers who were bound to their patrons by feelings of loyalty and obligations to provide labor or services in exchange for protection and privileges, such as access to land for subsistence farming (21). Collectively, household members and dependents made up the patron's "clientele" (*clientela*), and the "size of his *clientela* was the measure of a man" (22).

The structural hierarchies of capoeira and Candomblé disrupt these traditional patronage relations in several ways. On one hand, patrons or ogãs may be white and powerful, but they are still subordinate to community leaders, mestre/as and mães- and pais-de-santo. It is also important to recall that the system of enslavement in Brazil, as in the United States, made establishing familial relations exceedingly difficult for the enslaved (Harding 2000, 110). Thus, when enslaved and free Afro-Brazilians named their institutions in familial terms—in Candomblé but also in the Catholic *irmandades* (lay brotherhoods), mutual aid institutions—concepts of family took on meanings that "emphasized a compassionate mutuality" (110), departing from the authoritative punishment-benevolence model established by white patrons.[23] On the other hand, mestres occupying the position of authority in a group sometimes seem to perpetuate these historical models, wielding both "the threat of punishment and the promise of benevolence," entangling their students in "a powerful web of obligations owed and gifts expected" (Graham 1990, 24). Capoeira mestres often demand obedience and loyalty and punish transgressions, often through expulsion from the group—sometimes only threatened or temporary to teach a lesson, other times permanent.

However, the group's exchange of money again departs from the traditional patronage model, for while the students (clients) provide labor for the mestre, such as repairing instruments or preparing his grounds for the annual event, they also pay the mestre (patron). This alters the labor relations: the clients pay the patron for services (capoeira lessons), and in return the mestre-patron provides knowledge about capoeira, belonging to the group's affective community, and access to the mestre's axé. In addition to his income, the mestre also earns a reputation. Having a larger group, with more núcleos on more continents, adds to his prestige: the "size of his *clientela* [is] the measure of a [mestre]" (Graham 1990, 22). In these ways, capoeira's economy again appears more like that of Candomblé.

Baptista suggests that the numerous ways members contribute in Candomblé communities—from giving money, providing services, to donating goods, among other acts—constitute a kind of "hybrid" between commodity and gift exchanges, ultimately forming "a type of internal economy" unique to Candomblé (Baptista 2007, 14).[24] A similar economy functions in the capoeira group, where what is being exchanged—money, labor, wisdom, beer, commitments, or expressions of adoration—matters less than keeping the exchanges flowing, like the call and response in the roda. When wealthy white students, both Brazilian and foreign, contribute large sums of money, the sums "are not understood . . . as payment, but as a way of integrating, participating and redistributing the axé, the sacred force, the divine energy" (Baptista 2007, 14). What matters most is that by supporting Mestre Cláudio, his students and patrons ensure that he can continue cultivating and propagating axé. Everyone benefits from this unwritten arrangement, and although money changes hands, the value and meaning of these exchanges cannot be fully expressed in terms of external economic frameworks. Thus capoeira's economy could also be understood as an "economy of axé."[25] When capoeira students enter into economic relationships with the group, they do so because this enables them to access, experience, but also contribute to creating and redistributing the group's axé. I argue that in an economy of axé, money can also be seen as a force that, not unlike axé, is intimately linked to power and circulates and accumulates but also dissipates (is spent) and therefore must be constantly regenerated.

Money, also like axé, makes things happen. Money sustains the capoeira community and ensures the practice's continuation. This helps explain why Mestre Cláudio so often warns that "Capoeira gives, but it demands payment," reminding his students to reflect upon what they owe to capoeira, not to him personally.[26] Yet clearly giving money to mestres also sustains capoeira as mestres are the ones who keep capoeira's embodied knowledge alive in order to pass it on to other bodies.

When visitors enter the capoeira community, they step into these broader contexts, longer histories, and unspoken obligations that make up an economy of axé. However, as Sofie's tale and my own experience illustrate, especially when visitors come from outside of Brazil, they are not always aware of the nature of these existing relationships of exchange, expectations of help, and commitments to keep the exchanges flowing. Even Brazilian students sometimes struggle with fulfilling their compromisso when money is involved, as the following story shows.

Playing for Keeps?

In January 2023 I was back in Feira de Santana, staying at the roça for the weeks leading up to the group's annual event. During one Saturday roda, almost immediately when the roda began, a spectator threw a bill into the ring to initiate a money game. Yet instead of the common cobalt blue of a two real bill, the money radiated a bright powder blue: that of a one hundred real bill. Immediately spectators took note, someone asking, "Is that a hundred reais?" Another confirmed, excitement brimming in their voice. The players knelt at the berimbau, Boné (pseudonym) adjusting his tam, and Rato (pseudonym), his hair braided in a long narrow tail down his back, already eyeing the crumpled bill. Rato initiated the game by stepping over the bill into the ring as Boné lowered his torso onto an elbow in a quick *queda de rins*, knees bending, then extending both legs toward the bill, toes rolling over it and under Rato's face, blocking his path. Rato lifted his hands off the ground, keeping an arm between Boné's legs and his face, stepped over Boné's legs, and placed his foot on the ground between the money and Boné's face as Boné lowered his head to the ground. They both moved smoothly, rotating their bodies in tight concentric circles around the crumpled hundred real note, repeatedly reaching their feet to block their opponent's mouth from grabbing the bill. Rato stood up, deftly toed the bill, passing it to his other foot, which he swiftly swept behind him, shuttling the bill back toward the edge of the roda. With a quick pivot toward the bill, Rato reached his hands to the floor and lowered his mouth to the money as his legs swept up and over his body. He landed facing up to the sky, his knees and elbows deeply bent under his torso, supported just by feet and hands. Pushing up with his arms, he returned to an upright squat, money in his mouth. The game was over in a matter of fifteen seconds.

The crowd erupted in cheers and kept singing. As Rato stood up, he stuffed the bill into his pants pocket and returned to the foot of the berimbau to resume a regular game. I didn't notice it in the moment, but rewatching the video I can see Mestre Cláudio gesturing with his baqueta and saying something to Boné, shaking his head in disapproval. Perhaps the mestre felt Boné let the game end too soon, allowing such an easy win for Rato. The mestre often reminds students to "entertain the roda," so by failing to prolong the game, both players had truncated the fun. Perhaps the issue was that Rato "won" by moving the money with his feet, which technically violated the rules of touching the money only with one's mouth. In any case, Mestre Cláudio was displeased.

Later the next day I learned what had happened with the hundred reais. I had never thought about what happened to the money earned in money games, because it was usually a trivial amount, two, five, ten reais. Yet the next day, I happened upon Mestre Cláudio and Rato at a newly opened bar in the small village center near the mestre's roça. As I approached the table, half a dozen empty 600ml Heineken bottles signaled that they were well into their drinking session. I joined them and after ordering another bottle, they resumed their conversation. The situation seemed largely resolved by then, but it concerned the hundred reais that Rato had won in yesterday's game. Apparently, he had kept the money for himself, against Mestre Cláudio's insistence that he contribute the money toward the post-roda drinking session—adding it to the communal pot. Rato had not wanted to drink the day before, so he figured he would keep the money for himself. It seems that Mestre Cláudio had so disapproved of Rato's pocketing of the cash that he had threatened to expel Rato from the group. By the time I joined their table, they had resolved the disagreement: Rato was still in the group, and he had "given back" the money, or, as he clarified later to me, he "gave" it, not "gave back," still insisting it was his to give.

As we sat drinking together late that Sunday afternoon, the discussion turned more generally to money matters. Mestre Cláudio told us that only three people had called him regularly during the pandemic, asking how he was doing. He always told them he was fine, but they sent him money anyway. This was another instructive tale. I remember vividly during the pandemic trying to determine my own responsibility to the mestre. In the summer of 2020, I was taking regular Zoom lessons with the group, and there was talk suggesting we all should pay the mensalidade, as students in Feira did, even though we were remote. I agreed and calculated an amount, sending what I believe was the equivalent of more than two years of the monthly fee in

Brazil. The following year, the students organized a collection for the mestre for his birthday, and again I contributed as generously as I could. At the bar I felt an accusation in Mestre Cláudio's tale, sensing that he meant for me to reflect on my own failure to support him appropriately. I said sheepishly, "But I did send you money!" He answered immediately, "But you didn't call me!" It was true. My heart sank.

A cynical student might interpret this story through the lens of mandinga: the mestre was testing the loyalty of group members by seeing who would call him, and when he said he didn't need any help, the loyal would send him money anyway. Yet what if we take the tale at face value? Mestre Cláudio, who is used to traveling the world to participate in capoeira party after party, animating the festivities with his rural samba, charging the rodas with his axé, was suddenly forced to stay home on the roça in Feira's sparsely settled outskirts. Perhaps he was simply saying that he had been lonely, that those phone calls were like lifelines in that dark, quiet time. When Mestre Cláudio speaks of compromisso, about what one owes to capoeira, money is important, necessary, but it isn't everything. Sometimes hearing an old friend's voice means more.

Perhaps what upset the mestre about Rato's pocketing of the hundred reais was not the loss of help with paying for the rounds of beer. Rather, by keeping the cash, Rato had violated the community ethic, the unspoken expectation that you will contribute to the group. After all, even if Rato had won the money fairly (however that is defined), no one ever wins a money game on their own. Every game, every moment, every vibration of axé in the roda, is produced through participation and collaboration of everyone present. A successful roda, game, victory, is always a group effort. Despite being a member of the group for many years, Rato seemed to have forgotten this important point, and by pocketing the money, he had risked losing something incalculably more valuable: his membership in the Angoleiros do Sertão.

Rato is from Bahia, with deeply tanned skin, smooth brown hair, and a straight narrow nose. In the United States he might be perceived as nonwhite, though not Black, but in Bahia Rato is considered white. He has also lived for many years overseas, where he earns a currency that is consistently much stronger than the Brazilian real. At one point the mestre walked away from our table, and Rato turned to me. He asked if I ever "felt uncomfortable with all the sucking." I was momentarily confused, because "sucking" (*sugando*) was the same word Iaiá had used to describe foreigners like me who come to Bahia to "suck" up their culture and knowledge (see preface). Was he referring to *my* sucking? No, he insisted; he meant how the mestre and others were always sucking money out of me and other gringos. I told him that in truth it no longer made me uncomfortable, though it used to. I had come to accept it and sometimes see it as just and justified, as I argue in this chapter. But I asked if *he* felt uncomfortable, and he complained bitterly that he resented feeling treated like a gringo. He was Bahian! Because he lived abroad, he told me, everyone assumed he had tons of money, but he assured me he didn't. I wondered to myself, *Was he implying that he kept the money because he needed it, or because he was Bahian, not a gringo, and so was entitled to keep it?* Seeming to deny his racial and class privilege, Rato was deeply uncomfortable with being put in the category of "colonizer." Yet, ironically, by maintaining that the money was his to keep, Rato behaved more like a gringo who had not yet grasped what it meant to belong to the Angoleiros do Sertão and to owe something to capoeira.

Revalorizing Malandragem and Mandinga

Iê! Eu sou pobre de dinheiro	Iê! I am poor in terms of money
Porém não tenho tristeza	But I am not sad
Tem hora que eu me orgulho	There are times when I am proud
De ser filho da pobreza	To be a son of poverty
Porque lá no céu não entra	Because you can't take to heaven
Jóia, carro, nem beleza	Jewelry, cars, or beauty
Fazenda, gado e dinheiro	Farms, cattle, and money
Não me deixa preocupado	Don't worry me
Dinheiro também traz problema	Money also brings problems
Angústia, dor e pecado	Anguish, pain, and sin
Mesmo que no céu só entra	Even though the only ones to enter heaven
Aquele mais humilhado	Are the most humble
Não sou pobre porque tenho	I am not poor because I have
A paz de nosso Senhor	The peace of our Lord
Para mim pobre é aquele	For me, poor is the one
Que é escarnecedor	Who mocks [others]
É pobre de espírito	He is poor in spirit
Não tem carinho e nem amor	He has neither affection nor love
Camaradinho	Dear friend

Mestre Cláudio's "Ladainha of Poverty" appears on his first CD (Santo Amaro and Costa 2003). His lyrics express a familiar moral that money and material wealth cannot secure either happiness or (heavenly) redemption. He is proud of his lived experience of poverty and recognizes that with money also come challenges, potential conflicts, even suffering. Mestre Cláudio no longer sings this ladainha, as he mentioned to me in passing one day in 2015. Back when he wrote it, he told me, he was going through a truly difficult time, when he really had nothing. As we sat in his kitchen, in one of several structures he had built on his property lush with fruit and coconut trees, it was clear that this was no longer the case. Yet Mestre Cláudio remains "a son of poverty" in the sense that his lived and embodied experiences have left indelible marks on his body-spirit-mind, in ways he may or may not be conscious of. During one of our conversations in January 2023, Mestre Cláudio admitted to me that he used to use "malandragem" to get money out of gringos, but claimed he no longer does so because one, he no longer needs to, and two, it's exhausting. He explained that malandragem comes from "necessity," implying that nowadays he is economically secure, rendering the deception of gringos unnecessary. Yet such behaviors can endure, even when it seems they are no longer necessary, becoming a kind of habitus. Dona Antônia still cut off a piece of meat purchased by her daughter-in-law. Mestre Cláudio still got a bit more out of me on my most recent trip, even after I had again wired him a large sum before arriving. At the same time, these exchanges now feel more like a game that we both play.

Regardless of whether Mestre Cláudio continues to use malandragem consciously or not, or whether these minor tricks even qualify as malandragem in his mind, it was clear that he objected to the negative connotations of the deception narrative that pervades capoeira discourse. By insisting that malandragem came out of necessity, Mestre Cláudio redirected the focus from deception to its historical and economic contexts. Rather than emphasizing deception as the foundation of capoeira, therefore, we could better ask what constitute the conditions today that still render deception a necessary tactic for capoeira mestres' survival. We can also ask what other kinds of strategies and tactics are demanded by today's conditions and in what ways malandragem can be creatively adapted to address them.

After class one evening before the event in January 2023, Mestre Cláudio even more explicitly critiqued the negative associations of mandinga. As we sat in a haphazard circle on the floor, sweaty and spent but high off the training, Mestre Cláudio told a brief tale about another capoeira player he knew. The guy borrowed a capoeira book from another player but never gave it back. When Mestre Cláudio learned of this, he went to the guy and said something like, "What are you doing? Give the book back!" The guy responded, I imagine with a sly smile, "Capoeira is mandinga!" Everyone in the circle laughed.

But Mestre Cláudio remained serious. He said that this kind of behavior explained why mandinga had become a bad word (*pejorativo*). This kind of flippant remark reduced the complexity and nuance of mandinga to simple, negative behaviors such as taking (something) and not giving (it) back—breaking the cyclical flow of exchange. Actually, he went on, *"Mandinga é sabedoria!"* Mandinga is wisdom, not mere trickery or dishonesty. The guy in this story was not exhibiting wisdom, for there was no specialized knowledge or artistry needed to keep someone else's book.

Mandinga and related concepts belong to a broader foundation of knowledge created and sustained through capoeira practice. In a capoeira game and its aftermath, as in life, wisdom means knowing what to do, when, and how to do it. In Mestre Cláudio's teachings the "how" always involves intelligence and spirit. Many mestres say it includes playfulness (brincadeira), though it is still serious play, recalling Drewal's description of play "in the Yoruba sense" as "interactive exploration of the inner heads (*ori inu*) of the players, a creative, engaging, ongoing strategy for testing the stuff opponents are made of" (Drewal 1992, 19). Most significantly, Drewal adds, "The insight one gains in this kind of play is applicable to any life situation" (19). Famed scholar and mestre Nestor Capoeira confirms, too: "*Malícia*, in a broad sense, is the way that the player sees and plays with life, the world, and especially, with people—it is a kind of 'knowledge' or 'wisdom'" (2016, 271).[27] Playing with mandinga, therefore, not only requires wisdom but also generates wisdom and necessary knowledge. The wisdom of mandinga is vast, even infinite, but as the stories in this chapter show, capoeira players often leverage the knowledge generated in the roda to counter their uneven positions in the economic world, and they do so not only for personal gain but also to nourish their loved ones and cohere their community. As Mestre Cláudio sings in his "Ladainha of Poverty" above, those who ridicule others are poor in spirit, and the truly poor are those who have "neither affection nor love."

Conclusion

Playing with money, whether in money games or economic relations between mestres, group members, and gringos, is not fundamentally about either deception or capitalist entrepreneurship. Rather, money games reveal the creative strategies and wisdom Black community members have developed over centuries to counter their dehumanization and the exploitative labor practices they experienced in slavery and its afterlife. Mestre Cláudio and other mestres still deploy their wisdom to multiple ends: to survive, to thrive economically, to have some fun, and to provide for their families and dependents. Taken as individual acts, instances of deception may not seem to disrupt prevailing economic inequities and injustices. Yet as Kelley (1994) proposes, if we see them collectively and cumulatively, the power and politics of such acts comes to the fore. When Mestre Brabo forced the Europeans (colonizers) to experience hunger, he exposed their insatiability, fleetingly turning the relations of power on their head, reproducing and reorienting the hunger imposed upon the enslaved (Woodard 2014), to reserve precious portions of meat for those he held dear. When Mestre Cláudio found ways to gain more from my presence, he was likewise seeking to level the economic imbalance, intuiting that I would profit much more from being with him than I would ever pay him in cash.[28] Thus when a mestre plays with a gringa's money, or treats a Brazilian who lives abroad like a gringo, I see these as gestures toward reparation, however fleeting or incomplete. These money games, like games in the roda, require intelligence, wisdom, and finesse. They involve pushing against "rules" or expectations, sometimes stepping over them, other times ignoring or exaggeratedly adhering to them. Yet the point is not simply to break rules. Playing with money and mandinga, mestres leverage ancestral wisdom to play beautifully, with intelligence and spirit, with, within, and against the economic constraints of racial capitalism. Bending the rules so they can not only survive but also thrive, they create the conditions for sustaining the art form, the people, and the communities they love.

Epilogue

In the summer of 2020, as George Floyd's murder at the knee of a white policeman spurred protests in the United States, Brazil, and across the world, news media made much of the larger-than-ever numbers of white people joining the protests in support of the Black Lives Matter movement. However, seasoned Black activists were wary of celebrating white people's cross-racial solidarity, doubtful that it would last. In one "*live*," a live-streamed public discussion, in June 2020, Karine Teixeira Damasceno and Luciana Brito, both Brazilian historians of slavery who have spent considerable time in the States, spoke about the antiracism fight in the United States and Brazil. They warned that the media's focus on white participation in the protests threatened to obscure the depth and breadth of the problems. Damasceno said, "These white people going to the streets now, they are only thinking about one issue, police violence. But they're not talking about affirmative action. They're not talking about reparations."[1] Other participants in the live warned that too much attention to US Black movements threatened to obscure the struggles that have been waged and are ongoing in Africa and other places in the diaspora.

Now, four years after the uprising of summer 2020, Karine's prediction of white people's fair-weather allyship has become fact (Horowitz, Hurst, and Braga 2023). When I returned to Brazil to attend the group's annual encounter in January 2023, I also sensed none of the urgency I had witnessed in 2020 to discuss racial politics in society or within the capoeira community, or to consider capoeira's potential role in the struggle for valuing and protecting Black life. Although I was disappointed, I realized that this was also the nature of struggle. Movements wax and wane, and many individuals who went to the streets a few years ago, during the exceptional moment of the global pandemic, are now happy to resume their lives, attending capoeira events, collectively cultivating axé, and reveling in shared sintonia. This also speaks to the nature of ethnography: more a series of snapshots than a full picture. The book must end but the stories of people's lives continue, and of course the fight for racial justice is ongoing. I conclude the book with these broader continuities in mind, recalling the spiraling nature of time made manifest in capoeira's circular spaces of play and the cyclical calendar of weekly rodas, annual events, and generational knowledge transfer.

Over the years I have worked on this book, I have felt pulled between celebration and critique, energized by the genuinely radical potentials embedded in capoeira's wisdom but then pessimistic about the possibility of ever putting them into practice. If capoeira has the potential to raise practitioners' racial-political consciousness, then why does it so often fail to do so? If capoeira can fundamentally alter players' bodies, spirits, and minds, then why did I encounter so many white and non-Black practitioners who seemed content to enjoy Black expression but unwilling to ask themselves what they owe to Black communities? I admit that at times "I fell out of love with the [practice] I had poured hope into" (Shange 2019, 155). Yet instead of giving up hope, I remember the wider ebbs and flows of history, the centripetal and centrifugal forces of the roda, and the ways that capoeira contains heartbreaking contradictions along with the seeds of its own repair. I accept that asking big questions inevitably means foregoing neat, finite answers. When I set out to do this research in 2013, I wanted to find that capoeira radicalized its practitioners. Of course, it turned out to be not that simple.

In this epilogue, I draw out some of the promising concepts and potentials I encountered through my work with Mestre Cláudio and the Angoleiros do Sertão. Doing so, I emphasize that ultimately the book is not about Mestre Cláudio or his group. The problems and issues I've written about here transcend the community as they transcend capoeira. They also stretch beyond the period of my research (2013–2024), which saw new rallying cries in Black movements across hemispheres—#BlackLivesMatter, #ParemDeNosMatar, #VidasNegrasImportam—built upon centuries of struggle. Acknowledging the unfinished nature of this work, I consider what I have learned about capoeira as *A Beautiful Fight*.

Intention

If, as many practitioners describe it, capoeira is a tool (*ferramenta*) or an instrument, then what matters is how one uses it. While some practitioners leverage capoeira to fight racial injustice, others erase capoeira's Blackness and use the art form, for instance, to preach the Gospel of Jesus Christ (Schreiber 2017; William 2019, 158–66). As with learning a musical instrument or a dance practice, learning to play capoeira changes one's body, mind, and perhaps even spirit, but the ways in which practitioners change take many forms. Depending on who is teaching classes or leading a group, capoeira can be practiced as an instrument of Black liberation or as a tool for fostering apolitical color-blind belonging, among countless other aims.

This is where Mestre Cláudio's teachings about intention can be helpful. As described in chapter 1, neither infusing a roda with axé nor bringing bodies into sintonia happens automatically. To play with axé takes the right attitude and effortful intention. Mestre Cláudio described this attitude as "looking the horse in the eyes," and he demonstrated by focusing his gaze so intently that I felt as if his eyes were drilling into mine. This is how he directs the energy of the roda, sending axé to the players or dancers in the ring. As Rita put it, "When you are playing the instrument, give yourself! You must give yourself because whoever is playing depends on you! Give the best of yourself because whoever is playing depends on your best!" As Orikerê described it, "Axé is when you give your body, you sweat for it, you really throw yourself, break everything [*quebra tudo*]!" Learning to play with axé teaches practitioners how to channel their intention and give (of) themselves—to put their bodies on the line. If they choose to, they can apply this focused, full body-mind-spirited intention to the struggle for Black lives, dignity, and humanity.

Axé, Sintonia, and Ancestralidade

As the book has shown, axé can call diverse people together. Practitioners derive deep pleasure from being in the axé (*no axé*) and in sintonia, and these good feelings cohere a deep sense of affective community. Group members frequently express their love for one another, their gratitude for belonging to the Angoleiros do Sertão, and their sense of being a family. The participatory moving and musicking of capoeira summons what Durkheim called "collective effervescence" (Durkheim 2008), which both arises out of and produces group sociality, making "social worlds out of shared feeling" while "moving and sounding together" (Garcia-Mispireta 2023, 145).[2] Sensing axé and moving together in sintonia, practitioners may feel called to transcend their differences and appreciate their collective diversity. Yet despite sharing these moving experiences, group members diverged in how they interpretated capoeira's politics and their responsibilities to Black communities.

Many Black community members experienced their ancestralidade as summoning the past. Sensing, seeing, remembering, imagining, and fabulating their enslaved ancestors' suffering and resilience, these members felt called to continue the fight for racial justice and Black liberation in the present. In contrast, politically progressive white angoleiros viewed capoeira primarily as a resource for their personal benefit. They also understood capoeira's political significance for Brazil's Black movement, but they claimed to have no place in Black movement activism. However, as numerous Black community members attested, this fight cannot be waged exclusively by Black people. Dona Ivannide directly admonished white group members: "You need to assume the fight of antiracism!"

The ways in which axé, sintonia, and ancestralidade move practitioners suggest that other ways of responding to the call of axé are possible. One does not receive axé passively like a gift dropped in an outstretched hand. Rather, generating and receiving axé demand regular cultivation and propagation. Achieving sintonia requires responsiveness and receptivity, an active seeking to align frequencies. Experiencing axé and sintonia is therefore a choice. It requires intention. Receiving axé can also be empowering: opening oneself to axé's power to make something happen. What would it mean for white practitioners to attune their receptivity to the needs and demands of Black community members? In what ways could they direct their energies and align their frequencies to fight against racism and struggle for a better future?

The potential for accessing ancestralidade also offers possibilities. Many white practitioners claimed to be able to feel "the Black ancestralidade," yet none described envisioning the past, as their Black camaradas had. Still, this does not negate the possibility that they could access the past—only from a different perspective. I am not suggesting that white players envision a past enslavement, projecting themselves into the place of the enslaved, but rather that they confront their own real or imagined past. After all, capoeira practice provides ample opportunities for embodied reflection on one's relationship to slavery's past and its afterlife from numerous perspectives. Immersed in the sounds of the roda, practitioners sing songs, some of which directly reference slavery. For example, in our interview Hulluca, Mestre Cláudio's eldest son, recalled one corrido favored by Mestre Cláudio. He sang:

[*solo*] *Vou contar lhe uma história*	[call] I'm going to tell you a story
Muito tempo se passou	Much time has passed [since]
O nego fugia do engenho	The Black man escaped from the sugar mill

O branco corria a avisar o senhor	The white man ran to tell the master
Lá vai o nego!	There goes the Black man!
[*coro*] *Olha o nego senhá!*	[chorus] Look at the Black man, lady! [the master's wife]
[*solo*] *Lá vai o nego!*	[call] There goes the Black man!
[*coro*] *Olha o nego senhá!*	[chorus] Look at the Black man, lady!
[*solo*] *Ele é capoeira!*	[call] He is capoeira!
[*coro*] *Olha o nego senhá!*	[chorus] Look at the Black man, lady!

Hulluca interpreted:

> It's about a Black man who's enslaved and can't take it anymore and escapes the slave quarters. And the white man is always telling the master, running after the Black man. . . . When I'm playing and they sing this corrido, it's as if you're really calling attention, like, "Look at the Black man!" He's laughing! He's going! It brings this sensation [of seeing him run to his freedom]! And even though the white man tries to warn the master—"*Lá vai o nego!*"—no matter how much they try, they can't catch him. So it has power; we're like, "Let's go! We're going to go! We're going to follow him! We're going to manage to do things differently."

In the capoeira roda, white, Black, and non-Black camaradas sing this song alongside one another. At least in theory, this offers each player the opportunity to ask: How do I relate to this story? Who am I in this history? Hulluca derived a joyful kind of power from seeing the Black man run, using his body to seize his freedom. Hulluca also projected this sensation into the future: "We're going to follow him!" Following his lead, we're going to make something better. What other kinds of imagining might white and non-Black players undertake? What happens in white people's bodies when we invoke ghosts not only of heroic enslaved people but also of our ancestors: enslavers, colonizers, and the white man who ran to tell the master? Raul's brief embodiment of an aspiring slave owner in chapter 3 showed this was possible. However, I insist that there must be other ways of grappling with the violent past that is not past, ways that repair rather than reproduce its violence.

As Black community members explained to me, axé is ancestral, inseparable from the past-in-the-present, which means axé is inextricable from the enduring afterlife of slavery. My body could not enter into sintonia if other bodies in the past had not cultivated the ancestral energy, keeping its frequencies vibrating across time and space, through unimaginable suffering and rebellious joy. Ancestralidade is inseparable from the struggle not only to survive but also to dismantle white supremacist coloniality and, ultimately, to build something beautiful in its place. As Beatriz Nascimento put it, "The task is not merely to exist but make life more beautiful, and happier" (B. Nascimento 2023, 305). Surely white and non-Black community members share the responsibility to undertake this task. Could accessing ancestralidade move white people toward confronting their own presence in slavery's afterlife and recognizing that we also have a role to play in Black political movements? Figuring out the nature of these roles will take time, and it may be exhausting, but hasn't capoeira Angola taught us how to dig down to the last reserves of our physical, psycho-emotional, and mental resources to move, sing, play, and fight, even when we feel we have nothing left? Why else is the axé there to carry us through?

There is no definitive response to Dona Ivannide's call for white angoleiros to assume the fight of antiracism, no single action one can take to join the fight. Indeed, the ongoing nature of axé's regeneration echoes the unfinished nature of the struggle. It takes practice, repetition, and commitment. It takes compromisso.

Compromisso, Convivência, and Care

Whether a player realizes it at first or not, the act of sensing axé involves them in relations of obligation, of compromisso. As Orikerê put it, "Even though you might not be 'of axé,' the axé is in you. [If you play capoeira,] you're in the axé, the force, that current, that energy." Receiving axé involves the receiver in a dynamic, ongoing cycle of calls and responses, summoning practitioners to assume commitments to sustain the propagation of axé. While each practitioner follows a unique life trajectory, Mestre Cláudio's insistence that his students reflect on their compromisso with capoeira provides an opportunity for examining how far their responsibilities extend. Many dedicated group members are willing to commit their lives to capoeira Angola, moving across Brazil to be closer to Mestre Cláudio or making career choices that enable them to continue training. They understand that their responsibilities include showing up to trainings, rodas, and events and contributing financially. When students become sufficiently advanced, they may begin to teach their own students, keeping the art form alive in that way. Some of their núcleos are based in underserved Black communities, bringing capoeira's empowering lessons to the young Black people who need them most. Following from Mestre Cláudio's commitment to Black communities in rural Bahia, it seems that a compromisso with capoeira may extend even further, beyond trainings and rodas, to include Black communities more broadly. After all, these are the communities that have historically kept Candomblé, capoeira, and samba alive so that today "everyone" can join in.

This ethic of owing something to a community also emerges in the posture of convivência. Learning capoeira and samba, and participating in Candomblé, all require convivência, living-and-spending-time with elders and community members who have knowledge and experience with the practices. Spending time observing and absorbing ways of doing and being, practitioners become part of the community they are learning about. They learn to listen before speaking, assuming a posture of humility, recognizing how little they know. Convivência requires patience, a commitment of time, not unlike the unending curiosity of scholars, musicians, and artists who commit themselves to lifelong learning. Practitioners come to recognize that they have access to this knowledge only because those with more experience have agreed to teach them, and these teachers would not be here today were it not for a long line of ancestors who likewise taught younger generations with patience and care. Reflecting on the weight of this responsibility, the commitment to pass on the wisdom they are learning, practitioners must become like the elders from whom they have learned.

Discussing his responsibility as a white practitioner teaching a Black art form, one group member said, "I'm concerned about this. Sometimes even too much, thinking, 'I need to learn more first before I do this, before I play this instrument.' . . . I think the demand [*cobrança*, lit. charge for payment] ends up being even stronger [on me] . . . Because capoeira is Black culture, but it doesn't mean whites can't do it. But it means they have to be careful." Yet this same practitioner remained uninterested in capoeira's role in the Black movement or in politics more generally: "Sincerely, I don't concern myself a lot with [politics], to be truthful. I don't try to get involved with politics." This white Paulista practitioner understood that his commitment to passing on capoeira knowledge involved taking care, but he declined to examine how he might extend this care by embracing the political possibilities of capoeira.

However, another white Paulista has allowed his compromisso and convivência to shift his political thinking and actions. Afonso Mesquita had moved to Bahia in 2018 to be near Mestre Cláudio and participate more actively in the Angoleiros do Sertão. In a video-call interview in December 2022, he described to me how he had radically shifted how he understood his whiteness and his relationship to Blackness since moving to Bahia.[3] His convivência with the group and the rural Black community in Feira's peripheries had profoundly changed his understandings, especially during the period of intensive discussion of racial issues in 2020. Afonso told me that all the readings he had done, all he had studied and discussed about Blackness and racial politics prior to moving to Bahia, suddenly became part of his daily life. Speaking to me in English, Afonso explained, "I have learned that whiteness is a reality, and it does not depend on what you do or believe. It doesn't matter if I am, as a person, racist or not. This was my biggest insight, my biggest lesson. Because before I thought, 'I'm not a racist!'" But now he realized, "It's okay [to be not racist] but it's not enough. We are born, we grow up, and develop, and choose our life [path] and profession. And . . . every white person goes with the flow and every Black person goes against the flow." A society built to privilege white people was like a river: white people could drift along, passively being "not racist," and still be carried to their desired destinations. Black people, in contrast, had to fight against the current of a system that not only did not privilege them but also targeted them for exclusion and violence.

He went on: "We must understand that racial relations are white people problems. We made [the problems], as a historical group. You and me, we had nothing to do with it, but our ancestors made it. You are a white woman, I am a white man, our bloodline is European. . . . My ancestors were—I don't think my relatives were in the dominant class of society, but even so, we go with the flow. . . . So we as a social group made this difference and we have to do something about it. Simple."

By drawing a simple conclusion, Afonso was not denying the complexity of the problems or the myriad actions we must take. He acknowledged that each person could work only within their limited spheres of influence, whether in education, capoeira, music, or public health, for example. Yet his story illustrates some of the possibilities of compromisso, convivência, and ancestralidade. Reflecting on his ancestry, Afonso saw that he inherited the advantages built into the Brazilian system by European enslavers and colonizers, and he recognized that this instilled him with certain responsibilities. Moving to Bahia to deepen his compromisso with capoeira, he began to build closer relationships with community members, within and beyond the capoeira group. Indeed, he told me that some of these community members had taken him aside, on numerous occasions, and pointed out how his speech and actions were reproducing racist tropes. He has learned only because of this convivência, as he has built relationships of mutual care.

Afonso also understands that neither compromisso nor convivência have an end. Both continue to resound, like the calls and responses of capoeira rodas of the past, present, and future. Afonso expressed this sense of futurity and the ongoing nature of a convivência based on caring for one another: "We have to work, we have to prove ourselves, we have to *be* with Black people and fight for a future where racial relations don't have a substantial role in our society. But this is a future to be built. It's not reality now. . . . That's the movement of history. And maybe until our last days we have to do it."

It seemed Afonso was finding ways to respond to Dona Ivannide's call for white group members to join her in the fight against racism. He was committing to the process of defining his compromisso and determining his responsibilities as he lived in convivência with Black communities of Bahia's backlands.

Capoeira as a Beautiful Fight

If capoeira can transform a player's body, spirit, and mind, reorienting their senses and ways of knowing; if walking on their hands can shift how they see, hear, listen to, and understand the world; then can they apply these new ways of being beyond the boundaries of individual experience? If capoeira can possess its practitioners, moving and changing them in the process (I. Johnson 2020, 192), then surely players can also be possessed by capoeira's radical potentials to fight white supremacy and to value, protect, and care for Black lives. As I have argued with this book, however, realizing capoeira's potentials is neither automatic nor straightforward. Yet as a game that is always also a fight, capoeira offers tools for staying in the game and in the struggle. With intelligence, intention, commitment, and care, players can imagine and embody new ways of being human, mobilizing capoeira's wisdom toward creating a better, more beautiful future.

Glossary

Note: n.m. = *nome masculino*, masculine noun; n.f. = *nome feminino*, feminine noun, etc.

aboio (n.m.) A wistful melancholic song sung by cattle-drivers, often commenting on daily life.

agogô (n.m.) A double bell used in Candomblé (made of metal) and capoeira (either metal or, in the Angoleiros do Sertão, made of two Brazil nut casings secured to a wooden rod).

ancestralidade (n.f.) Ancestry; can also signify a profound consciousness of one's descent from enslaved Africans.

angoleiro/a (n.m./f.) A practitioner of capoeira Angola. I use "angoleiro" (lowercase) to refer to any Angola practitioner and "Angoleiro" (capitalized) to refer to a member of the Angoleiros do Sertão group.

apelido (n.m.) Nickname. In capoeira, commonly given by mestre to student.

atabaque (n.m.) A drum used in Candomblé, a barrel shape with curved sides and tapered opening at bottom. In Candomblé three sizes are used, from large to small: *rum*, *(rum)pi*, and *lê*. One atabaque is also played in the capoeira bateria.

àṣẹ (n.) Yoruba term for sacred force, the power to make things happen. See *axé*.

aú (n.m.) A cartwheel movement in capoeira. In capoeira Angola, often performed with bent knees close to chest.

axé (n.m.) Sacred force; ancestral energy cultivated in Candomblé. Good energy. A greeting. A genre of pop music in Bahia (*axé music*).

bananeira (n.f.) Literally, "banana tree." A handstand movement in capoeira.

baqueta (n.f.) A wooden stick used to strike the berimbau wire. Also a generic drumstick.

bate-papo (n.m.) An informal chat or discussion session.

bateria (n.f.) The capoeira percussion ensemble consisting of three *berimbaus*, two *pandeiros*, *reco-reco*, *agogô*, and *atabaque*.

berimbau (n.m.) A bowed resonator gourd instrument of African provenance, consisting of hollow calabash gourd (*cabaça*) tied with string to a wooden rod (*verga*), which is strung into a bow with wire from car tires (*arame*). Played while clutching a *caxixi* in the same hand that holds the *baqueta*. The other, supporting hand balances the *berimbau* on the pinky finger and holds a coin against the wire to raise the pitch.

berra-boi (n.m.) The larger, lowest-pitched berimbau.

bumbo (n.m.) The large double-ended bass drum played in Mestre Cláudio's *samba rural*.

branco/a (n.m./f./adj.) White person; white. When used as a noun, (i.e., "whites") not considered offensive as it would be in English.

brincar (v.) To play around, joke.

Caboclo (n.m.) An entity (spirit) summoned in many Candomblé houses and in Umbanda. Also an ethnic-racial term referring to mixed-race rural dwellers (often assumed to be of Indigenous and European descent but often including African descent whether acknowledged or not). In this book, I capitalize the entity (Caboclo) to disambiguate it from the ethnic-racial category (caboclo).

camarada (n.m.) A friend and comrade, appears often as "*camará*" or "*camaradinho*" in the call-and-response praise section of the *ladainha* capoeira song.

Candomblé (n.m.) A generic term for Afro-Brazilian religions of various denominations or *nações*, "nations."

capoeira (n.f.) An Afro-Brazilian fight-game movement form played to live music. Historically, a *capoeira* (n.m.) was also a practitioner of capoeira.

capoeira Angola (n.f.) A style of capoeira considered more "traditional" and closer to the form's African roots.

capoeira contemporânea (n.f.) A catchall term for contemporary capoeira styles that are neither *Angola* nor *Regional*. Some groups claim to merge the two.

capoeira Regional (n.f.) A capoeira style developed by Mestre Bimba in the 1930s that incorporated elements from other martial arts. Colloquially, angoleiros tend to refer to all contemporary non-Angola forms as "Regional."

capoeirista (n.m. or f.) Contemporary term for a capoeira practitioner.

caxixi (n.m.) A rattle made of woven cane filled with seeds.

chama (n.f.) A call.

chamar (v.) To call.

compromisso (n.m.) A commitment, obligation, or promise.

contramestre/a (n.m./f.) A highly advanced capoeira player one rank below *mestre/a.*

convivência (n.f.) The act of living together. Also a means of transmitting knowledge in Afro-Brazilian traditions.

corrido (n.m.) Literally, "running." A call-and-response song sung to accompany capoeira play. May have a faster tempo than the *ladainha.*

cultura popular (n.f.) Literally, "popular culture." Refers to traditional cultural practices of "the people" (*o povo*), the lower and working classes in Brazil, as opposed to commercially produced cultural products. Often implies Afro-Brazilian popular culture. Compare with *música popular brasileira (MPB).*

espírito (n.m.) Spirit.

ferramenta (n.f.) Tool, instrument.

festa (n.f.) A party. Also refers to public festive Candomblé ceremonies.

força (vital) (n.f.) (Vital) force. Common definition of *axé. Força* can mean force, energy, power, or strength.

ginga/gingar (n.f./v.) *Gingar* literally means "to sway," but in capoeira *ginga* refers to the basic movement from which all other movements (kicks, defenses, etc.) can follow. At its most basic: from a wide-legged stance, step back with the right foot, then step forward with the right foot; then step back with the left foot and forward with the left foot; repeat. However, to perform the *ginga* also involves arm movements and individual expression.

gringo/a (n.m./f.) In Brazil, refers to white foreigners regardless of nationality; sometimes includes non-white foreigners, too.

gunga (n.m.) The middle-sized and pitched *berimbau.*

Iaiá/iaiá (n.f.) Capitalized, it is an *apelido* (nickname). In lower case, it is a term of endearment, commonly heard in songs of *cultura popular*, that enslaved people used to refer to the master's daughter.

índio/a (n.m./f./adj.) Literally, "Indian." Refers to Indigenous people in Brazil. Generally, self-identifying as Indigenous means that the person belongs to an existing Indigenous ethnic group and community. Someone who claims only to have, for instance, an "Indian grandmother," usually would not identify as Indigenous in Brazil.

jogar (v.) To play (a game).
jogo (n.m.) A game.
jogo bonito (n.m./adj.) A beautiful game, referring to an ideal capoeira game that combines style and wit.
ladainha (n.f.) Literally, "litany." The reflective opening song of a capoeira *roda*, usually sung at a slower tempo.
luta (n.f.) A fight, struggle.
mãe-de-santo (n.f.) A Candomblé priestess or female religious leader.
malandragem (n.f.) The characteristic of a *malandro*. In capoeira, trickery.
malandro (n.m.) A streetwise hustler who neither has nor wants employment.
malícia (n.f.) Literally, "malice." In capoeira, cunning, trickery.
mandinga (n.f.) Witchcraft, magic. In capoeira, trickery.
matrizes africanas (n.f.) Literally, "African matrices." Afro-Brazilian practices and cultural expressions.
mensalidade (n.f.) Monthly fee.
mestiçagem (n.f.) Literally, "miscegenation." Racial mixture.
mestiço/a (adj.) Racially mixed.
mestre/a (n.m./f.) A master practitioner and teacher of capoeira or any other practice of *cultura popular*.
militante (n.m.) A militant; political activist.
movimento negro (n.m.) Generic term for Black political movements in Brazil, groups of which may or may not belong to the national organization Movimento Negro Unificado (the Unified Black Movement).
mulato/a (n.m./f. and adj.) Mulatto/a. Describes mixed-race person (of Black and white parentage) with medium to light brown skin. Considered offensive and racist owing to its derivation from the word for "mule." Applied to women (*mulata*) invokes stereotypes of sexual availability.
música popular brasileira (MPB) (n.f.) Commercially produced popular music in Brazil, including diverse genres and styles.
nação (n.f.) Literally, "nation." In Candomblé, refers to various traditions within the religion, named after different African ethnicities of origin. Differentiated by language use, liturgy, and ways of playing instruments and conducting rituals.
negro/a (n.m./f./adj.) Black person; Black. Refers to an often-politicized African-descended identity. When used as a noun, (i.e., "Blacks") not considered offensive as it would be in English. When interlocutors

spoke of "negros" or "negras," I translated this as Black people, Black folks, or Black men/women depending on context.

núcleo (n.f.) Group. In capoeira, a satellite school affiliated with a larger group.

ogã (n.m.) In Candomblé, a non-initiated member who either performs ritual functions (such as sacrifices or playing instruments for ceremonies) or protects and/or aids the house and community. If in the latter role, often a white person with wealth and power.

orixá (n.m.) Divinity, divine entity of Candomblé.

pai-de-santo (n.m.) A Candomblé priest or male religious leader.

pandeiro (n.m.) Hand drum similar to North American tambourine, played in capoeira, *samba de roda,* and other Brazilian music styles.

pardo/a (n.m./f./adj.) Brown person; Brown. A Brazilian census category of "color or race."

Paulista (n.m./f.) Resident of São Paulo state.

Paulistano/a (n.m./f.) Resident of São Paulo city.

periferia (n.f.) Literally, "periphery." Usually majority-Black communities that are marginalized, socioeconomically disadvantaged, and deprived of basic infrastructure. Often but not always located far from the city centers.

povo (n.m.) The people; Brazil's majority Black lower and working classes.

preto/a (n.m/f./adj.) Black person; Black (color), now reclaimed formerly derogatory term for a Black person.

queda de rins (n.f.) Literally, "fall on the kidneys." Capoeira movement of balancing on two hands, propping up the torso on one bent elbow, legs either extended in the air or bent.

quilombo (n.m.) Historical community founded by fugitives from slavery, now inhabited by their descendants.

rabo de arraia (n.m.) Literally, "stingray's tail." Capoeira movement with backside facing one's opponent, bent all the way at the waist so that the head is upside down, kicking one leg up behind in an arc.

real/reais (n.m) The Brazilian currency, singular and plural.

reco-reco (n.m.) Scraper instrument played in capoeira. In Mestre Cláudio's roda, it is made from a large oblong notched gourd, played by scraping a wooden stick across the grooves. Can also be made of bamboo.

referência (n.f.) Literally, "reference." Role model; someone respected and emulated.

resistência (n.f.) Resistance, opposition; physical endurance or stamina.

roça (n.f.) A rural plot of land. Also can refer to the location of a Candomblé *terreiro.*

roda (n.f.) Literally, "wheel." Both the event and circular space of capoeira play or samba dancing.

samba de roda (n.m.) Afro-Brazilian singing, drumming, dancing form. The style from the Recôncavo region of Bahia was recognized in 2008 by UNESCO as intangible cultural heritage, but there are numerous other regional styles throughout Bahia and the northeast of Brazil.

samba rural (n.m.) Rural samba; the term Mestre Cláudio uses for the style of *samba de roda* he plays with his group. Unlike *samba de roda* of the Recôncavo, Mestre Cláudio's *samba rural* does not use guitar-like instruments (*violas*); verses and choruses are sung without harmony; and the group does not dress in a "folkloric" style but usually wears capoeira clothes as the *samba* often follows a capoeira *roda*.

sentido (n.m.) Sense, meaning, feeling, direction. An important element in a capoeira game, according to Mestre Cláudio's teaching.

sertão (n.m.) The semi-arid "backlands," rural or remote areas of the interior of Bahia and northeastern Brazil.

sintonia (n.f.) Literally, "syntony." The alignment of frequencies. Colloquially, being in sync or feeling the same vibe.

tambor (n.m.) Generic term for drum.

terreiro (n.m.) A parcel of land. In Candomblé refers to both the house and grounds of the Candomblé temple.

timbal (n.m.) The straight-sided tapered barrel drum played in Mestre Cláudio's *samba rural*. Louder and higher-pitched than the *atabaque*.

toque (n.m.) A rhythmic pattern.

treinar (v.) To train, practice, or work out.

treinel (n.m.) An accomplished capoeira player who is teaching their own students. In capoeira Angola the only rank above student before *contramestre*.

Umbanda (n.f.) An Afro-Brazilian religion combining Candomblé, Spiritism, and Catholicism.

vadiação, vadiagem (n.f.) Vagrancy. The act of being idle, loafing about. Also the act of playing capoeira.

vadio (n.m.) An idler, vagabond. See *vagabundo*.

vagabundo (n.m.) A vagabond, idler.

viola (n.f.) The smallest, highest-pitched berimbau that also plays the most elaborate rhythmic variations.

Notes

Introduction

1. The Brazilian national style of soccer playing is referred to as "*o jogo bonito*" (the beautiful game). However, this overlap of terminology does not point to an isolated relationship between soccer and capoeira, but rather may gesture toward a broader system of embodied knowledge generated across multiple Brazilian movement practices (Rosa 2015). All translations are my own unless otherwise noted.

2. For a discussion of capoeira as a "blurred genre" after Geertz, see Downey (2002, 490).

3. O Movimento Negro Unificado (MNU) (the Unified Black Movement) was founded in 1978, in the waning days of Brazil's latest military dictatorship. While the MNU exists today, colloquially the "Black movement" refers to numerous formal and informal groups fighting racism and racialized violence in Brazil.

4. The shorthand "*Regional*" comes from Mestre Bimba's Luta Regional Baiana (Regional Bahian Fight), which he created in the 1930s, though only a few groups still practice Bimba's style today. See Assunção (2005, 134). Works that discuss both styles include L. Reis (1997) and Höfling (2019).

5. On how Bahian artists, including capoeiristas, leverage Africanness in their practices, see Díaz (2021).

6. Much capoeira literature presents capoeira as a practice of resistance, freedom, or liberation. See, e.g., Lewis (1992); Browning (1995); Abib (2004); Araújo (2015); Marriage (2019); Griffith (2023). For a succinct overview of resistance in/as capoeira, see also Wesolowski (2023, 112–13).

7. Assunção addresses what he calls capoeira's "competing master narratives," though some of the controversies have since been resolved. Most notably, Mestre Moraes and other prominent proponents of the view that capoeira originated in Africa and arrived in Brazil fully formed have retracted this opinion, in part due to Mestre Cobra Mansa's and Matthias Assunção's collaborative project for which they visited Angola in search of capoeira's roots. They produced a documentary of the voyage and concluded that capoeira did not come directly from Africa but was

more likely an amalgam, created in Brazil, of multiple African dance, fight, and game styles (Assunção 2013). This is the view I also find most supportable, especially given that cultural expressions are always evolving. As Mestre Cláudio puts it, "Capoeira was created by Africans in Brazil."

8. Candomblé's resistance is often described as resistance to both annihilation and assimilation, thereby preserving African/Afro-Brazilian culture (Braga 1995).

9. Cultura popular in Latin America is therefore a false cognate of popular (or pop) culture as it is discussed in North America. Cultura popular is closer to, though not always synonymous with, folk or folkloric culture (Hutchinson 2011). Note also that "cultura popular," referring to the people's culture that includes multiple music, dance, performance, and artistic practices, is differentiated in Brazil from *música popular*, which refers to Brazil's commercial popular music genre *música popular brasileira* (MPB) (Sandroni 2011).

10. See Celina de Sá's forthcoming monograph on capoeira in Senegal.

11. This goes against decades of discourse about capoeira Regional as "whitened" and capoeira Angola as closer to its traditional African roots (i.e., still Black) (Magalhães Filho 2012, 34). Höfling (2019) also counters this overly simple and inaccurate racialized reading of the styles over the course of their development.

12. Mestre Cláudio's claim echoes Pierre Verger, the French photographer who lived in Bahia and whose images of Black life there have become iconic, cited by Abdias do Nascimento. Verger wrote: "If it is true that the slaves were Europeanized through the contact with their masters, it is equally true that the same Portuguese masters in turn went through a process of Africanization through their contact with their slaves" (A. Nascimento 1989, 69).

13. See this book's preface, where I address further how reflecting on my positionality has shaped this study. For an extended discussion on research ethics, see Kurtz (2024b).

14. Maureen Mahon draws on Dorinne Kondo to distill "the dialectic of resistance and complicity" often present in cultural works and practices, which is also at the heart of this book (Mahon 2014, 329). Like Mahon, I am committed to grappling with the contradictions and ambiguities of resistance, as cautioned by Sherry Ortner (2006) among others.

15. For an overview of capoeira's history in both Rio and Bahia, see Assunção (2005). On nineteenth century capoeira in Rio de Janeiro, see Soares (2001). In Bahia, see Abreu (2005).

16. Practitioners have reclaimed some terms: *vadiagem* and *vadiação* (vagrancy) share a root with *vadio* and mean "playing capoeira," as in the lyric "*Vamos vadiar!*" (Let's play capoeira!).

17. The *abertura* began in 1974 and continued until 1985 when Brazil inaugurated a civilian president (M. Mitchell 1985, 115).

18. Iaiá is Urania's *apelido* (nickname) and also a term of endearment commonly heard in capoeira songs that enslaved people used to refer to the master's daughter.

19. Compounding Brazil's racial violence is the dramatic spread of evangelical

churches that demonize Afro-Brazilian culture and actively encourage their congregants to terrorize Candomblé practitioners and vandalize their property (Boaz 2021).

20. The periphery (*periferia*) in Brazil refers to usually majority-Black communities that are not only spatially marginalized but also socioeconomically disadvantaged and often deprived of basic infrastructure.

21. See, e.g., Sansone (2003) and P. Pinho (2010). See also the prominent debate between North American political scientist Michael Hanchard and French sociologists Pierre Bourdieu and Loïc Wacquant, the latter two who accused Hanchard of "disseminating US cultural imperialism" through his scholarship on race and Black movement activism in Brazil (Hanchard 2003, 5).

22. Keisha-Khan Perry cited Luiza Bairros, who was an activist, academic, and minster of the secretariat for Policies Promoting Racial Equality in Brazil.

23. The other census categories are *amarela* (yellow), *branca* (white), *indígena* (Indigenous), and *sem declaração* (no declaration) (IBGE 2013). The adjectives appear in the feminine because they modify the feminine nouns "*cor ou raça*" (color or race).

24. The Black movement has also achieved several significant victories, passing laws establishing affirmative action policies in the nation's public universities (Martins, Medeiros, and Nascimento 2004) and mandating the teaching of African and Afro-Brazilian history in schools (Pereira 2011), passed in 2002 and 2003, respectively. These changes have surely impacted national consciousness of racial identity, which may help explain why more Afro-descendants are readily self-identifying as negro/a.

25. See Carvalho (1999) for an analysis of Black identity expression and racial terms in Brazilian popular song lyrics across eras and genres.

26. Regarding the two who declined to self-identify, one had pale skin, wore their hair in locks, and said they had both African and Indian ancestors, but claimed not to know what that made them. Another said their parents were both white, but they came out "moreno/a" (tanned-hued skin and silky, wavy brown hair), perhaps explained by their Indian great-grandmother, but they preferred to identify as "just human."

27. Community members also acknowledged the existence of colorism (*colorismo*) in Brazil, whereby dark-skinned Black people are more likely to experience racism in their daily lives than lighter-skinned Black people. However, this should not be confused with the debunked "mulatto escape hatch" theory, for Black people across the color spectrum still suffer disproportionate disadvantages compared to white people (Salata 2020).

28. The Herderian idea of national identity rooted in an authentic folk culture has influenced numerous nations in search of their national character from the nineteenth century onward. The Brazilian state has claimed as national culture numerous Black practices and genres, including capoeira (Wesolowski 2012), samba (Raphael 1990; Vianna 1999; McCann 2004; Sandroni 2021), and Black popular culture/music more generally (Perrone 2002; Davis 2009; O. Pinho 2020).

29. Abidas do Nascimento points to Brazil's related mestiçagem and whitening ideologies as evidence that the ultimate goal of the state is to eliminate Black people from the nation (1989). Vargas explores genocidal anti-Blackness in both Brazil and the United States, attending to the wide spectrum of symbolic and actual violence inflicted upon Black communities (Vargas 2008).

30. Freyre's publication of *Casa Grande e Senzala* in 1933 was perhaps the most pivotal moment in formulating mestiçagem ideology, but other intellectuals of the time were also working with notions of mixture, such as proto-ethnomusicologist Mário de Andrade (1972). However, Andrade, despite being mixed race himself, was more ambivalent than Freyre regarding the value of expressly African elements.

31. As a result of decades of Black activists' organizing, the new Brazilian constitution of 1988 outlawed racial discrimination, thereby officially acknowledging that racism exists in the country, though only as individual acts of prejudice (Andrews 1991, 185). Still, the belief in Brazil's exceptional lack of racism endures in the popular imaginary and in courts of law (Twine 1998; Sheriff 2001; M. Machado, Silva, and Santos 2020; Schucman and Melo 2022).

32. White consumption of Black cultural practices has been examined through, e.g., nineteenth-century white working-class men's "love and theft" of Black culture (Lott 1993), white hipsters' hypersexualization of Black jazz musicians in the 1940s (Monson 1995), whites passing as Black (Dreisinger 2008), and white rock musicians adopting Black political discourses in the 1960s (Burke 2021), among other dynamics. Scholars have also examined the ways in which sounds, music, and performance practices are racialized (Eidsheim 2019) and have thereby shaped racial politics in the United States and its popular music industry (Stoever 2016; M. D. Morrison 2024). Numerous texts have addressed cultural appropriation as a core concern in North American popular culture (Ziff and Rao 1997; Hartman 1997; J. Butler 1993; Tate 2003) and beyond the Americas (Born and Hesmondhalgh 2000; E. P. Johnson 2003; Sterling 2010). I address the racial politics of Brazil's popular music history in chapter 3, but for an extensive reflection on cultural appropriation in Brazil, see William (2020).

33. For discussions of appropriation in popular media, see, e.g., Brooks (2008), Morris (2019), Jackson (2019), Mohamed (2021), M. Collins (2024).

34. Works tackling the racial politics and interracial tensions in multiracial communities of music-movement practice are less common but include A. Harrison (2009) and Ahlgren (2018). Much research on multiracial musical communities focuses on religious contexts, including in communities of Afro-Brazilian religions, providing a fruitful point of comparison with capoeira as I explore in chapter 3. See, e.g. Amaral and da Silva (1993), Prandi (1997), Burdick (2013), Gidal (2016), França (2018), Campanaro (2021).

35. Given how Lipsitz contends "that the artificial construction of whiteness almost always comes to possess white people themselves unless they develop anti-racist identities, unless they disinvest and divest themselves of their investments in white supremacy," this book could be understood as addressing the tension between being possessed by whiteness (and the political power and privilege that accompany

it) and being possessed by capoeira's political power to resist white supremacy (Lipsitz 2006, viii).

36. See, e.g., Hamera (2007), Turino (2008), Miller (2008), Cruz Banks (2010), Garrett and Oja (2021), Griffith (2023), Romero et al. (2023), Garcia-Mispireta (2023).

37. Garcia-Mispireta finds that the vague belonging fostered in dance club parties also masks inequities, exclusions, and violence. Though the scene and its affect differ from capoeira rodas, I make a similar argument that the group's strong cohesion hides tensions that often go unaddressed (Garcia-Mispireta 2023).

38. Savannah Shange (2019) reaches a similar conclusion in her ethnography about a public high school in San Francisco as a "progressive dystopia," and she applies an abolitionist approach to argue for alternative pathways to Black freedom.

39. I follow Omi and Winant (2014) and others in using "racialization" to refer to "relational process[es] . . . constructed through social interaction as well as structurally through institutions, law, and government" rather than considering race as only a "personal characteristic" (Hurtado 2019, 76). In other words, racialization is something done to people, and something people do to themselves, in a range of different ways in different contexts. However, this does not undermine the deeply personal meanings, attachments, and understandings people ascribe to their racialization.

40. While Black Brazilian feminist activists and scholars have long theorized intersectional oppressions in their own terms, they are now more than ever collaborating with Black feminists in the north and seeking to realize the benefits of working in solidarity with one another (Alvarez and Caldwell 2016; Caldwell et al. 2018; Mitchell-Walthour 2020). For example, Black Brazilians' adoption of #VidasNegrasImportam is a direct translation of #BlackLivesMatter, but activists also originate their own movements speaking to urgent issues on the ground in Brazil, such as #ParemDeNosMatar [#StopKillingUs], which protests Brazil's alarming rates of femicide, especially the killing of Black women. In Brazil as in the United States, many of these movements are founded and led by Black women, as is also the case in Feira de Santana, Bahia.

41. I follow Wynter, who builds on Aníbal Quijano and others, in using "coloniality" to mean a broad, *longue durée* project of "demarcating human differences" (Wynter 2003, 263).

42. For statements of similar definitions of Black studies, the Black radical tradition, Black feminism, and related fields in critical ethnic studies, see, e.g., Kelley (2002), C. Robinson (2000), P. Collins (2000), Combahee River Collective (2014), Critical Ethnic Studies Editorial Collective (2016). Black studies, of course, encompasses diverse approaches, viewpoints, and schools of thought. However, most Black studies scholarship contends with Black people's lived experience and ultimately aims to make a better world for Black and other subjugated peoples.

43. This is not a comprehensive list, but scholars who have influenced my thinking include Burnim (1985), Rose (1994), Mahon (2004), Ramsey (2004, 2022), Wong (2004), Maultsby (2005), Gaunt (2006), Lipsitz (2006), Monson (2010),

Burdick (2013), Maultsby and Burnim (2016), Ndaliko (2016), Shonekan (2018), Jones (2020), Redmond (2020), Harris (2022), and M. Morrison (2024).

44. These scholars have also presented on "Black Ethnomusicology" panels at recent meetings of the Society for Ethnomusicology.

45. One explanation—but not excuse—for this may be that ethnomusicologists are still often housed in conservative music departments (and conservatories). As Wong noted, ethnomusicologists "are far more likely to be advocates in the classroom than in their scholarly work" (2006, 262). Well-meaning white ethnomusicologists may already see themselves as the most progressive voices in the room, not the ones who need to do better.

46. Another serious problem Harris addresses is the pipeline issue: the underrepresentation of Black scholars in music fields. I see these issues as related. Centering Black and critical ethnic studies in ethnomusicology curricula and scholarship could help create an environment and, eventually, a field where scholars and prospective students from historically marginalized groups felt they belonged. See also Ramsey (2022, 43–89).

47. I echo Danielle Brown's critique: "Changing the system does mean that people of color must be at the forefront of telling their stories until some sort of equity is reached" (Brown 2020). On Black scholars and artists theorizing their practices, see DeFrantz and Gonzalez (2014).

48. See also (Kurtz 2024b), where I elaborate more reflexively on the political responsibilities of ethnographers.

49. See Kurtz (2024a), in which I question the seemingly automatic reflex among many ethnomusicologists still to privilege European continental theory as what counts as "theory." For a good overview of the debates, see also Hood and Hutchinson (2020).

50. I asked every interviewee how they wanted to be identified in my text and, notably, all interviewees wanted me to use their real names or apelidos. I have honored their preferences and used pseudonyms only when I felt that my critique of their ideas or behavior exceeded what they likely expected when agreeing to be interviewed. Outside of interviews, I also assigned pseudonyms when requested by the person I wrote about or when describing speech or behavior that I deemed sensitive. In chapters 3 and 4, for instance, I assigned pseudonyms to members whom I critique most forcefully, because my intention is not to single out individuals but to reveal how colonialist, white supremacist logics pervade even well-intentioned actors' ways of thinking and doing. Use of pseudonyms is indicated in the text at the name's first mention and in the list of cited interviews following the bibliography. Interviews were conducted in Portuguese unless otherwise noted, and all translations are mine unless otherwise noted.

51. Wesolowski (2023) also elaborates the concept of convivência as capoeira's special form of sociality. I use the term more narrowly to signal a specific mode of knowledge transmission in Afro-Brazilian cultural contexts. See also Kurtz (2024b).

52. I have also been influenced by anthropologist Kim TallBear, who proposes

a radical feminist-Indigenous practice of "standing with," which requires working with a community one "cares for, challenges, critiques, and is generous with" (TallBear 2014, 3), and American studies scholars Tomlinson and Lipsitz, who suggest that researchers allow "disagreements to be seen as evidence of problems yet to be solved" while adopting a posture of talking less and listening more (Tomlinson and Lipsitz 2013, 11–12).

53. Black women and Black feminist scholars have pioneered work considering the seemingly invisible—and invisibilized—spheres of Black women's lives, and my choices of theory and methods have been influenced by their work across multiple (overlapping) fields including anthropology (Twine 1998; Caldwell 2007; Perry 2013; Hordge-Freeman 2015; Smith 2016); music and performance studies (J. Johnson 2012; Mengesha and Padmanabhan 2019; I. Johnson 2022); political science/theory/philosophy (Wynter 2003; McKittrick 2015; Gonzalez 1984; Mitchell-Walthour 2018; Carneiro 2003; Cardoso 2014; M. Nascimento 2018; B. Nascimento 2023; Smith and Leu 2023); history (Hartman 1997; K. Butler 1998; Harding 2000; Mustakeem 2016) and English/literature studies (Sharpe 2016; Campt 2017).

54. See Kurtz (2020), where I address how Black angoleiras originate tactics to navigate their underrepresentation and *machismo* in capoeira.

55. Catherine Appert (2017, 464) similarly found that cultivating relationships with other women can be a way to "extend the field site outward beyond music and to imagine a reconstituted field site that articulates across spheres of being, relating, and knowing."

56. For literature on musical cultures of northeastern Brazil that also describes how musicians negotiate stereotypes of the region, see, e.g., Silvers (2018) and Sharp (2014).

Chapter 1

1. I notate transcriptions in 2/4 staff notation, which is standard among many samba and capoeira scholars (Sandroni and Sant'Anna 2006; Iyanaga 2013; Díaz 2017). However, the transcriptions do not include variations or microtiming. Note also that instrumentalists learn aurally, not from notation.

2. Abusada's apelido does not mean "abused" but rather "brave" and "courageous" (see chapter 2).

3. The nações refer to the ethnic African origins of Candomblé denominations, not necessarily the ethnic ancestry of practitioners. Nations are differentiated by the details of their rituals: languages used, rhythms played, how instruments are played, which entities are venerated, and other liturgical elements. Ketu and Nagô are Yorùbá, Jeje is Fon/Ewe, and Angola and Congo are Bantu.

4. As explained in the introduction, "cultura popular" is the people's culture, more akin to folk expressions than to commercial cultural products.

5. For examples of works addressing capoeira, Candomblé, and samba, see Pinto (1991), who addresses their music largely in parallel to one another; Abib

(2004), who discusses capoeira and Rio-style samba as manifestations of cultura popular; Cristina Rosa (2015), who examines the "*ginga* [swaying movement] aesthetic" across samba de roda, capoeira Angola, and concert dance in Brazil; and Browning (1995) who addresses shared movement aesthetics and resistance in samba, Candomblé, and capoeira. See also chapter 4 of Mika Lior's dissertation, which compares the religious Caboclo samba with Rio's secular style of samba (2021, 183–234). Varela claims that capoeira Angola's "religious foundations" lie in the ways that mestres have their students "worship" ancestors and dead mestres in tandem with the orixás (2019, 85–122), though I have not encountered this in my research. I have found Flávia Diniz's work on the "musical transit" between capoeira Angola and Candomblé particularly helpful (2010).

6. Henry (2008) recognizes the diasporic reach of "West African àsé" in his monograph exploring how popular musicians and other cultural actors in Bahia have reinvented, negotiated, appropriated, altered, and secularized axé through their use of Candomblé's rhythms, themes, and symbols (all Henry's terms).

7. Remarkably, given how significant axé transmitted through sound-movement is to African matrix spaces, the confluence of axé-sound-movement has received scant attention in the literature. This may be because participant-scholars immersed in Afro-Brazilian cultural environments find it self-evident. Yet as a result, the profound sensory-affective relationships among the forms have gone largely unnoted—though they are clearly central to practitioners' experience.

8. A wide range of involvement with Candomblé exists in groups today. Grupo Nzinga in Salvador incorporates (new to capoeira) songs from Candomblé in various African "Bantu" languages (see Diniz 2010). In contrast, Mestre João Grande, the foremost elder of capoeira Angola, openly maintains ties with Candomblé but strictly prohibits singing songs that derive from or even reference Candomblé in the capoeira roda. There are also evangelical capoeira groups who demonize and seek to erase all references to Afro-Brazilian culture (William 2020, 158-166). Following capoeira rodas with samba de roda is a common practice, but rarely do groups take the samba as seriously as Mestre Cláudio does.

9. Mestre Cláudio uses these names for the berimbaus, but other groups may call them respectively gunga, *médio*, and viola.

10. Practitioners of capoeira and Candomblé also speak about the related concept of *aprendizagem* (apprenticeship). See Downey (2005) and Griffith (2016).

11. See Boaz (2021), who addresses the dramatic increase in violent acts of "religious racism" against Candomblé practitioners and their property as Evangelicalism spreads exponentially in Brazil. Also see Prandi (2004).

12. Diniz (2010) notes that Caboclo sects have made outsized contributions to capoeira Angola and samba. Referring to capoeira, samba, and Candomblé, F. Silva also notes that "in some way, the caboclo is in all of these manifestations, which are interlinked principally by way of the people who realize them" (2018, 93). However, not all groups acknowledge or celebrate these linkages.

13. At stake here are the politics of African purity that have embroiled Candomblé communities and scholarship. Yorùbá Candomblés (Nagô, Keto, Ijexá

nations) have long claimed to be more authentically and purely African than their Bantu or Fon/Ewe counterparts, which were considered impure and "degenerate" (Capone 2010, 184), and anthropologists have historically helped formulate and corroborate these claims (173–201). In this context, the Caboclo, as a non-African Indigenous Brazilian, has been seen as a threat to African purity, relegated to "the lowest rung on the ladder of Candomblés" (Capone 2010, 183–84). See also Matory (2005) and J. T. dos Santos (1995). Despite official condescension toward Caboclo cults (Béhague 1999, 44), however, the popularity of Caboclos, their festas, and their incorporation into Candomblé houses of all denominations continues to grow (J. T. dos Santos 1995, 20; Lior 2021, 34), likely in part due to the spread of Umbanda since the 1930s (Prandi 2004).

14. Example 5 uses what I believe may be the Cabula toque (see Iyanaga 2013, 271), but I did not encounter this toque in Mestre Cláudio's group.

15. I also join recent calls to develop more robust theories and methods for analyzing music-dance ethnographically (Stepputat and Seye 2020), but I argue for centering African diasporic perspectives in particular.

16. See also Elferen (2021), who argues that timbre is responsible for such "immediate and intense responses" (1).

17. Mestre Cláudio seems to be using the terms "Caboclos" and "orixás" interchangeably, which contradicts much of the literature but perhaps reflects a practice more common than recognized (see also Iyanaga 2013, 326).

18. Opipari also found a diversity of uses, meanings, and "subtleties" of axé in her ethnography of Candomblé practitioners in São Paulo (2010, 81–105), noting that axé's "vast field of meanings and uses" has prompted her and other scholars to compare it with *mana*, the Polynesian and Melanesian concept of spiritual force, whose meanings have been famously debated in anthropological literature (81).

19. Not only is there no consensus around definitions of axé, but the subject is contentious. As a white North American non-practitioner of Candomblé, I have no authority to explain what axé is: that is the provenance of Candomblé mães- and pais-de-santo. However, I have felt compelled to discuss axé because it is so central to capoeira practitioners' experience. Note also that non-Yorùbá sects have similar concepts of vital force but use different terms.

20. Browning also found that axé was "not restricted to the context of the candomblé. The power-to-make-things-happen can exist within a secular rhythm," referring to samba de roda (1995, 27).

21. Juana Elbein dos Santos (2012 [1976]), a white Argentinian anthropologist initiate living in Brazil (Capone 2010, 7), has written perhaps the most exhaustive and most cited description of àse in her classic monograph on the "most traditional" Nagô terreiro, *Ilê Àse Òpó Àfònjá*. The terreiro's founder, Mãe Aninha, set the precedent for privileging contemporary information on Yorùbá practices (in Nigeria) over that which had been passed down by practitioners in Brazil (Matory 2005, 26).

22. Compromisso may be synonymous and used interchangeably with terms such as *obrigação* (obligation), *comprometimento* (commitment) and *comprometer-se* (commit oneself) and responsibility (*responsabilidade*).

23. In chapter 4, I address the financial aspect of compromisso. Mestre Cláudio ended his lecture in Recife with an emotional appeal about older mestres dying in poverty, a recurring concern for him and many other mestres of his generation, having witnessed older tradition bearers dying without access to proper health care, basic amenities, or the dignity of a proper burial. See also Kurtz (2025) for an extensive discussion of compromisso as an ethical practice among the Angoleiros do Sertão.

24. Pernalonga declined to identify racially.

Chapter 2

1. In one session I gave a book talk, describing each chapter and the arguments I make in this book and answering group members' questions.

2. Sharpe (2016) examines the afterlife of slavery—enduring conditions of anti-Blackness that render premature Black death the norm—through the metaphors of "the wake," "the ship," and "the hold," echoing Bethânia's lyrics. Also see Thompson (2014), which argues that the Middle Passage was foundational to Black popular music and dance in North America.

3. See also Smith (2016), Alves (2018), and Villenave (2021).

4. While I find some of Oliveira's theorizing productive, his philosophy ultimately renders ancestralidade so expansive a concept, equating it with many things, from "tradition" to "the body" (2005, 125), that it cannot be easily connected to community members' use of the term. Oliveira also makes oversimplifying generalizations about "African culture," including both the continent of Africa and Afro-Brazil, collapsing the diversity of Afro-Brazilian practices and the wide range of philosophies, worldviews, and cultural practices of Africans on the continent. Nevertheless, Oliveira's work has been celebrated and widely cited, demonstrating that his focus on ancestralidade as a deeply significant subject resonates profoundly with scholars and scholar-practitioners of Afro-Brazilian culture.

5. Downey discusses the "corporeality of sound" of the berimbau and also notes a synesthesia in the ways capoeira players hear the physical qualities of the berimbau in its sound (2002, 495–97). His interlocutors also spoke about the berimbau entering their "blood." While he stated that the "sound of the roda . . . draws the past into the present," his reference was more literal: an aged Mestre Pastinha was remembering his own lived past while listening to a roda. See also Díaz's theorization of "listening with the body" (Díaz Meneses 2016).

6. With "forgotten" past, I refer to Toni Morrison's observation that authors of narratives, such as Frederick Douglass and Harriet Jacob, "were silent about many things, and they 'forgot' many other things," by which she meant "their interior life," while enslaved (1995, 92).

7. For some notable studies on music and memory see, e.g., Kay Shelemay's work on how Syrian Jewish songs evoke, carry, and preserve memories that are individual, conscious, unconscious, "familial, spatial/geographic, communal, and affective" (1998, 5). Steven Feld (2012) wrote about Kaluli songs that evoke strong emotions of grief, loss, and nostalgia as well as bird sounds that are heard as "talk"

from the dead (30). See also Lipsitz (1990). In Brazilian music studies, Dent (2009) analyzes the poetics of memory in country music of central southern Brazil as a means to grappling with anxieties about modernity, and Sharp (2014) explores how *samba de coco* musicians in rural Pernambuco state leverage both nostalgia and apocalypse in their performances and to build their careers. Performance and dance studies scholars have explored memory, both historical and personal (Taylor 2003), especially in studies of African diasporic forms (Gilroy 1993; Feldman 2006; Suárez, Conrado, and Daniel 2018; Wolf 2019). Several scholars have embraced the metaphor of the palimpsest to express the trans-temporality of Mexican experimental theater performance (Hellier-Tinoco 2018) or the ways that hip hop in Senegal connects to collective memory and layers "discourse, story, memory, and sound" (Appert 2018, 19). Christen Smith also develops the concept of "palimpsestic embodiment" (2016), arguing, "Violence against the black body is a haunting: a series of performative repetitions that mimic, reflect, and refract memory across time and space" (156).

8. The earliest written mentions of capoeira are found in police documents of the early nineteenth century, but they contain almost no description of capoeira play (movements, sounds, rituals, etc.) and police encountered capoeira only in public spaces, not private (Assunção 2005, 71–73). The earliest artist's rendition, Rugendas's engraving from 1835, provides some sense of how capoeira may have been played (upright, light on the feet, fists clenched, accompanied by pandeiro) but is, of course, limited as an isolated illustration made by an outside observer (see Assunção 2005, 72–79).

9. See Hartman's "A Note on Method" in *Scenes of Subjection* (1997, 10–14) and Hartman (2008b) for fuller elaborations of her thinking on methods for approaching the archive of slavery. See also the many scholars who have taken up Hartman's critical fabulation and thought. A comprehensive acknowledgment is too long to include here, but I am influenced by the ways that the following scholars have theorized Blackness, temporality, and slavery's enduring violence: Christina Sharpe (2016); Tina Campt (2017); Colbert, Jones Jr., and Vogel (2020); Christen Smith (2016); and Tavia Nyong'o (2018), who has offered a profound and extensive rumination on "afro-fabulation" as "a theory and practice of black time and temporality" (5), analyzing performances of afro-fabulation that "operate as a queer hack of the codes of an anti-black world" (4).

10. Beatriz Nascimento's writings have only recently been translated to English (B. Nascimento 2023), thus when citing this English-language volume, I use the translators' translations. When citing Portuguese texts, translations are my own.

11. Activist-scholar Abdias do Nascimento (no relation) also theorized the quilombo in his essay "Quilombismo" (1980), which summoned Black Brazilians to embark upon a "radical transformation of existing socioeconomic and political structures" (160) by drawing on their specific historical experience "utilizing critical and inventive knowledge of our own social and economic institutions, battered as they have been by colonialism and racism. In sum, to reconstruct in the present a society directed toward the future, but taking into account what is still useful and positive in the stores of our past" (160). As far as I am aware, Abdias and Beatriz

did not cite one another. See also Henson (2024), who draws on Beatriz's work in his ethnographic study of Salvador's hip hop spaces as "emergent quilombos."

12. See also Feldman, who writes that in Cruz's choreographic method "the body itself represents a kind of 'Africa' where lost ancestral memories are stored" (2006, 67).

13. I gesture again to Rachel Harding's (2000) "alternative spaces of blackness."

14. A *cotista* is a student who benefited from university affirmative action policies (quotas) intended for students of low-income backgrounds and/or African descent.

15. See chapter 1 for a discussion of "sintonia," an alignment of frequencies, which roughly translates to being on the same wavelength.

16. *Ginga* is the basic movement of capoeira, a swaying step out of which one can transition to any other movement. *Bananeira*, literally "banana tree," is a handstand, and *aú* is a capoeira cartwheel, which in capoeira Angola is often performed with knees bent and tucked close to the body.

17. Other scholars have noted the nonlinear nature of time in African matrix practices (Machado and Araújo 2015; Abib 2004; E. Oliveira 2003), but whereas these authors posit that time is "circular" in these spaces, that is not how my interlocutors seemed to experience it. Rather, when they spoke of ancestralidade, it seemed to merge time concepts, perhaps rendering it more of a hybrid of old and new, past and present (Júnior 2004, 150).

18. Neither Bolinha nor his sister mentioned that Dona Pomba was white, which I later confirmed. While Dona Pomba's whiteness may seem to complicate Rua Nova's history of Black self-determination, it also reveals the complexity of racial politics on the ground. It shows, for instance, that white individuals can act against white supremacist systems, even as the systems remain intact, but that such acts can still have profound repercussions for future generations. Moreover, by emphasizing how Black residents built, sustained, and experienced their neighborhood, both Bolinha and his sister were careful to avoid making Rua Nova's history a story of white saviorhood. See chapter 4 for discussion of the complexities of white patronage of Black cultural and economic activities.

19. See also the Brazilian Wikipedia page about Feira de Santana. Rua Nova is mentioned there only under the headings "Poverty and inequality," "Security and criminality," and "poor neighborhoods," portraying the neighborhood as one of the poorest and most violent areas of the city ("Feira de Santana" 2021).

20. In a rapid aside Abusada explained that her air quotes referred to her teachers' use of the term: "I use the term 'enslavement' [*escravização*] because 'slavery' [*escravidão*] makes it seem like it was something they wanted. The Black people didn't want to be there! They were there because they were forced to be there. That's why I say 'enslavement.'"

Chapter 3

1. See the start of chapter 2, where I describe the incident in more detail.

2. Hordge-Freeman (2015) has written about the ways in which Afro-

Brazilians negotiate racialization, racial stigma, and resulting disparities in affection within their families. In Black Brazilian families, as in Black families across the diaspora, members of one family often present diverse ranges of skin tones and phenotypical characteristics. For a psychological approach to the topic, see Schucman (2023).

3. Camouflaged forms of racism are not unique to Brazil. Covert, indirect, or color-blind forms of racism (both systemic and among individuals) are the norm in the post–civil rights era United States (P. Collins 2004; Bonilla-Silva 2014; Alexander 2012). Moreover, Brazil's cordial racism coexists with brutal violence against Black people at the hands of police (Smith 2016; Alves 2018). Thus the existence of veiled racism should not be mistaken as evidence that racisms in Brazil are milder or subtler than in the United States (cf. Telles 2004).

4. See, e.g., Hanchard (1994), Twine (1998), Caldwell (2007), Williams (2013), and Perry (2013). Also see musicologist Guthrey Ramsey's account of experiencing police brutality (Ramsey 2022, 96–98) and the personal accounts of Hordge-Freeman, Smith, and Perry in Reiter and Oslender (2014). While these testimonies all describe experiences of racism, from violent to subtle, they also reveal the complexity, nuance, dynamism, and variation among positionalities and experiences. Black Brazilian scholars have also written, e.g., on Black women's experiences of exclusion in academia (M. Reis 2022) and Black women musicians' experiences of domestic violence (Nascimento Luz 2020).

5. The symbolic eating of Black bodies pervades Brazilian culture, surfacing in the names of food items such as peanut brittle, *pé de moleque* (Carvalho-Neto 1978), which means "foot of a little Black boy." Brazilian Portuguese slang also underscores the sexual connotations of "eating," as the verb *comer* (to eat) also means "to fuck." See also Woodard (2014), which examines white slaveholders' sexual desire for and cannibalism of Black men in the United States.

6. Robinson's concept of "hungry listening" (2020) includes both white settlers' desires to grasp and their inability to hear Indigenous music/sound and thus the inability to be satiated. For an examination of the complex relationships between Indigenous peoples' land, forced labor, African humans turned chattel, and various forms of genocide and dispossession, see King, Navarro, and Smith (2020).

7. Like Bonilla-Silva (2021), my focus is not on "racists," a term that often evokes a minority of subjects with extreme anti-Black, white supremacist views. While these views have become more mainstream in recent years (Silva and Larkins 2019), that is not the case within the Angoleiros do Sertão.

8. While the group has white non-Brazilian members, they all live abroad (mostly in Europe) and I had little opportunity to interact with them. A significant amount of recent capoeira literature focuses on white non-Brazilians, though only some of it addresses practitioners' racial attitudes. See, e.g., Griffith (2016, 88–92) on how foreign capoeira students visiting Salvador consider Black Brazilian men the most authentic carriers of the tradition.

9. Beija-flor was one of the few members who declined to self-identify racially, though she said her parents are white and she is identified as white on her birth certificate. She has tanned, light-brown skin and medium-brown, shiny, wavy hair.

She said that her great-grandmother was Indian and admitted that her skin color was "morena," but she preferred to identify as "just human."

10. Ideas about the authentic spirit of poor, dark-skinned Brazilians as a resource available for whites to mine and appropriate have been institutionalized even in a prestigious university dance program in São Paulo state (Höfling 2016).

11. See also P. Pinho (2010, 183–215) for an analysis of the ways Black culture, especially the work of bloco afro Ilê Aiyê, has been commodified and objectified in Salvador, often with the collaboration of Ilê Aiyê's leaders.

12. See also Fanon on white people projecting their desire and fears onto Black men: "The black man is nothing but biological. Black men are animals" (2008, 143).

13. In early 2017, protests were taking place across Brazil under the hashtag #ForaTemer! (Out with Temer!) against the government of Michel Temer (of the center-right Brazilian Democratic Movement [PMDB]), who as vice president under Dilma Rousseff, of the leftist Worker's Party (PT), had helped orchestrate her impeachment and removal from office.

14. Throughout I translate "liberdade" as both liberty and freedom, using the terms synonymously, following political philosophers such as Barnor Hesse.

15. See, e.g., Machado and Araújo, who contrast a European "analytical logic or instrumental reason" with "a logic based on African ontology," though they note that they coexist in the same spaces (2015, 104). Machado and Araújo draw extensively on the ideas of Eduardo de Oliveira (see, e.g., 2003, 2005). See also Lewis (1992), who argued that capoeira's inverted movements (like handstands and cartwheels) symbolize the desires of the oppressed to invert social relations (turn the masters into slaves). I disagree.

16. A passage from Hesse's article, citing Césaire, is eerily similar to Carlão's view: "Cesaire [*sic*] paraphrases the exemplariness of Mannoni's liberal-colonial views in the following way: 'The Negroes can't even imagine what freedom is. They don't want it, they don't demand it. It's the white agitators who put that into their heads. And if you gave it to them, they wouldn't know what to do with it'" (Hesse 2014, 295).

17. Quilombo of Palmares was an autonomous society formed by fugitives from slavery with an estimated population of 11,000 (French 2009, 77) to upward of 30,000 (A. do Nascimento and Nascimento 1992, 123). Palmares existed for most of the seventeenth century, and Zumbi was its leader at the time of its demise. Listen also to Mestre Moraes's ladainha "Rei Zumbi de Palmeras" (Moraes and GCAP 1996).

18. I find that white/non-Black capoeira students often occupy a position comparable to that of ethnomusicologists. For instance, in Ted Solís's *Performing Ethnomusicology* (2004), Gage Averill adopts Hood's framing of the ethnomusicologist as "apprentice," which resonates with Griffith's theorization of capoeira "apprenticeship pilgrims" (2016). Like Marmota, many of the authors in Solís's volume express angst at representing a culture to which they don't belong, but none of them advocates ceasing to do so.

19. White people in Brazil have contributed to the Black movement with their

antiracism scholarship. For example, among others, Elisa Larkin Nascimento, a North American scholar-activist who has lived in Brazil for decades and was the partner of the late Abdias do Nascimento, has published extensively on racial politics in Brazil. Lia Vainer Schucman has contributed critical analyses of whiteness and race in Brazil in her scholarship and social media postings.

20. Afonso asked me pointedly in both our interviews to use his full name and not a pseudonym.

Chapter 4

1. An exception is communications scholar Robitaille's dissertation (2013), which considered capoeira mestres as neoliberal entrepreneurs and examined capoeira's economy through the lens of resource, building on Yúdice's (2004) concept of the "expediency of culture."

2. For works on trickster figures, see, for example, Levine (1977) discussing Brer Rabbit and other folktales, Gates (1988) on the significance of the Signifying Monkey and his tales, and more recent literature that evaluates the importance of trickster figures: for African American literature confronting the traumas of slavery and racism (Lussana 2018; Marshall 2019) and for African theater (Shipley 2015). In Brazil, Exu (the messenger orixá of the crossroads), the Malandro, and the Caboclo are all trickster archetypes.

3. Lussana also argues for a reassessment of trickery in an article that revisits overlooked Brer Rabbit tales to show how they valorized "friendship, altruism, and commitment to vulnerable members of the community" (2018, 123).

4. I have used pseudonyms and fictionalized aspects of this account of Sofie's tale to preserve the anonymity of those involved. Any resemblance to known people or mestres is coincidental.

5. Thanks to Adanna Kai Jones for her suggestion of the concept of "stretching."

6. Similar extended kinship relations exist in Candomblé, too, where it is not uncommon for initiates or members to live for extended periods at the terreiro.

7. I thank Saroya Corbett for bringing this story and text to my attention.

8. Kelley's (1994) broader argument is that Black workers' tactics reveal that we must look beyond organized political or union movements to gain a full picture of Black labor resistance practices.

9. Meats are among the preferred foods of the orixás and, when prepared for ritual offerings, literally become axé (see chapter 1).

10. In contemporary capoeira Angola rodas, the "Tico-Tico" song and game are unique, for "Tico-Tico" is also accompanied by its own toque and thus is one of the only times where the change in toque still signals a major shift in the game and way of playing.

11. J. Lowell Lewis (1992) also privileges malícia in his study as a concept "at the heart of the practice of traditional capoeira," which includes a "notion of double-dealing or cunning, a lesson learned in slavery" (33).

12. Like capoeira, Candomblé was also outlawed by the Penal Code of 1890

as a "crime against public health," as the religion was intentionally conflated with "(black) magic" and practices of "(faith) healing" (*curandeirismo*) (J. Oliveira 2010). Contemporary dictionaries define mandinga as "*feitiçaria*" (magic, witchcraft, or sorcery) ("mandinga," n.d.; "feitiçaria," n.d.).

13. In the literature, the street-smart malandro of Rio de Janeiro is often claimed as the capoeirista's archetype (Capoeira 2002, 47–56; Abib 2004, 71), but I find the Caboclo a more relevant archetype for capoeira in Bahia, especially in the Angoleiros do Sertão (see chapter 1).

14. In addition to the texts cited here by Downey, Varela, and Lewis, see also Fuggle (2008), Willson (2001), and Díaz (2017). I am not alone in my critique, at least concerning Varela's monograph. In her review, Brazilian capoeira scholar-practitioner Cristina Rosa writes that Varela settles on "a narrow translation of mandinga as a 'logic of deception.' In doing so, I fear, the narrative may mislead readers into perceiving capoeira as unethical and an untrustworthy practice where people cheat to gain power, rather than a martial art whose knowledge and ways of knowing differ from or exceeds [*sic*] Western social norms" (C. Rosa 2019, 114).

15. On mistrust see also Varela (2017, 6, 65, 85), and on valuing distrust see Lewis (1992, 33, 193, 198).

16. Many have discussed how capoeira is a form of play as theorized by Huizinga and other play theorists. See, e.g., Lewis (1992), Wesolowski (2007), and Capoeira (2016).

17. As Brazil emerged from dictatorship in the 1980s, the Rouanet Law was established in 1991 as the nation's primary public mechanism for funding the arts, which it remains to this day (Moreira 2023, 49). However, the law works by incentivizing private investment in artistic projects, requiring artists to translate their project into corporate terms, with the result that most of the funded projects are concentrated in the wealthy cities of São Paulo and Rio de Janeiro in southeast Brazil (50–51).

18. Robitaille (2013), writing about capoeira Regional, calls this the "batizado circuit." "*Batizados*," literally baptisms, are often enormous, on a much larger scale than capoeira Angola events, with hundreds or even thousands of participants. The large scale means that guest teachers are well compensated.

19. See also Butler (1998, 137–38) and Harding (2000, 116–22).

20. Many mestres in Brazil have sought degrees in (physical) education or physical therapy as a means toward certification and validation of their knowledge. If they are unable to secure a position teaching at a school, they may seek employment at a gym or health club. However, these kinds of positions still offer little job security.

21. Prominent ogãs in the 1930s included folklorist Edison Carneiro, Ruth Landes's main informant (Landes 1994, 145) and in the 1950s and '60s, visual artist Carybé, author Jorge Amado, and singer-songwriter Vinicius de Moraes (França 2018, 66).

22. Carybé, Amado, and Moraes were also given the title "*conselheiros da corte*," court advisors, of their Candomblé terreiro (França 2018, 66).

23. Butler also argues that Afro-Brazilian patronage was more "limited in scope" and Black patrons of the brotherhoods did not "have access to . . . the same means of coercive force wielded by the traditional patrons" (1998, 23). The irmandades and "protection societies" are powerful historical examples of the ways in which Black Brazilians created their own mutual aid institutions (Butler 1998, 141–60).

24. Baptista (2007) discusses Mauss's concept of the gift, as does Foster (2019). Robitaille briefly addresses gift exchange and concludes by identifying a "coexistence of economies" (2013, 173) in capoeira, arguing that the capoeira business cannot be seen only as "a neoliberal enterprise but also as an extension and adaptation of the more traditionally organized groups in Brazil" (173) whose relations "are based on loyalty, obligations, hierarchy, trust and respect" (175).

25. As in chapter 1, I am not suggesting a one-to-one equivalence between Candomblé and capoeira and their economic structures, but rather allowing Candomblé's economy to frame an understanding of capoeira's. Candomblé's "economy of axé" is quite distinct in many ways—for instance, its demand for and small-scale self-production of ritual objects, clothing, food, herbs, among many other specialized products (J. Carvalho 2011).

26. In Candomblé many exchanges are understood as being made between client/initiate and orixá (such as offerings or sacrifices made to please the orixá in exchange for protection). While there is no direct correlate of orixá in capoeira, by positioning capoeira as the object of students' obligations and compromissos, Mestre Cláudio (albeit ambiguously) renders capoeira as an entity, too.

27. Nestor explains further: "In a more restricted sense, *malícia* is what permits a player to anticipate the attacks of the other; and also 'to deceive' the opponent, pretending that they are going to do something, when, in truth, they are preparing another thing. We could ask what 'wisdom' has to do with 'deceiving the other': it is that, to deceive the other, it is necessary to know how the other is, and how he is going to act; and, on the other hand, to know our [own] potentialities of action and weakness" (2016, 271).

28. See Kurtz (2024b) for a more detailed discussion of what I have gained from my research with Mestre Cláudio and what I might owe in return.

Epilogue

1. I have recreated this quote from my notes; it may not be verbatim.

2. With this last phrase, Garcia-Mispireta cites Turino (1993, 111). Whereas Garcia-Mispireta suggests that in minimal electronic music-dance parties the synchronized activity creates a sense of community yet to be (2023, 145), I find that capoeira rodas can both strengthen existing community bonds and create them in the moment; and this community can endure after the roda ends, but it depends upon the continued renewing of axé in future rodas.

3. In both our interviews, Afonso Mesquita expressed his wishes that I use his full name.

Bibliography

Abib, Pedro Rodolpho Jungers. 2004. *Capoeira Angola: cultura popular e o jogo dos saberes na roda*. EDUFBA.

Abib, Pedro Rodolpho Jungers. 2009. *Mestres e capoeiras famosos da Bahia*. EDUFBA.

Abiodun, Rowland. 1994. "Understanding Yoruba Art and Aesthetics: The Concept of Ase." *African Arts* 27 (3): 68–103. https://doi.org/10.2307/3337203.

Abreu, Frederico José de. 2005. *Capoeiras: Bahia, século XIX Vol. 1*. Instituto Jair Moura.

Afolabi, Niyi. 2009. *Afro-Brazilians: Cultural Production in a Racial Democracy*. University of Rochester Press.

Afolabi, Niyi. 2016. *Ilê Aiyê in Brazil and the Reinvention of Africa*. Springer.

Agawu, Kofi. 2003. *Representing African Music: Postcolonial Notes, Queries, Positions*. Routledge.

Ahlgren, Angela K. 2018. *Drumming Asian America: Taiko, Performance, and Cultural Politics*. Oxford University Press.

Ahmed, Sara. 2000. *Strange Encounters: Embodied Others in Post-Coloniality*. Routledge.

Ahmed, Sara. 2004. "Declarations of Whiteness: The Non-Performativity of Anti-Racism." *Borderlands E-Journal* 3 (2). https://rbb85.wordpress.com/2014/08/24/declarations-of-whiteness/.

Alexander, Michelle. 2012. *The New Jim Crow: Mass Incarceration in the Age of Colorblindness*. New Press.

Alvarez, Sonia E., and Kia Lilly Caldwell. 2016. "Promoting Feminist Amefricanidade: Bridging Black Feminist Cultures and Politics in the Americas." *Meridians: Feminism, Race, Transnationalism* 14 (1): v–xi.

Alves, Jaime Amparo. 2018. *The Anti-Black City: Police Terror and Black Urban Life in Brazil*. University of Minnesota Press.

Amanda Seales TV, dir. 2023. *Side Effects of African American Studies with Dr. Robin D. G. Kelley | Small Doses Podcast*. https://www.youtube.com/watch?v=U4_6ZnuaJJo.

Amaral, Rita de Cássia, and Vagner Gonçalves da Silva. 1993. "A cor do axé: brancos e negros no candomblé de São Paulo." *Estudos Afro-Asiáticos* 25: 99–124.

Amico, Stephen. 2020. "'We Are All Musicologists Now'; or, the End of Ethnomusicology." *Journal of Musicology* 37 (1): 1–32. https://doi.org/10.1525/jm.2020.37.1.1.

Anderson, Elizabeth. 2010. *The Imperative of Integration*. Princeton University Press.

Anderson, Warwick, Ricardo Roque, and Ricardo Ventura Santos. 2019. *Luso-Tropicalism and Its Discontents: The Making and Unmaking of Racial Exceptionalism*. Berghahn Books.

Andrade, Mário de. 1972 [1928]. *Ensaio sobre a música brasileira*. 3rd ed. Vila Rica.

Andrade, Oswald de. 1991. "Cannibalist Manifesto." Translated by Leslie Bary. *Latin American Literary Review* 19 (38): 38–47.

Andrews, George Reid. 1991. *Blacks & Whites in São Paulo, Brazil, 1888–1988*. University of Wisconsin Press.

Appert, Catherine M. 2017. "Engendering Musical Ethnography." *Ethnomusicology* 61 (3): 446–67. https://doi.org/10.5406/ethnomusicology.61.3.0446.

Appert, Catherine M. 2018. *In Hip Hop Time: Music, Memory, and Social Change in Urban Senegal*. Oxford University Press.

Araújo, Rosângela Costa. 2015. *É preta, Kalunga: a capoeira Angola como prática política entre os angoleiros baianos—anos 80–90 [It's Black, Kalunga: Capoeira Angola as a political practice among Bahian angoleiros—in the 80s and 90s]*. Fundação Gregório de Mattos.

Assunção, Matthias, dir. 2013. *Jogo de corpo: capoeira e ancestralidade*. Documentary.

Assunção, Matthias Röhrig. 2005. *Capoeira: The History of an Afro-Brazilian Martial Art*. Routledge.

Assunção, Matthias Röhrig. 2007. "History and Memory in Capoeira Lyrics from Bahia, Brazil." In *Cultures of the Lusophone Black Atlantic*, edited by Nancy Priscilla Naro, Roger Sansi-Roca, and David H. Treece, 199–217. Studies of the Americas. Palgrave Macmillan US. https://doi.org/10.1057/9780230606982_10.

Balaguer, Gabriela. 2016. "Capoeira Angola e suas relações com o mito da democracia racial brasileira." *Semina: Ciências Sociais e Humanas* 37 (2): 133–50. https://doi.org/10.5433/1679-0383.2016v37n2p133.

Balaguer, Gabriela. 2017. "Exercícios da branquitude: o estrangeiro, os brasileiros e os angoleiros." PhD diss., Instituto de Psicologia, Universidade de São Paulo. https://repositorio.usp.br/item/002919270.

Baptista, José Renato de Carvalho. 2007. "The Gods Sell When They Give: The Meanings of Money in Candomblé Exchange Relations." *Mana* 3 (SE): 1–26.

Barbosa, Maria José Somerlate. 2005. "Capoeira: a gramática do corpo e a dança das palavras." *Luso-Brazilian Review* 42 (1): 78–98. https://doi.org/10.1353/lbr.2005.0019.

Béhague, Gerard. 1984. "Patterns of Candomblé Music Performance: An Afro-Brazilian Religious Setting." In *Performance Practice: Ethnomusicological Perspectives*, edited by Gerard Béhague, 222–54. Series: Contributions in Intercultural and Comparative Studies, No. 12. Greenwood.

Béhague, Gerard. 1999. "Expressões musicais do pluralismo religioso afro-baiano: a negoçiação de identidade." *Brasiliana: Revista Quadrimestral da Academia Brasileira de Música* 1 (1): 40–47.

Béhague, Gerard. 2006. "Regional and National Trends in Afro-Brazilian Religious Musics: A Case of Cultural Pluralism." *Latin American Music Review* 27 (1): 91–103. https://doi.org/10.1353/lat.2006.0022.

Berg, Ulla D., and Ana Y. Ramos-Zayas. 2015. "Racializing Affect: A Theoretical Proposition." *Current Anthropology* 56 (5): 654–77. https://doi.org/10.1086/683053.

Bishop-Sanchez, Kathryn. 2021. *Creating Carmen Miranda: Race, Camp, and Transnational Stardom*. Vanderbilt University Press.

Boaz, Danielle N. 2021. *Banning Black Gods: Law and Religions of the African Diaspora*. Penn State University Press.

Bonilla-Silva, Eduardo. 2014. *Racism without Racists: Color-Blind Racism and the Persistence of Racial Inequality in America*. 4th ed. Rowman & Littlefield.

Bonilla-Silva, Eduardo. 2021. "What Makes Systemic Racism Systemic?" *Sociological Inquiry* 91 (3): 513–33. https://doi.org/10.1111/soin.12420.

Born, Georgina, and David Hesmondhalgh. 2000. *Western Music and Its Others: Difference, Representation, and Appropriation in Music*. University of California Press.

Bourdieu, Pierre. 2000. "Making the Economic Habitus: Algerian Workers Revisited." Translated by Richard Nice and Loïc Wacquant. *Ethnography* 1 (1): 17–41. https://doi.org/10.1177/14661380022230624.

Bowen, Larnies A., Ayanna Legros, Tianna Paschel, Geísa Mattos, Kleaver Cruz, and Juliet Hooker. 2017. "A Hemispheric Approach to Contemporary Black Activism." *NACLA Report on the Americas* 49 (1): 25–35. https://doi.org/10.1080/10714839.2017.1298240.

Braga, Júlio Santana. 1995. *Na gamela do feitiço: repressão e resistência nos candomblés da Bahia*. EDUFBA.

Brito, Celso de, and Daniel Granada. 2020. *Cultura, política e sociedade: estudos sobre a capoeira na contemporaneidade*. EDUFPI, Universidade Federal do Piauí. https://dataspace.princeton.edu/handle/88435/dsp0108612r689.

Brooks, Daphne A. 2008. "Amy Winehouse and the (Black) Art of Appropriation." *The Nation*. September 10. https://www.thenation.com/article/archive/amy-winehouse-and-black-art-appropriation/.

Brown, Danielle. 2020. "An Open Letter on Racism in Music Studies." *My People Tell Stories* (blog). June 12. https://www.mypeopletellstories.com/blog/open-letter.

Browning, Barbara. 1995. *Samba Resistance in Motion*. Indiana University Press.

Burdick, John. 2013. *The Color of Sound: Race, Religion, and Music in Brazil*. New York University Press.

Burke, Patrick. 2021. *Tear Down the Walls: White Radicalism and Black Power in 1960s Rock*. University of Chicago Press.

Burnim, Mellonee. 1985. "Culture Bearer and Tradition Bearer: An Ethnomusicologist's Research on Gospel Music." *Ethnomusicology* 29 (3): 432–47. https://doi.org/10.2307/851798.

Butler, Judith. 1993. "Gender Is Burning: Questions of Appropriation and Subversion." In *Bodies That Matter: On the Discursive Limits of "Sex,"* 121–41. Psychology Press.

Butler, Kim D. 1998. *Freedoms Given, Freedoms Won: Afro-Brazilians in Post-Abolition, São Paulo and Salvador*. Rutgers University Press.

Caldwell, Kia Lilly. 2007. *Negras in Brazil Re-Envisioning Black Women, Citizenship, and the Politics of Identity*. Rutgers University Press.

Caldwell, Kia Lilly, Wendi Muse, Tianna S. Paschel, Keisha-Khan Y. Perry, Christen A. Smith, and Erica L. Williams. 2018. "On the Imperative of Transnational Solidarity: A U.S. Black Feminist Statement on the Assassination of Marielle Franco." *The Black Scholar* (blog). March 23. https://www.theblackscholar.org/on-the-imperative-of-transnational-solidarity-a-u-s-black-feminist-statement-on-the-assassination-of-marielle-franco/.

Campanaro, Priscila Kikuchi. 2021. "Branquitude e religião: uma análise autoetnográfica sobre ser uma mulher branca no candomblé." *Mandrágora* 27 (2): 91–113. https://doi.org/10.15603/ma27291-113.

Campt, Tina M. 2017. *Listening to Images*. Reprint ed. Duke University Press.

Capoeira, Nestor. 2002. *Capoeira: Roots of the Dance-Fight-Game*. North Atlantic Books.

Capoeira, Nestor. 2016. "Capoeira: a malícia e a filosofia da malandragem." In *Capoeira em múltiplos olhares: estudos e pesquisas em jogo*, edited by Antonio Liberac Cardoso Simões Pires, Paulo Magalhães, Franciane Figueiredo, and Sara Abreu, 261–78. Editora UFRB.

Capone, Stefania. 2010. *Searching for Africa in Brazil: Power and Tradition in Candomblé*. Translated by Lucy Lyall Grant. Duke University Press.

Cardoso, Ângelo Nonato Natale. 2006. "A Linguagem dos tambores." PhD diss., Universidade Federal da Bahia. https://repositorio.ufba.br/handle/ri/9112.

Cardoso, Cláudia Pons. 2014. "Amefricanizando o feminismo: o pensamento de Lélia Gonzalez." *Revista Estudos Feministas* 22 (3): 965–86. https://doi.org/10.1590/S0104-026X2014000300015.

Carneiro, Sueli. 2003. "Enegrecer o feminismo: a situação da mulher negra na América Latina a partir de uma perspectiva de gênero." In *Racismos contemporâneos*, 49–58. Takano Editora.

Carvalho, José Jorge de. 1999. "The Multiplicity of Black Identities in Brazilian Popular Music." In *Black Brazil: Culture, Identity, and Social Mobilization*, edited by Larry Crook and Randal Johnson, 261–95. UCLA Latin American Center Publications.

Carvalho, José Jorge de. 2011. "A economia do axé: os terreiros de religião de matriz afrobrasileira como fonte de segurança alimentar e rede de circuitos econômicos e comunitários." In *Alimento: direito sagrado. pesquisa socioeconômica e cultural de povos e comunidades tradicionais de terreiros*, edited by Luana Lazzeri Arantes and Monica Rodrigues, 37–62. Ministério do Desenvolvimento Social e Combate à Fome.

Carvalho-Neto, Paulo de. 1978. "Folklore of the Black Struggle in Latin America." *Latin American Perspectives* 5 (2): 53–88. https://doi.org/10.1177/0094582X7800500205.

Césaire, Aimé. 2016. "From Discourse on Colonialsim (1955)." In *I Am Because We Are: Readings in Africana Philosophy*, edited by Fred Lee Hord, Mzee Lasana Okpara, and Jonathan Scott Lee, 196–205. University of Massachusetts Press.

Chada, Sonia. 2006. *A música dos caboclos nos candomblés baianos*. Série Fundação Gregório de Mattos. EDUFBA.

Chávez, Luis, and Russell P. Skelchy. 2019. "Decolonization for Ethnomusicology and Music Studies in Higher Education." *Action, Criticism, and Theory for Music Education* 18 (3): 115–43.

Christian, Barbara. 1987. "The Race for Theory." *Cultural Critique* (6): 51–63. https://doi.org/10.2307/1354255.

Colbert, Soyica Diggs. 2017. *Black Movements Performance and Cultural Politics*. Rutgers University Press.

Colbert, Soyica Diggs, Douglas A. Jones Jr., and Shane Vogel, eds. 2020. *Race and Performance after Repetition*. Duke University Press.

Coletto, Diego. 2010. *The Informal Economy and Employment in Brazil: Latin America, Modernization, and Social Changes*. Springer.

Collins, Marcus. 2024. "Why Country's Resistance to Beyoncé Is Cultural Appropriation." *Forbes*. February 16. https://www.forbes.com/sites/marcuscollins/2024/02/16/why-countrys-resistance-to-beyonce-is-cultural-appropriation/.

Collins, Patricia Hill. 2000. *Black Feminist Thought: Knowledge, Consciousness, and the Politics of Empowerment*. Routledge.

Collins, Patricia Hill. 2004. *Black Sexual Politics: African Americans, Gender, and the New Racism*. Taylor and Francis.

Combahee River Collective. 2014. "A Black Feminist Statement." *Women's Studies Quarterly* 42 (3/4): 271–80.

"compromisso" n.d. In *Dicionário Priberam: Dicionário Online de Português Contemporâneo*. Priberam Informática S.A. Accessed May 12, 2021. https://dicionario.priberam.org/compromisso.

Costa, Alexandre Emboaba da. 2014. *Reimagining Black Difference and Politics in Brazil: From Racial Democracy to Multiculturalism*. Springer.

Costa, Alexandre Emboaba da. 2016. "The (Un)Happy Objects of Affective Community." *Cultural Studies* 30 (1): 24–46. https://doi.org/10.1080/09502386.2014.899608.

Costa, Ana de Lourdes Ribeiro da. 1991. "Espaços negros: cantos e lojas em Salvador no século XIX." *Revista Caderno CRH* 4: 18–34.

Costa, Eliane Silvia, and Lia Vainer Schucman. 2022. "Identidades, identificações e classificações raciais no brasil: o pardo e as ações afirmativas." *Estudos e Pesquisas em Psicologia* 22 (2): 466–84.

Couto, Solange. 2021. "Tradição, ancestralidade e inclusão social através da cultura popular afrocentrada na Bahia." In *Narrativas negras: escrevendo nossas histórias*, edited by Daniel Pintto, 192–205. Editora Vecchio.

Cox, Aimee Meredith. 2020. "Can Anthropology Get Free?" *Transforming Anthropology* 28 (2): 118–20. https://doi.org/10.1111/traa.12186.

Critical Ethnic Studies Editorial (C.E.S.E.) Collective. 2016. *Critical Ethnic Studies: A Reader*. Edited by Nada Elia, David M. Hernández, Jodi Kim, Shana L. Redmond, Dylan Rodríguez, and Sarita Echavez See. Duke University Press.

Crook, Larry. 1993. "Black Consciousness, Samba Reggae, and the Re-Africanization of Bahian Carnival Music in Brazil." *The World of Music* 35 (2): 90–108.

Crook, Larry, and Randal Johnson, eds. 1999. *Black Brazil: Culture, Identity, and Social Mobilization*. UCLA Latin American Center Publications.

Cruz Banks, Ojeya. 2010. "Critical Postcolonial Dance Pedagogy: The Relevance of West African Dance Education in the United States." *Anthropology & Education Quarterly* 41 (1): 18–34. https://doi.org/10.1111/j.1548-1492.2010.01065.x.

Csordas, Thomas J. 1999. "Embodiment and Cultural Phenomenology." In *Perspectives on Embodiment: The Intersections of Nature and Culture*, edited by Gail Weiss and Honi Fern Haber, 143–62. Routledge.

Damasceno, Karine Teixeira. 2022. *Mal ou bem procedidas: transgressões de regras sociais e jurídicas em Feira de Santana, Bahia, 1890–1920*. EDUFBA.

Damasceno, Karine Teixeira. 2023. *Para serem donas de si: mulheres negras lutando em família*. EDUFBA.

DaMatta, Roberto. 1992. *Carnivals, Rogues, and Heroes: An Interpretation of the Brazilian Dilemma*. 1st ed. Translated by John Drury. University of Notre Dame Press. Originally published 1979.

Daniel, Yvonne. 2005. *Dancing Wisdom: Embodied Knowledge in Haitian Vodou, Cuban Yoruba, and Bahian Candomblé*. University of Illinois Press.

Davies, Carole Boyce, ed. 2008. *Encyclopedia of the African Diaspora: Origins, Experiences, and Culture*. ABC-CLIO.

Davis, Darién J. 2009. *White Face, Black Mask: Africaneity and the Early Social History of Popular Music in Brazil*. Michigan State University Press.

Decânio Filho, Angelo Augusto. 2002. *Transe capoeirano: um estudo sobre estrutura do ser humano e modificações de estado de consciência durante a prática da capoeira*. CEPAC—Coleção S. Salamão.

DeFrantz, Thomas. 2004. "The Black Beat Made Visible: Hip Hop Dance and Body Power." In *Of the Presence of the Body: Essays on Dance and Performance Theory*, edited by Andre Lepecki, 64–81. Wesleyan University Press.

DeFrantz, Thomas, and Anita Gonzalez, eds. 2014. *Black Performance Theory*. Duke University Press.

Dent, Alexander Sebastian. 2009. *River of Tears: Country Music, Memory, and Modernity in Brazil*. Duke University Press.

Desmond, Jane C. 1993. "Embodying Difference: Issues in Dance and Cultural Studies." *Cultural Critique* (26): 33–63. https://doi.org/10.2307/1354455.

Dias, Adriana Albert. 2006. *Mandinga, manha & malícia: uma história sobre os capoeiras na capital da Bahia (1910–1925)*. EDUFBA.

Díaz, Juan Diego. 2017. "Between Repetition and Variation: A Musical Performance of Malícia in Capoeira." *Ethnomusicology Forum* 26 (1): 46–68. https://doi.org/10.1080/17411912.2017.1309297.

Díaz, Juan Diego. 2021. *Africanness in Action: Essentialism and Musical Imaginations of Africa in Brazil*. Oxford University Press.

Díaz Meneses, Juan Diego. 2016. "Listening with the Body: An Aesthetics of Spirit Possession Outside the Terreiro." *Ethnomusicology* 60 (1): 89–124. https://doi.org/10.5406/ethnomusicology.60.1.0089.

Diniz, Flávia Cachineski. 2010. "Capoeira Angola: identidade e trânsito musical." Master's thesis, Universidade Federal da Bahia, Escola de Música.

Diniz, Flávia, Ricardo Pamfilio de Sousa, and Angela Lühning. 2015. "Capoeira, música e religião." In *Uma coleção biográfica: os mestres Pastinha, Bimba e Cobrinha Verde no Museu Afro-Brasileiro da UFBA*, edited by Joseania Miranda Freitas, 189–209. EDUFBA.

Downey, Greg. 2002. "Listening to Capoeira: Phenomenology, Embodiment, and the Materiality of Music." *Ethnomusicology* 46 (3): 487–509. https://doi.org/10.2307/852720.

Downey, Greg. 2005. *Learning Capoeira: Lessons in Cunning from an Afro-Brazilian Art*. Oxford University Press.

Downey, Greg. 2008. "Scaffolding Imitation in Capoeira: Physical Education and Enculturation in an Afro-Brazilian Art." *American Anthropologist* 110 (2): 204–213. https://doi.org/10.1111/j.1548-1433.2008.00026.x.

Dreisinger, Baz. 2008. *Near Black: White-to-Black Passing in American Culture*. University of Massachusetts Press.

Drewal, Margaret Thompson. 1992. *Yoruba Ritual: Performers, Play, Agency*. Indiana University Press.

Du Bois, W.E.B. 1986. *W.E.B. Du Bois: Writings: The Suppression of the African Slave-Trade / The Souls of Black Folk / Dusk of Dawn / Essays and Articles*. Library of America.

Dunkley, D. A., and Stephanie Shonekan, eds. 2018. *Black Resistance in the Americas*. Routledge.

Dunn, Christopher. 1992. "Afro-Bahian Carnival: A Stage for Protest." *Afro-Hispanic Review* 11 (1/3): 11–20.

Dunn, Christopher. 2001. *Brutality Garden: Tropicália and the Emergence of a Brazilian Counterculture*. University of North Carolina Press.

Dunn, Christopher. 2016. *Contracultura: Alternative Arts and Social Transformation in Authoritarian Brazil*. University of North Carolina Press.

Durkheim, Emile. 2008. *The Elementary Forms of Religious Life*. Oxford University Press.

Eidsheim, Nina Sun. 2019. *The Race of Sound: Listening, Timbre, and Vocality in African American Music*. Duke University Press.

Elferen, Isabella Anna Maria Van. 2021. *Timbre: Paradox, Materialism, Vibrational Aesthetics*. Bloomsbury Academic.

Emerson, Robert M., Rachel I. Fretz, and Linda L. Shaw. 2011. *Writing Ethnographic Fieldnotes*. 2nd ed. University of Chicago Press.

Enriquez, Falina. 2022. *The Costs of the Gig Economy: Musical Entrepreneurs and the Cultural Politics of Inequality in Northeastern Brazil*. University of Illinois Press.

Escóssia, Fernanda da. 2016. "A cada 23 minutos, um jovem negro é assassinado no Brasil, diz CPI." *BBC News Brasil*, June 6. https://www.bbc.com/portuguese/brasil-36461295.

Fanon, Frantz. 2008. *Black Skin, White Masks*. Translated by Richard Philcox. Grove Press.

"Feira de Santana." 2021. In *Wikipédia, a enciclopédia livre*. https://pt.wikipedia.org/w/index.php?title=Feira_de_Santana&oldid=62196390.

"feitiçaria." n.d. In *Dicionário Priberam: Dicionário Online de Português Contemporâneo*. Priberam Informática S.A. Accessed July 6, 2023. https://dicionario.priberam.org/feitiçaria.

Feld, Steven. 2012. *Sound and Sentiment: Birds, Weeping, Poetics, and Song in Kaluli Expression*. 3rd ed. Duke University Press.

Feldman, Heidi Carolyn. 2006. *Black Rhythms of Peru: Reviving African Musical Heritage in the Black Pacific*. Wesleyan University Press.

Ferreira, Natália Rizzatti, and Christiano Key Tambascia. 2021. "Capoeira em Feira de Santana (1970–1990)." *Revista EntreRios do Programa de Pós-Graduação em Antropologia* 4 (2): 126–58. https://doi.org/10.26694/rer.v4i2.12771.

Floyd, Samuel A. 1995. *The Power of Black Music: Interpreting Its History from Africa to the United States*. Oxford University Press.

Folha de S. Paulo / Datafolha. 1995. *Racismo cordial: a mais completa análise sobre o preconceito de cor no Brasil*, edited by Cleusa Turra and Gustavo Venturi. Editora Atica.

Foster, Susan Leigh. 2019. *Valuing Dance: Commodities and Gifts in Motion*. Oxford University Press.

França, Jonas. 2018. "Elementos para um debate sobre os brancos e a branquitude no candomblé: identidades, espaços e responsabilidades." *Revista Calundu* 2 (2): 55–81. https://doi.org/10.26512/revistacalundu.v2i2.15706.

French, Jan Hoffman. 2009. *Legalizing Identities: Becoming Black or Indian in Brazil's Northeast*. University of North Carolina Press.

Freyre, Gilberto. 2003 [1933]. *Casa-grande e senzala: formação da família brasileira sob o regime da economia patriarcal*. 48th ed. Global Editora.

Fuggle, Sophie. 2008. "Discourses of Subversion: The Ethics and Aesthetics of Capoeira and Parkour." *Dance Research: The Journal of the Society for Dance Research* 26 (2): 204–222.

Garcia, Luis Fellipe. 2020. "Only Anthropophagy Unites Us—Oswald de Andrade's Decolonial Project." *Cultural Studies* 34 (1): 122–42. https://doi.org/10.1080/09502386.2018.1551412.

Garcia, Luis-Manuel. 2015. "Beats, Flesh, and Grain: Sonic Tactility and Affect in Electronic Dance Music." *Sound Studies* 1 (1): 59–76. https://doi.org/10.1080/20551940.2015.1079072.

Garcia-Mispireta, Luis Manuel. 2023. *Together, Somehow: Music, Affect, and Intimacy on the Dancefloor*. Duke University Press.

Garrett, Charles, and Carol J. Oja. 2021. *Sounding Together: Collaborative Perspectives on U.S. Music in the 21st Century*. Ann Arbor: University of Michigan Press.

Gates, Henry Louis. 1988. *The Signifying Monkey: A Theory of Afro-American Literary Criticism*. Oxford University Press.

Gaunt, Kyra Danielle. 2006. *The Games Black Girls Play: Learning the Ropes from Double-Dutch to Hip-Hop*. New York University Press.

Gelbert, Laura. 2014. "Unesco declara roda de capoeira patrimônio imaterial da humanidade." ONU News. November 26. https://news.un.org/pt/story/2014/11/1493921.

Geurts, Kathryn Linn. 2002. *Culture and the Senses: Bodily Ways of Knowing in an African Community*. University of California Press.

Gidal, Marc. 2016. *Spirit Song: Afro-Brazilian Religious Music and Boundaries*. Oxford University Press.

Gilroy, Paul. 1993. *The Black Atlantic: Modernity and Double Consciousness*. Harvard University Press.

Gonzalez, Lélia. 1984. "Racismo e sexismo na cultural brasileira." *Revista Ciências Sociais Hoje*, 223–44.

Gonzalez, Lélia. 1985. "The Unified Black Movement: A New Stage in Black Political Mobilization." In *Race, Class, and Power in Brazil*, edited by Pierre-Michel Fontaine, 120–34. University of California Center for Afro-American Studies.

Gottschild, Brenda D. 1998. *Digging the Africanist Presence in American Performance: Dance and Other Contexts*. Praeger.

Graham, Richard. 1990. *Patronage and Politics in Nineteenth-Century Brazil*. Stanford University Press.

Griffith, Lauren Miller. 2016. *In Search of Legitimacy: How Outsiders Become Part of the Afro-Brazilian Capoeira Tradition*. Berghahn Books.

Griffith, Lauren Miller. 2023. *Graceful Resistance: How Capoeiristas Use Their Art for Activism and Community Engagement*. University of Illinois Press.

Hagedorn, Katherine J. 2001. *Divine Utterances: The Performance of Afro-Cuban Santería*. Smithsonian Institution Press.

Hahn, Tomie. 2007. *Sensational Knowledge: Embodying Culture through Japanese Dance*. Wesleyan University Press.

Hale, Charles R., and Lynn Stephen, eds. 2013. *Otros saberes: Collaborative Research on Indigenous and Afro-Descendant Cultural Politics*. Global Indigenous Politics. School for Advanced Research Press.

Hamera, Judith. 2007. *Dancing Communities: Performance, Difference, and Connection in the Global City*. Studies in International Performance. Palgrave Macmillan.

Hanchard, Michael. 2003. "Acts of Misrecognition: Transnational Black Politics, Anti-Imperialism and the Ethnocentrisms of Pierre Bourdieu and Loïc Wacquant." *Theory, Culture & Society* 20 (4): 5–29. https://doi.org/10.1177/02632764030204002.

Hanchard, Michael George. 1994. *Orpheus and Power: The Movimento Negro of Rio de Janeiro and São Paulo, Brazil, 1945–1988*. Princeton University Press.

Haraway, Donna. 1988. "Situated Knowledges: The Science Question in Feminism and the Privilege of Partial Perspective." *Feminist Studies* 14 (3): 575–99. https://doi.org/10.2307/3178066.

Harding, Rachel E. 2000. *A Refuge in Thunder: Candomblé and Alternative Spaces of Blackness*. Indiana University Press.

Harris, Deonte L. 2022. "On Race, Value, and the Need to Reimagine Ethnomusicology for the Future." *Ethnomusicology* 66 (2): 213–35. https://doi.org/10.5406/21567417.66.2.03.

Harrison, Anthony Kwame. 2009. *Hip Hop Underground: The Integrity and Ethics of Racial Identification.* Temple University Press.

Harrison, Faye Venetia. 1991. *Decolonizing Anthropology: Moving Further toward an Anthropology for Liberation.* Association of Black Anthropologists.

Hartman, Saidiya. 1997. *Scenes of Subjection: Terror, Slavery, and Self-Making in Nineteenth-Century America.* Oxford University Press.

Hartman, Saidiya. 2008a. *Lose Your Mother: A Journey along the Atlantic Slave Route.* Farrar, Straus and Giroux.

Hartman, Saidiya. 2008b. "Venus in Two Acts." *Small Axe: A Caribbean Journal of Criticism* 12 (2): 1–14. https://doi.org/10.1215/-12-2-1.

Hedegard, Danielle. 2013. "Blackness and Experience in Omnivorous Cultural Consumption: Evidence from the Tourism of Capoeira in Salvador, Brazil." *Poetics* 41 (1): 1–26. https://doi.org/10.1016/j.poetic.2012.11.003.

Hellier-Tinoco, Ruth. 2018. *Performing Palimpsest Bodies: Postmemory Theatre Experiments in Mexico.* Intellect Books.

Henriques, Julian. 2010. "The Vibrations of Affect and Their Propagation on a Night Out on Kingston's Dancehall Scene." *Body & Society* 16 (1): 57–89.

Henry, Clarence Bernard. 2008. *Let's Make Some Noise: Axé and the African Roots of Brazilian Popular Music.* University Press of Mississippi.

Henson, Bryce. 2024. *Emergent Quilombos: Black Life and Hip-Hop in Brazil.* University of Texas Press.

Hesse, Barnor. 2014. "Escaping Liberty: Western Hegemony, Black Fugitivity." *Political Theory* 42 (3): 288–313. https://doi.org/10.1177/0090591714526208.

Höfling, Ana Paula. 2016. "Pedagogy of the Possessed: Re-Thinking the Dancer-Researcher-Performer (BPI) Method in Dance Curricula in Brazil." *Revista Brasileira de Estudos da Presença* 6 (2): 287–308. https://doi.org/10.1590/2237-266058130.

Höfling, Ana Paula. 2019. *Staging Brazil: Choreographies of Capoeira.* Wesleyan University Press.

Hood, Made Mantle, and Sydney Hutchinson. 2020. "Beyond the Binary of Choreomusicology: Moving from Ethnotheory towards Local Ontologies." *The World of Music* 9 (2): 69–88.

hooks, bell. 1992. "Eating the Other: Desire and Resistance." In *Black Looks: Race and Representation*, 21–39. South End Press.

Hordge-Freeman, Elizabeth. 2015. *The Color of Love: Racial Features, Stigma, and Socialization in Black Brazilian Families.* University of Texas Press.

Hordge-Freeman, Elizabeth. 2022. *Second-Class Daughters.* Cambridge University Press.

Horowitz, Juliana Menasce, Kiley Hurst, and Dana Braga. 2023. "Support for the Black Lives Matter Movement Has Dropped Considerably from Its Peak in 2020." *Pew Research Center's Social & Demographic Trends Project* (blog). June 14. https://www.pewresearch.org/social-trends/2023/06/14/support-for-the-black-lives-matter-movement-has-dropped-considerably-from-its-peak-in-2020/.

Howes, David. 2019. "Multisensory Anthropology." *Annual Review of Anthropology* 48 (1): 17–28. https://doi.org/10.1146/annurev-anthro-102218-011324.

Hurtado, Aída. 2019. "'Race' in Search of a Discipline." *Equity & Excellence in Education* 52 (1): 75–88. https://doi.org/10.1080/10665684.2019.1634501.

Hutchinson, Sydney. 2011. "*Típico, Folklórico* or *Popular*? Musical Categories, Place, and Identity in a Transnational Listening Community." *Popular Music* 30 (2): 245–62. https://doi.org/10.1017/S0261143011000055.

IBGE, ed. 2013. *Atlas do censo demográfico 2010*. Rio de Janeiro, RJ, Brasil. https://biblioteca.ibge.gov.br/index.php/biblioteca-catalogo?view=detalhes&id=264529.

Ickes, Scott, and Bernd Reiter. 2018. *The Making of Brazil's Black Mecca: Bahia Reconsidered*. Michigan State University Press.

Isfahani-Hammond, Alexandra. 2008. *White Negritude: Race, Writing, and Brazilian Cultural Identity*. New Concepts in Latino American Cultures. Palgrave Macmillan.

Iyanaga, Michael Zenryu. 2013. "New World Songs for Catholic Saints: Domestic Performances of Devotion and History in Bahia, Brazil." PhD diss., University of California Los Angeles.

Iyer, Vijay. 2002. "Embodied Mind, Situated Cognition, and Expressive Microtiming in African-American Music." *Music Perception: An Interdisciplinary Journal* 19 (3): 387–414. https://doi.org/10.1525/mp.2002.19.3.387.

Jackson, Lauren Michele. 2019. *White Negroes: When Cornrows Were in Vogue . . . and Other Thoughts on Cultural Appropriation*. Beacon Press.

Johnson, E. Patrick. 2003. *Appropriating Blackness: Performance and the Politics of Authenticity*. Duke University Press.

Johnson, Imani Kai. 2012. "Music Meant to Make You Move: Considering the Aural Kinesthetic." *Sounding Out!* (blog). June 18. https://soundstudiesblog.com/2012/06/18/music-meant-to-make-you-move-considering-the-aural-kinesthetic/.

Johnson, Imani Kai. 2020. "Black Culture without Black People: Hip-Hop Dance beyond Appropriation Discourse." In *Are You Entertained?* edited by Simone C. Drake and Dwan K. Henderson, 191–206. Duke University Press.

Johnson, Imani Kai. 2022. *Dark Matter in Breaking Cyphers: The Life of Africanist Aesthetics in Global Hip Hop*. Oxford University Press.

Johnson, Jasmine Elizabeth. 2012. "Dancing Africa, Making Diaspora." PhD diss., University of California, Berkeley.

Johnson, Paul Christopher. 2002. *Secrets, Gossip, and Gods: The Transformation of Brazilian Candomblé*. Oxford University Press.

Jones, Alisha Lola. 2020. *Flaming?: The Peculiar Theopolitics of Fire and Desire in Black Male Gospel Performance*. Oxford University Press.

Jung, Moon-Kie, and João Helion Costa Vargas, eds. 2021. *Antiblackness*. Duke University Press.

Júnior, Luis Vitor Castro. 2004. "Capoeira angola: olhares e toques cruzados entre historicidade e ancestralidade." *Revista Brasileira de Ciências do Esporte* 25 (2). http://revista.cbce.org.br/index.php/RBCE/article/view/232.

Kapchan, Deborah. 2015. "Body." In *Keywords in Sound*, edited by David Novak and Matt Sakakeeny, 33–43. Duke University Press.

Keil, Charles. 2005. "Motion and Feeling through Music." In *Music Grooves: Essays and Dialogues*, 2nd ed., edited by Charles Keil and Steven Feld, 53–76. Fenestra Books.

Kelley, Robin D. G. 1994. *Race Rebels: Culture, Politics, and the Black Working Class*. Free Press.

Kelley, Robin D. G. 2002. *Freedom Dreams: The Black Radical Imagination*. Beacon Press.

King, Tiffany Lethabo. 2019. *The Black Shoals: Offshore Formations of Black and Native Studies*. Duke University Press.

King, Tiffany Lethabo, Jenell Navarro, and Andrea Smith. 2020. *Otherwise Worlds: Against Settler Colonialism and Anti-Blackness*. Duke University Press.

Kurtz, Esther Viola. 2018. "Moving and Sounding Towards Freedom: Capoeira Angola As a Practice of Afro-Brazilian Racial Consciousness." PhD diss., Brown University.

Kurtz, Esther Viola. 2020. "*Guerreira* Tactics: Women Warriors' Sonic Practices of Refusal in Capoeira Angola." *Women and Music* 24 (1): 71–95.

Kurtz, Esther Viola. 2024a. "Community in Syntony: Theorizing Axé in Capoeira Angola and Rural Samba of Backland Bahia, Brazil." *Ethnomusicology* 68 (1): 118–49. https://doi.org/10.5406/21567417.68.1.08.

Kurtz, Esther Viola. 2024b. "Responding to the Call of *Compromisso*: Reflections on Research Ethics from the Ground of Capoeira Angola." *Conversations Across the Field of Dance Studies* 43. https://doi.org/10.3998/conversations.5951.

Kurtz, Esther Viola. 2025. "Call, Response, and *Compromisso*: Ethical Practice in Capoeira of Backland Bahia, Brazil." *Journal of the Society for American Music*. 19 (1): 1–22.

Lacerda, Alice Pires de. 2021. "Políticas culturais para a capoeira no Brasil: a avaliação dos mestres quanto à participação social." *Políticas Culturais em Revista* 14 (2): 11–31. https://doi.org/10.9771/pcr.v14i2.43409.

Landes, Ruth. 1994 [1947]. *The City of Women*. University of New Mexico Press.

Levine, Lawrence W. 1977. *Black Culture and Black Consciousness: Afro-American Folk Thought from Slavery to Freedom*. Oxford University Press.

Lewis, John Lowell. 1992. *Ring of Liberation: Deceptive Discourse in Brazilian Capoeira*. University of Chicago Press.

Lior, Mika Lillit. 2021. "Circling With/In The Saint: Bahian Candomblé's Feminist Poiesis and Dark Horse Kinetics." PhD diss., University of California Los Angeles.

Lipsitz, George. 1990. *Time Passages: Collective Memory and American Popular Culture*. University of Minnesota Press.

Lipsitz, George. 2006. *The Possessive Investment in Whiteness: How White People Profit from Identity Politics*. Revised, expanded ed. Temple University Press.

Lipsitz, George. 2011. *How Racism Takes Place*. Temple University Press.

Lott, Eric. 1993. *Love and Theft: Blackface Minstrelsy and the American Working Class*. Oxford University Press.

Lühning, Angela. 1990. "Música: coração do candomblé." *Revista USP*, no. 7 (November), 115–24. https://doi.org/10.11606/issn.2316-9036.v0i7p115-124.

Lussana, Sergio. 2018. "Reassessing Brer Rabbit: Friendship, Altruism, and Community in the Folklore of Enslaved African-Americans." *Slavery & Abolition* 39 (1): 123–46. https://doi.org/10.1080/0144039X.2017.1323705.

Machado, Marta Rodriguez de Assis, Márcia Regina de Lima Silva, and Natália Neris da Silva Santos. 2020. "Anti-Racism Legislation in Brazil: The Role of the Courts in the Reproduction of the Myth of Racial Democracy." *Revista de Investigações Constitucionais* 6 (January): 267–96. https://doi.org/10.5380/rinc.v6i2.70080.

Machado, Sara, and Janja Araújo. 2015. "Capoeira Angola, corpo e ancestralidade: por uma educação libertadora." *Horizontes* 33 (December). https://doi.org/10.24933/horizontes.v33i2.256.

Machado, Sara Abreu da Mata. 2016. "Baobá na encruzilhada: ancestralidade, capoeira Angola e permacultura." PhD diss., Universidade Federal da Bahia.

Madison, D. Soyini. 2007. "Co-Performative Witnessing." *Cultural Studies* 21 (6): 826–31. https://doi.org/10.1080/09502380701478174.

Magalhães Filho, Paulo Andrade. 2012. *Jogo de discursos: a disputa por hegemonia na tradição da capoeira Angola baiana*. EDUFBA.

Mahon, Maureen. 2004. *Right to Rock: The Black Rock Coalition and the Cultural Politics of Race*. Duke University Press.

Mahon, Maureen. 2014. "Music, Power, and Practice." *Ethnomusicology* 58 (2): 327–33. https://doi.org/10.5406/ethnomusicology.58.2.0327.

Mahon, Maureen. 2019. "Constructing Race and Engaging Power through Music." In *Theory for Ethnomusicology: Histories, Conversations, Insights*, 2nd ed., edited by Harris Berger and Ruth Stone, 99–113. Routledge.

"mandinga." n.d. In *Dicionário Priberam: Dicionário Online de Português Contemporâneo*. Priberam Informática S.A.. Accessed October 9, 2024. https://dicionario.priberam.org/mandinga.

Marriage, Zoë. 2019. *Cultural Resistance and Security from Below: Power and Escape through Capoeira*. Routledge.

Marshall, Emily Zobel. 2019. *American Trickster: Trauma, Tradition, and Brer Rabbit*. Rowman & Littlefield.

Martins, Sérgio da Silva, Carlos Alberto Medeiros, and Elisa Larkin Nascimento. 2004. "Paving Paradise: The Road from 'Racial Democracy' to Affirmative Action in Brazil." *Journal of Black Studies* 34 (6): 787–816.

Matory, James Lorand. 2005. *Black Atlantic Religion: Tradition, Transnationalism, and Matriarchy in the Afro-Brazilian Candomblé*. Princeton University Press.

"matriz." n.d. In *Dicionário Priberam: Dicionário Online de Português Contemporâneo*. Priberam Informática S.A. Accessed July 5, 2021. https://dicionario.priberam.org/matriz.

Mattos, Amana, and Giovana Xavier. 2016. "Activist Research and the Production of Non-Hegemonic Knowledges: Challenges for Intersectional Feminism." *Feminist Theory* 17 (2): 239–45. https://doi.org/10.1177/1464700116645880.

Mattos, Geísa, and Izabel Accioly. 2023. "'Tornar-se negra, tornar-se branca' e os riscos do 'antirracismo de fachada' no Brasil contemporâneo." *Latin American and Caribbean Ethnic Studies* 18 (2): 244–55. https://doi.org/10.1080/17442222.2021.2015950.

Maultsby, Portia. 2005. "Africanisms in African-American Culture." In *Africanisms in American Culture*, edited by Joseph E. Holloway, 326–55. Indiana University Press.

Maultsby, Portia K., and Mellonee V. Burnim, eds. 2016. *Issues in African American Music: Power, Gender, Race, Representation*. Routledge.

McCallum, Cecilia. 2005. "Racialized Bodies, Naturalized Classes: Moving through the City of Salvador da Bahia." *American Ethnologist* 32 (1): 100–117.

McCann, Bryan. 2004. *Hello, Hello Brazil: Popular Music in the Making of Modern Brazil*. Duke University Press.

McKittrick, Katherine. 2006. *Demonic Grounds: Black Women and the Cartographies of Struggle*. University of Minnesota Press.

McKittrick, Katherine, ed. 2015. *Sylvia Wynter: On Being Human as Praxis*. Duke University Press.

Mengesha, Lilian G., and Lakshmi Padmanabhan. 2019. "Introduction to Performing Refusal/Refusing to Perform." *Women & Performance: A Journal of Feminist Theory* 29 (1): 1–8. https://doi.org/10.1080/0740770X.2019.1574527.

Miller, Kiri. 2008. *Traveling Home: Sacred Harp Singing and American Pluralism*. University of Illinois Press.

Mitchell, Gladys L., and Elizabeth Hordge-Freeman, eds. 2016. *Race and the Politics of Knowledge Production: Diaspora and Black Transnational Scholarship in the United States and Brazil*. Palgrave Macmillan.

Mitchell, Michael. 1985. "Blacks and the *Abertura Democrática*." In *Race, Class, and Power in Brazil*, edited by Pierre-Michel Fontaine, 95–119. University of California Center for Afro-American Studies.

Mitchell-Walthour, Gladys. 2020. "Afro-Brazilian Women YouTubers' Use of African-American Media Representations to Promote Social Justice in Brazil." *Journal of African American Studies* 24 (1): 149–63. https://doi.org/10.1007/s12111-020-09458-7.

Mitchell-Walthour, Gladys L. 2018. *The Politics of Blackness: Racial Identity and Political Behavior in Contemporary Brazil*. Cambridge University Press.

Mohamed, Maryam. 2021. "Bruno Mars Defends Himself against Cultural Appropriation Accusations." CNN. March 7. https://www.cnn.com/2021/03/07/entertainment/bruno-mars-cultural-appropriation-breakfast-club-trnd/index.html.

Monson, Ingrid. 1995. "The Problem with White Hipness: Race, Gender, and Cultural Conceptions in Jazz Historical Discourse." *Journal of the American Musicological Society* 48 (3): 396–422. https://doi.org/10.2307/3519833.

Monson, Ingrid. 2010. *Freedom Sounds: Civil Rights Call Out to Jazz and Africa*. Oxford University Press.

Moreira, João Fernandes da Luz. 2023. "Practices of Cultural Democracy: The *Cultura Viva* Program in Brazil." Master's thesis. Universidade Católica Portuguesa. https://repositorio.ucp.pt/handle/10400.14/40526.

Morris, Wesley. 2019. "Why Is Everyone Always Stealing Black Music?" *New York Times*, August 14, sec. Magazine. https://www.nytimes.com/interactive/2019/08/14/magazine/music-black-culture-appropriation.html.

Morrison, Matthew D. 2024. *Blacksound: Making Race and Popular Music in the United States*. University of California Press.

Morrison, Toni. 1995. "The Site of Memory." In *Inventing the Truth: The Art and Craft of Memoir*, 2nd ed., edited by William Zinsser, 83–102. Houghton Mifflin.

Morrison, Toni. 2004. *Beloved*. Reprint ed. New York: Vintage.

Munanga, Kabengele. 2020. *Rediscutindo a mestiçagem no Brasil: identidade nacional versus identidade negra*. 5th ed. São Paulo, SP: Autêntica.

Mustakeem, Sowande M. 2016. *Slavery at Sea: Terror, Sex, and Sickness in the Middle Passage*. University of Illinois Press.

Nascimento, Abdias do. 1980. "Quilombismo: An Afro-Brazilian Political Alternative." *Journal of Black Studies* 11 (2): 141–78.

Nascimento, Abdias do. 1989. *Brazil, Mixture or Massacre?: Essays in the Genocide of a Black People*. Translated by Elisa Larkin Nascimento. Revised, subsequent ed.: Majority Press.

Nascimento, Abdias do, and Elisa Larkin Nascimento. 1992. *Africans in Brazil: A Pan-African Perspective*. Africa World Press.

Nascimento, Beatriz. 2021. *Uma história feita por mãos negras*. Edited by Alex Ratts and Alceu Chiesorin Nunes. Rio de Janeiro: Zahar.

Nascimento, Beatriz. 2023. *The Dialectic Is in the Sea: The Black Radical Thought of Beatriz Nascimento*. Edited and translated by Christen A. Smith, Bethânia N. F. Gomes, and Archie Davies. Princeton University Press.

Nascimento, Gabriela Rodrigues do. 2021. "Etnomusicologia negra: um olhar feminino sobre a produção de conhecimento das mulheres negras." In *Anais do X Encontro Nacional da Associação Brasileira de Etnomusicologia*. Universidade Federal Rio Grande do Sul. https://www.even3.com.br//anais/xenabet/399891-etnomusicologia-negra--um-olhar-feminino-sobre-a-producao-de-conhecimento-das-mulheres-negras.

Nascimento, Maria Beatriz. 2018. *Beatriz Nascimento, quilombola e intelectual: possibilidades nos dias da destruição*. União dos Coletivos Pan-Africanistas. Editora Filhos da África.

Nascimento Luz, Gabriela Rodrigues do. 2020. "'Música entre lágrimas': um estudo etnomusicológico sobre mulheres musicistas vítimas de violência doméstica." Master's thesis, Instituto de Artes, Programa de Pós-Graduação em Música, Universidade Federal do Rio Grande do Sul. https://lume.ufrgs.br/handle/10183/214309.

Ndaliko, Chérie Rivers. 2016. *Necessary Noise: Music, Film, and Charitable Imperialism in the East of Congo*. Oxford University Press.

Nketia, J. H. Kwabena. 1965. "The Interrelations of African Music and Dance." *Studia Musicologica Academiae Scientiarum Hungaricae* 7 (1/4): 91–101. https://doi.org/10.2307/901416.

Nyong'o, Tavia. 2018. *Afro-Fabulations: The Queer Drama of Black Life*. New York University Press.

Oliveira, Eduardo David de. 2003. *Cosmovisão africana no Brasil: elementos para uma filosofia afrodescendente*. Publicação Ibeca.

Oliveira, Eduardo David de. 2005. "Filosofia da ancestralidade: corpo e mito na filosofia da educação brasileira." PhD diss., Universidade Federal do Ceará.

Oliveira, Josivaldo Pires de. 2006. *No tempo dos valentes: os capoeiras na cidade da Bahia*. Quarteto Editora.

Oliveira, Josivaldo Pires de. 2010. "'Adeptos da mandinga': candomblés, curandeiros e repressão policial na Princesa do Sertão (Feira de Santana-BA, 1938–1970)." PhD diss., Universidade Federal da Bahia.

Oliveira, Josivaldo Pires de, and Luiz Augusto Pinheiro Leal. 2009. *Capoeira, identidade e gênero: ensaios sobre a história social da capoeira no Brasil*. EDUFBA.

Oliveira, Miriam de. 2018. "Black gospel: um estudo etnomusicológico com o grupo Family Soul do Rio Grande do Sul." Master's thesis, Universidade Federal do Rio Grande do Sul. https://lume.ufrgs.br/handle/10183/180666.

Oliveira, Roberta Gondim de, Ana Paula da Cunha, Ana Giselle dos Santos Gadelha, Christiane Goulart Carpio, Rachel Barros de Oliveira, and Roseane Maria Corrêa. 2020. "Racial Inequalities and Death on the Horizon: COVID-19 and Structural Racism." *Cadernos de Saúde Pública* 36 (September). https://doi.org/10.1590/0102-311X00150120.

Omi, Michael, and Howard Winant. 2014. *Racial Formation in the United States*. 3rd ed. New York: Routledge.

Opipari, Carmen. 2010. *O candomblé: imagens em movimento*. EDUSP.

Ortner, Sherry B. 2006. "Introduction: Updating Practice Theory." In *Anthropology and Social Theory: Culture, Power, and the Acting Subject*, 1–18. Duke University Press.

Packman, Jeff. 2010. "Singing Together/Meaning Apart: Popular Music, Participation, and Cultural Politics in Salvador, Brazil." *Latin American Music Review / Revista de Música Latinoamericana* 31 (2): 241–67.

Packman, Jeff. 2021. *Living from Music in Salvador: Professional Musicians and the Capital of Afro-Brazil*. Wesleyan University Press.

Parés, Luis Nicolau. 2013. *The Formation of Candomblé: Vodun History and Ritual in Brazil*. University of North Carolina Press.

Paschel, Tianna S. 2009. "Re-Africanization and the Cultural Politics of Bahianidade." *Souls* 11 (4): 423–40. https://doi.org/10.1080/10999940903417334.

Pereira, Amilcar Araujo. 2011. "A Lei 10.639/03 e o movimento negro: aspectos da luta pela 'reavaliação do papel do negro na história do Brasil'." *Cadernos de História* 12 (17): 25–45. https://doi.org/10.5752/P.2237-8871.2011v12n17p25.

Perrone, Charles A. 2002. "Nationalism, Dissension, and Politics in Contemporary Brazilian Popular Music." *Luso-Brazilian Review* 39 (1): 65–78.

Perry, Keisha-Khan Y. 2013. *Black Women against the Land Grab: The Fight for Racial Justice in Brazil*. University of Minnesota Press.

Phillips-Silver, Jessica, and Peter Keller. 2012. "Searching for Roots of Entrainment and Joint Action in Early Musical Interactions." *Frontiers in Human Neuroscience* 6: 1–11. https://doi.org/10.3389/fnhum.2012.00026.

Pinho, Osmundo. 2020. "Race and Cultural Politics in Bahia." In *Oxford Research Encyclopedia of Latin American History*. https://doi.org/10.1093/acrefore/9780199366439.013.946.

Pinho, Patricia de Santana. 2009. "White but Not Quite: Tones and Overtones of Whiteness in Brazil." *Small Axe: A Caribbean Journal of Criticism* 13 (2): 39–56. https://doi.org/10.1215/07990537-3697250.

Pinho, Patricia de Santana. 2010. *Mama Africa: Reinventing Blackness in Bahia*. Duke University Press.

Pinho, Patricia de Santana. 2018. *Mapping Diaspora: African American Roots Tourism in Brazil*. University of North Carolina Press.

Pinto, Tiago de Oliveira. 1991. *Capoeira, Samba, Candomblé: Afro-brasilianische Musik im Recôncavo, Bahia*. Museum für Völkerkunde Berlin.

Piper, Daniel. 2007. "Caboclo Ritual Dance 'Brings the Juke-Joint to the Church.'" *ReVista: Harvard Review of Latin America* (Fall): 57.

Pires, Antônio Liberac Cardoso Simões. 2004. *A capoeira na Bahia de Todos os Santos: um estudo sobre cultura e classes trabalhadoras (1890–1937)*. Fundação Federal do Tocantins, NEAB.

Prandi, Reginaldo. 1997. "The Expansion of Black Religion in White Society: Brazilian Popular Music and Legitimacy of Candomblé." Paper presented at the Twentieth International Congress of the Latin American Studies Association, Guadalajara, Mexico, April 17–19, 1997.

Prandi, Reginaldo. 2004. "O Brasil com axé: candomblé e umbanda no mercado religioso." *Estudos Avançados* 18 (52): 223–38. https://doi.org/10.1590/S0103-40142004000300015.

Rabelo, Miriam C. M. 2020. "Obrigações e a construção de vínculos no candomblé." *Mana* 26 (1): 1-31. https://doi.org/10.1590/1678-49442020v26n1a201.

Radano, Ronald Michael, and Philip Vilas Bohlman, eds. 2000. *Music and the Racial Imagination*. University of Chicago Press.

Ramsey, Guthrie P. 2004. *Race Music: Black Cultures from Bebop to Hip-Hop*. University of California Press.

Ramsey, Guthrie P. 2022. *Who Hears Here?: On Black Music, Pasts and Present*. University of California Press.

Raphael, Alison. 1990. "From Popular Culture to Microenterprise: The History of Brazilian Samba Schools." *Latin American Music Review* 11 (1): 73–83.

Ratts, Alex. 2007. *Eu sou atlântica: sobre a trajetoria de vida de Beatriz Nascimento*. Instituto Kuanza / Imprensa oficial do estado de São Paulo.

Redmond, Shana L. 2016. "'As Though It Were Our Own': Against a Politics of Identification." In *Critical Ethnic Studies: A Reader*, edited by Critical Ethnic Studies Editorial Collective, Nada Elia, David M. Hernández, Jodi Kim, Shana L. Redmond, Dylan Rodríguez, and Sarita Echavez See, 19–42. Duke University Press.

Redmond, Shana L. 2020. *Everything Man: The Form and Function of Paul Robeson*. Duke University Press.

Rego, Waldeloir. 1968. *Capoeira Angola: ensaio sócio-etnográfico*. Editôra Itapua.

Reis, Leticia Vidor de Sousa. 1997. *O mundo de pernas para o ar: a capoeira no Brasil.* Publisher Brasil.

Reis, Maíra Lopes dos. 2022. "'A universidade não é um espaço feito para gente, mas a gente está ocupando': mulheres camponesas na licenciatura em educação do campo da Universidade Federal do Recôncavo da Bahia-UFRB," PhD diss., Universidade Federal da Bahia. https://repositorio.ufba.br/handle/ri/36613.

Reiter, Bernd, and Ulrich Oslender, eds. 2014. *Bridging Scholarship and Activism: Reflections from the Frontlines of Collaborative Research.* Michigan State University Press.

Robinson, Cedric J. 2000. *Black Marxism: The Making of the Black Radical Tradition.* University of North Carolina Press.

Robinson, Dylan. 2020. *Hungry Listening: Resonant Theory for Indigenous Sound Studies.* University of Minnesota Press.

Robitaille, Laurence. 2013. "Capoeira as a Resource: Multiple Uses of Culture under Conditions of Transnational Neoliberalism." PhD diss., York University. https://yorkspace.library.yorku.ca/xmlui/handle/10315/29815.

Rodrigues, Yasmin. 2017. "E os 'brancos' do candomblé'?" *Geledés Instituto da Mulher Negra* (blog). October 19, 2017. https://www.geledes.org.br/e-os-brancos-do-candomble/.

Romero, Brenda M., Susan M. Asai, David A. McDonald, Andrew G. Snyder, and Katelyn E. Best, eds. 2023. *At the Crossroads of Music and Social Justice.* Indiana University Press.

Romo, Anadelia. 2022. *Selling Black Brazil: Race, Nation, and Visual Culture in Salvador, Bahia.* University of Texas Press.

Rosa, Cristina F. 2015. *Brazilian Bodies and Their Choreographies of Identification: Swing Nation.* Palgrave Macmillan.

Rosa, Cristina F. 2019. "Sergio González Varela, Power in Practice: The Pragmatic Anthropology of Afro-Brazilian Capoeira." *Dance Research* 37 (1): 113–15. https://doi.org/10.3366/drs.2019.0258.

Rosa, Pedro Fernando Acosta da. 2020. "Sopapo poético e etnomusicologia negra: agência, performance, musicalidade e protagonismo negro em Porto Alegre." PhD diss., Universidade Federal do Rio Grande do Sul. https://lume.ufrgs.br/handle/10183/213597.

Rose, Tricia. 1994. *Black Noise: Rap Music and Black Culture in Contemporary America.* Wesleyan University Press.

Sá, Celina de. forthcoming. *Diaspora Without Displacement: The Coloniality and Promise of Capoeira in Senegal.* Durham, NC: Duke University Press.

Salata, André. 2020. "Race, Class, and Income Inequality in Brazil: A Social Trajectory Analysis." *Dados* 63 (October). https://doi.org/10.1590/dados.2020.63.3.213.

Samuels, David W. 2004. *Putting a Song on Top of It: Expression and Identity on the San Apache Reservation.* University of Arizona Press.

Sandroni, Carlos. 2011. "Farewell to MPB." In *Brazilian Popular Music and Citizenship*, edited by Idelber Avelar and Christopher Dunn, 64–73. Duke University Press.

Sandroni, Carlos. 2021 [2001]. *A Respectable Spell: Transformations of Samba in Rio de Janeiro*. Translated by Michael Iyanaga. University of Illinois Press.

Sandroni, Carlos, and Márcia G. de Sant'Anna, eds. 2006. *Samba de roda do Recôncavo baiano*. Dossiê IPHAN 4. Instituto do Patrimônio Histórico e Artístico Nacional.

Sansone, Livio. 2003. *Blackness without Ethnicity: Constructing Race in Brazil*. Palgrave Macmillan.

Santa Barbara, Reginilde Rodrigues. 2007. "O caminho da autonomia na conquista da dignidade: sociabilidades e conflitos entre lavadeiras em Feira de Santana—Bahia (1929–1964)." PhD diss., Universidade Federal da Bahia.

Santa Barbara, Urania do Carmo Rodrigues. 2019. "'Jogo de dentro, jogo de fora': uma leitura Foucaultiana das práticas histórico-discursivas, dos cantos e do corpo na capoeira angola." Master's thesis, Universidade Estadual de Feira de Santana.

Santos, Flávia Santana. 2016a. "Relatório final de produção do paradidático 'Um quilombo urbano chamado Rua Nova.'" Relatório Técnico Final: Universidade Federal do Recôncavo da Bahia. https://www.ufrb.edu.br/mphistoria/images/Disserta%C3%A7%C3%B5es/Turma_2014/Fl%C3%A1via_Santana/01-Relat%C3%B3rio_Final__de_Produ%C3%A7%C3%A3o_do_Paradid%C3%A1tico__Um_Quilombo_Urbano_Chamado_Rua_Nova.pdf.

Santos, Flávia Santana. 2016b. *Um quilombo urbano chamado Rua Nova*. Fundação de Amparo à Pesquisa do Estado da Bahia. https://www.ufrb.edu.br/mphistoria/images/Disserta%C3%A7%C3%B5es/Turma_2014/Fl%C3%A1via_Santana/03-Miolo_do_Livro.pdf.

Santos, Jocélio Teles dos. 1995. *O dono da terra: o Caboclo nos candomblés da Bahia*. Editora Sarah Letras.

Santos, Juana Elbein dos. 2012 [1976]. *Os Nàgô e a morte: Pàde, Àsèsè e o culto Égun na Bahia*. 14th ed. Editora Vozes.

Santos, Sales Augusto dos. 2006. "Who Is Black in Brazil? A Timely or a False Question in Brazilian Race Relations in the Era of Affirmative Action?" Translated by Obianuju C. Anya. *Latin American Perspectives* 33 (4): 30–48.

Schneider, Rebecca. 2018. "That the Past May Yet Have Another Future: Gesture in the Times of Hands Up." *Theatre Journal* 70 (3): 285–306.

Schreiber, Mariana. 2017. "'Capoeira gospel' cresce e gera tensão entre evangélicos e movimento negro." BBC News Brasil. October 14. https://www.bbc.com/portuguese/brasil-41572349.

Schucman, Lia. 2020. *Entre o encardido, o branco e o branquíssimo: branquitude, hierarquia e poder na cidade de São Paulo*. Veneta.

Schucman, Lia Vainer. 2023. *Famílias inter-raciais: tensões entre cor e amor*. Fósforo.

Schucman, Lia Vainer, and Willamys Da Costa Melo. 2022. "White Supremacy, Brazil Style: As White Brazilians Continue to Dominate Powerful Positions, Persistent Myths of Meritocracy and Racial Democracy Disguise the Structural Racism Driving Their Privilege." *NACLA Report on the Americas* 54 (2): 197–202. https://doi.org/10.1080/10714839.2022.2084991.

Scott, David. 2000. "Interview: The Re-Enchantment of Humanism: An Interview with Sylvia Wynter." *Small Axe: A Caribbean Journal of Criticism* 4 (2): 119–207.

Scott, James C. 1987. *Weapons of the Weak: Everyday Forms of Peasant Resistance*. Yale University Press.

"sentido." n.d. In *Dicionário Priberam: Dicionário Online de Português Contemporâneo*. Priberam Informática S.A. Accessed October 10, 2022. https://dicionario.priberam.org/sentido.

Shange, Savannah. 2019. *Progressive Dystopia: Abolition, Antiblackness, and Schooling in San Francisco*. Duke University Press.

Sharp, Daniel B. 2014. *Between Nostalgia and Apocalypse: Popular Music and the Staging of Brazil*. Wesleyan University Press.

Sharpe, Christina. 2016. *In the Wake: On Blackness and Being*. Duke University Press.

Shelemay, Kay Kaufman. 1998. *Let Jasmine Rain Down: Song and Remembrance among Syrian Jews*. University of Chicago Press.

Sheriff, Robin E. 2001. *Dreaming Equality: Color, Race, and Racism in Urban Brazil*. Rutgers University Press.

Shipley, Jesse Weaver. 2015. *Trickster Theatre: The Poetics of Freedom in Urban Africa*. Indiana University Press.

Shonekan, Stephanie. 2018. "Black Mizzou: Music and Stories One Year Later." In *Black Lives Matter and Music: Protest, Intervention, Reflection*, edited by Fernando Orejuela and Stephanie Shonekan, 14–33. Indiana University Press.

Silva, Antonio José Bacelar da, and Erika Robb Larkins. 2019. "The Bolsonaro Election, Antiblackness, and Changing Race Relations in Brazil." *Journal of Latin American and Caribbean Anthropology* 24 (4): 893–913. https://doi.org/10.1111/jlca.12438.

Silva, Fábio Alex Ferreira da. 2018. "'Eu vou ali e volto já, daqui a pouco tô no mesmo lugar': performances e agências sociorrituais no culto aos Caboclos em Santo Amaro." Master's thesis, Universidade Federal do Recôncavo da Bahia. https://ufrb.edu.br/pgcienciassociais/images/Disserta%C3%A7%C3%B5es/2018/disserta%C3%A7%C3%A3o_F%C3%A1bio_Alex_Ferreira_da_Silva_vers%C3%A3o_final.pdf.

Silvers, Michael B. 2018. *Voices of Drought: The Politics of Music and Environment in Northeastern Brazil*. University of Illinois Press.

Skidmore, Thomas E. 1993. *Black into White: Race and Nationality in Brazilian Thought*. Duke University Press.

Smith, Christen, Archie Davies, and Bethânia Gomes. 2021. "'In Front of the World': Translating Beatriz Nascimento." *Antipode* 53 (1): 279–316. https://doi.org/10.1111/anti.12690.

Smith, Christen A. 2016. *Afro-Paradise: Blackness, Violence, and Performance in Brazil*. University of Illinois Press.

Smith, Christen A., and Lorraine Leu. 2023. *Black Feminist Constellations: Dialogue and Translation across the Americas*. University of Texas Press.

Smith, Christen A., Erica L. Williams, Imani A. Wadud, and Whitney N. L. Pirtle.

2021. "Cite Black Women: A Critical Praxis (A Statement)." *Feminist Anthropology* 2 (1): 10–17. https://doi.org/10.1002/fea2.12040.

Snyder, Andrew. 2022. *Critical Brass: Street Carnival and Musical Activism in Olympic Rio de Janeiro.* Wesleyan University Press.

Soares, Carlos Eugênio Líbano. 1994. *A negregada instituição: os capoeiras no Rio de Janeiro.* Prefeitura da Cidade do Rio de Janeiro, Secretaria Municipal de Cultura, Departamento Geral de Documentação e Informação Cultural, Divisão de Editoração.

Soares, Carlos Eugênio Líbano. 2001. *A capoeira escrava e outras tradições rebeldes no Rio de Janeiro, 1808–1850.* Editora de UniCamp.

Sodré, Muniz. 1988. "À sombra do retrato." In *Escravos brasileiros do século XIX na fotografia de Christiano Jr.*, edited by Paulo Cesar de Azevedo and Mauricio Lissovsky, xvii–xxi. Ex Libris.

Solís, Ted, ed. 2004. *Performing Ethnomusicology: Teaching and Representation in World Music Ensembles.* University of California Press.

Sousa, Rayron Lennon Costa, and Risoleta Viana de Freitas. 2021. "A genealogia negro-brasileira contemporânea de autoria feminina na literatura de Conceição Evaristo: tempo, temporalidade e ancestralidade em *Olhos d'água* (2018)." *Revista Criação & Crítica*, no. 29 (May), 198–217. https://doi.org/10.11606/issn.1984-1124.i29p198-217.

Souza, Elizandra. 2023. "Diasporic Memories: Black Women Writers' Lived Experiences and Ancestralities." In *Black Feminist Constellations: Dialogue and Translation across the Americas*, edited by Christen A. Smith and Lorraine Leu, translated by Christen A. Smith, 276–84. University of Texas Press.

Sovik, Liv Rebecca. 2009. *Aqui ninguém é branco.* Aeroplano.

Spivak, Gayatri Chakravorty. 2010. "Can the Subaltern Speak?" In *Can the Subaltern Speak? Reflections on the History of an Idea*, edited by Rosalind C. Morris, 21–78. Columbia University Press.

Stepputat, Kendra, and Elina Seye. 2020. "Introduction: Choreomusical Perspectives." *The World of Music* 9 (1): 7–24.

Sterling, Marvin D. 2010. *Babylon East: Performing Dancehall, Roots Reggae, and Rastafari in Japan.* Duke University Press.

Stoever, Jennifer. 2016. *Sonic Color Line.* New York University Press.

Stroud, Sean. 2008. *The Defence of Tradition in Brazilian Popular Music: Politics, Culture and the Creation of* Música Popular Brasileira. Ashgate Publishing.

Suárez, Lucía M., Amélia Vitória de S. Conrado, and Yvonne Daniel, eds. 2018. *Dancing Bahia: Essays on Afro-Brazilian Dance, Education, Memory, and Race.* Intellect.

"syntony." n.d. In *Merriam-Webster Inc.* Accessed February 15, 2018. https://www.merriam-webster.com/dictionary/syntony.

TallBear, Kim. 2014. "Standing With and Speaking as Faith: A Feminist-Indigenous Approach to Inquiry." *Journal of Research Practice* 10 (2): 17.

Tate, Greg. 2003. *Everything but the Burden: What White People Are Taking from Black Culture.* Harlem Moon/Broadway Books.

Tatum, Beverly Daniel. 2019. "Together and Alone? The Challenge of Talking about Racism on Campus." *Daedalus* 148 (4): 79–93.

Taylor, Diana. 2003. *The Archive and the Repertoire: Performing Cultural Memory in the Americas*. 2nd printing ed. Duke University Press.

Telles, Edward, and Tianna Paschel. 2014. "Who Is Black, White, or Mixed Race? How Skin Color, Status, and Nation Shape Racial Classification in Latin America." *American Journal of Sociology* 120 (3): 864–907. https://doi.org/10.1086/679252.

Telles, Edward E. 2004. *Race in Another America: The Significance of Skin Color in Brazil*. Princeton University Press.

Thomas, Deborah A. 2016. "Time and the Otherwise: Plantations, Garrisons and Being Human in the Caribbean." *Anthropological Theory* 16 (2–3): 177–200. https://doi.org/10.1177/1463499616636269.

Thompson, Katrina Dyonne. 2014. *Ring Shout, Wheel About: The Racial Politics of Music and Dance in North American Slavery*. University of Illinois Press.

Tinhorão, José Ramos. 2001. *Cultura popular: temas e questões*. Editora 34.

Tomlinson, Barbara, and George Lipsitz. 2013. "American Studies as Accompaniment." *American Quarterly* 65 (1): 1–30. https://doi.org/10.1353/aq.2013.0009.

Travae, Marques. 2017. "'I Love Being Black!'—Popular White Singer Daniela Mercury Heavily Criticized for Honoring Legendary Afro-Brazilian Singer in Blackface and Afro Wig." *Black Brazil Today* (blog). March 10. https://blackbraziltoday.com/popular-white-singer-daniela-mercury-heavily-criticized/.

Treece, David. 1997. "Guns and Roses: Bossa Nova and Brazil's Music of Popular Protest, 1958–68." *Popular Music* 16 (1): 1–29. https://kclpure.kcl.ac.uk/ws/portalfiles/portal/149142194/Treece_Guns_and_Roses.pdf.

Treuke, Stephan. 2020. "Structures of Opportunity and Constraints on Socioeconomic Integration in Three Segregated Favelas of Salvador, Brazil." *Latin American Research Review* 55 (2): 227–41. https://doi.org/10.25222/larr.626.

Turino, Thomas. 1993. *Moving Away from Silence: Music of the Peruvian Altiplano and the Experience of Urban Migration*. University of Chicago Press.

Turino, Thomas. 2008. *Music as Social Life: The Politics of Participation*. University of Chicago Press.

Twine, France Winddance. 1998. *Racism in a Racial Democracy: The Maintenance of White Supremacy in Brazil*. Rutgers University Press.

Varela, Sergio González. 2017. *Power in Practice: The Pragmatic Anthropology of Afro-Brazilian Capoeira*. Berghahn Books.

Varela, Sergio González. 2019. *Capoeira, Mobility, and Tourism: Preserving an Afro-Brazilian Tradition in a Globalized World*. Rowman & Littlefield.

Vargas, João H. Costa. 2004. "Hyperconsciousness of Race and Its Negation: The Dialectic of White Supremacy in Brazil." *Identities* 11 (4): 443–70. https://doi.org/10.1080/10702890490883803.

Vargas, João H. Costa. 2008. *Never Meant to Survive: Genocide and Utopias in Black Diaspora Communities*. Transformative Politics. Rowman & Littlefield.

Vatin, Xavier. 2005. *Rites et musiques de possession à Bahia*. Editions L'Harmattan.

Vatin, Xavier. 2013. "Música e possessão para além da eficácia simbólica?" In *Para além da eficácia simbólica: estudos em ritual, religião e saúde*, edited by Fátima Tavares and Francesca Bassi, 243–60. EDUFBA.

Vianna, Hermano. 1999. *The Mystery of Samba: Popular Music and National Identity in Brazil*. Edited and translated by John Charles Chasteen. Latin America in Translation/en Traducción/em Tradução. University of North Carolina Press.

Villenave, Sabrina. 2021. *Disappearances and Police Killings in Contemporary Brazil: The Politics of Life and Death*. Routledge.

Wafer, James William. 1991. *The Taste of Blood: Spirit Possession in Brazilian Candomblé*. University of Pennsylvania Press.

Weheliye, Alexander G. 2014. *Habeas Viscus: Racializing Assemblages, Biopolitics, and Black Feminist Theories of the Human*. Duke University Press.

Weinstein, Barbara. 2015. *The Color of Modernity: São Paulo and the Making of Race and Nation in Brazil*. Duke University Press.

Wesolowski, Katya. 2007. "Hard Play: Capoeira and the Politics of Inequality in Rio de Janeiro." PhD diss., Columbia University.

Wesolowski, Katya. 2012. "Professionalizing Capoeira: The Politics of Play in Twenty-First-Century Brazil." *Latin American Perspectives* 39 (2): 82–92. https://doi.org/10.1177/0094582X11427892.

Wesolowski, Katya. 2023. *Capoeira Connections: A Memoir in Motion*. University of Florida Press.

William, Rodney. 2020. *Apropriação cultural*. Editora Jandaíra.

Williams, Erica Lorraine. 2013. *Sex Tourism in Bahia: Ambiguous Entanglements*. University of Illinois Press.

Willson, Margaret. 2001. "Designs of Deception: Concepts of Consciousness, Spirituality, and Survival in Capoeira Angola in Salvador, Brazil." *Anthropology of Consciousness* 12 (1): 19–36. https://doi.org/10.1525/ac.2001.12.1.19.

Winant, Howard. 1992. "Rethinking Race in Brazil." *Journal of Latin American Studies* 24 (1): 173–92. https://www.cambridge.org/core/journals/journal-of-latin-american-studies/article/abs/rethinking-race-in-brazil/798A341619AFA46395FEEC0A73F06441.

Wolf, Juan Eduardo. 2019. *Styling Blackness in Chile: Music and Dance in the African Diaspora*. Indiana University Press.

Wong, Deborah. 2004. *Speak It Louder: Asian Americans Making Music*. Routledge.

Wong, Deborah. 2006. "Ethnomusicology and Difference." *Ethnomusicology* 50 (2): 259–79.

Wong, Deborah. 2021. "Witnessing: A Methodology." In *Transforming Ethnomusicology Volume I: Methodologies, Institutional Structures, and Policies*, edited by Beverley Diamond and Salwa El-Shawan Castelo-Branco, 187–201. Oxford University Press.

Woodard, Vincent. 2014. *The Delectable Negro: Human Consumption and Homoeroticism within US Slave Culture*. New York University Press.

Wynter, Sylvia. 2003. "Unsettling the Coloniality of Being/Power/Truth/Freedom: Towards the Human, After Man, Its Overrepresentation—An Argument." *CR:*

The New Centennial Review 3 (3): 257–337. https://doi.org/10.1353/ncr.2004.0015.

Yúdice, George. 2004. *The Expediency of Culture*. Duke University Press.

Zambrano, Pilar Echeverry. 2018. "Pedagogies of the Body within African Matrix Education of Salvador, Brazil: Perspectives and Challenges of an Emancipatory Project." In *Dancing Bahia: Essays on Afro-Brazilian Dance, Education, Memory, and Race*, edited by Lucía M. Suárez, Amélia Vitória de S. Conrado, and Yvonne Daniel, 75–94. Intellect.

Ziff, Bruce H., and Pratima V. Rao. 1997. "Introduction to Cultural Appropriation: A Framework for Analysis." In *Borrowed Power: Essays on Cultural Appropriation*, 1–27. Rutgers University Press.

Zonzon, Christine Nicole. 2014. "Algumas versões da malícia." *Revista de Humanidades e Letras* 1 (1): 45–81.

Zonzon, Christine Nicole. 2016. "Mulher na capoeira: interfaces entre género e reafricanização da tradição no processo de legitimação da capoeira Angola." In *Capoeira em múltiplos olhares: estudos e pesquisas em jogo*, edited by Antonio Liberac Cardoso Simões Pires, Paulo Magalhães, Franciane Figueiredo, and Sara Abreu, 403–414. Editora UFRB.

Cited Interviews

Abusada. Paraguaçu Paulista, SP, March 19, 2016; video call, March 26, 2017

Beija-Flor (pseud.). São Paulo state. 2016.

Binho. Feira de Santana, BA, April 3, 2016.

Bolinha. Feira de Santana, BA, February 11, 2017.

Carlão (pseud.). São Paulo state. 2017.

Costa, Mestre Cláudio. Mantiba, Feira de Santana, BA, July 4, 2013; in car to Salvador, BA, July 10, 2013.

Damasceno, Karine Teixeira. Salvador, BA, May 6, 2016.

Hulluca. In car to Salvador, BA, January 9, 2023.

Iaiá. Feira de Santana, BA, March 14, 2016.

Igor and Papagaio (joint interview). Feira de Santana, BA, April 8, 2016.

Lantier, Rita Eloá Gonçalves. Salvador, BA, August 25, 2015.

Marmota (pseud.). São Paulo state. 2016.

Mateu (pseud.). São Paulo state. 2016.

Mesquita, Afonso. Mantiba, Feira de Santana, BA, January 18, 2017; video call, December 12, 2022.

Orikerê. São Felix, BA, March 10, 2016.

Pernalonga. Feira de Santana, BA, February 23, 2016.

Sadan, Fabio. Feira de Santana, BA, January 15, 2023.

Santa Bárbara, Ivannide Rodrigues. Feira de Santana, BA, August 18, 2015; May 9, 2016.

Discography

Bethânia, Maria. 2003. *Brasileirinho.* Biscoito Fino, compact disc.

Moraes, Mestre, and GCAP. 1996. *Grupo de Capoeira Angola Pelourinho—Capoeira Angola from Salvador, Brazil.* Smithsonian Folkways SF CD 40465, compact disc.

Santo Amaro, M. Felipe de, and M. Cláudio Costa. 2003. *Angoleiros do Sertão e do Recôncavo*, compact disc.

Videography

Templo Escola Filhos do Mar, dir. 2016. "Quem Vem Lá Sou Eu." May 26. YouTube video, 1:43. https://www.youtube.com/watch?v=fw5Cf4Gqcbc.

Umbanda let's talk, dir. 2017. "PONTOS DE BOIADEIRO—Quem Vem Lá?—Que Barulho é Esse?—Camarada Meu." July 23. YouTube video, 2:40. https://www.youtube.com/watch?v=i5IR3_JAHKE&t=61s.

Wesle Pereira, dir. 2015. "Ponto de Boiadeiro Quem Vem Lá Sou Eu." August 28. YouTube video, 1:13. https://www.youtube.com/watch?v=aOk-RAowg7E.

Index

Note: Page numbers in italics indicate figures and musical examples.